EVANGELICAL CHRISTIANITY IN THE
UNITED STATES AND GREAT BRITAIN

Evangelical Christianity in the United States and Great Britain

Religious Beliefs, Political Choices

J. Christopher Soper
Assistant Professor of Political Science
Pepperdine University, Malibu

NEW YORK UNIVERSITY PRESS
Washington Square, New York

© J. Christopher Soper 1994

First published in the U.S.A. in 1994 by
NEW YORK UNIVERSITY PRESS
Washington Square
New York, N.Y. 10003

Library of Congress Cataloging-in-Publication Data
Soper, J. Christopher.
Evangelical Christianity in the United States and Great Britain :
religious beliefs, political choices / by J. Christopher Soper.
p. cm.
Includes bibliographical references and index.
ISBN 0–8147–7987–5
1. Evangelicalism—Great Britain—History. 2. Evangelicalism–
United States—History. 3. Great Britain—Politics and
government—20th century. 4. United States—Politics and
government—20th century. 5. Abortion—Religious aspects–
–Evangelicalism. 6. Temperance—Great Britain—History.
7. Temperance—United States—History. I. Title.
BR1642.G7S67   1994
270.8' 2—dc20   93–36638
                                                        CIP

Printed in Hong Kong

To Jane Katharine and Katharine Elizabeth,
with love and gratitude

Contents

List of Tables

Preface

Evangelical Christians have been politically involved since the founding of their religious movement over two centuries ago. This book focuses on two of the more prominent issues which caused evangelicals to become politically active: temperance and abortion. The book rests on the claim that evangelical political mobilization and activism cannot be understood unless the content and meaning of their ideology is plumbed. Through an analysis of evangelical political mobilization in Great Britain and the United States, I show how group norms encouraged believers to engage in collective political action in ways that would not have occurred without shared religious beliefs and cultural values. I hope that it will attract the attention of those who are convinced, as I am, that ideology and culture belong at the centre of the study of social movements and political science.

This book began as a dissertation at Yale University and became a book while I was teaching at Pepperdine University. I am grateful for the assistance and support of my colleagues and absolve them of any responsibility for my errors. David Mayhew and Rogers Smith gave liberally of their time and talents in thoughtful readings of draft chapters. Byron Shafer assisted me with setting up interviews with British evangelical activists and helped interpret my findings during a six-month stay at Oxford University. I am particularly indebted to David Plotke who convinced me that a study of evangelical social movements had merit in a political science department. David patiently discussed ideas with me on social movements and political participation and I am grateful for his intellectual and personal support. Friends and scholars at Pepperdine University have been particularly supportive as I have made the transition from student to professor. Dan Caldwell, Steve Monsma, Stan Moore and Robert Williams deserve special praise for being interested and enthusiastic about my research. Special thanks are also due to Ken Wald for his painstaking review of an earlier draft of this book.

My wife, Jane, read my manuscript more times than I could or would dare to count. Her technical and emotional support did more for my professional and personal life than I will ever be able to relate in words. She richly deserves this dedication.

J. Christopher Soper

1 Introduction

Don Treshman, the head of the Texas-based evangelical pro-life group Rescue America, went to Britain in April 1993 to bring the combative tactics of American anti-abortion groups to a nation where the debate around abortion has been relatively free of such confrontation. Treshman soon found himself under heavy criticism from the British Government – which tried to deport him – and newspaper editorials – which condemned his visit. Even the well-established British pro-life groups, which shared his religious opposition to elective abortion, were unsympathetic to his intimidating style and aggressive political tactics.[1]

Treshman's visit to Britain underscored important similarities and differences between the political involvement of religious groups in Britain and America. In ideological and organizational terms, American and British groups are, and have been, quite similar. Both nations have witnessed the formation of religiously-based political organizations to change public policy on such moral issues as abortion and pornography, in contemporary politics, and drinking, in the past. In each case, religious values were the impetus for the mobilization of political organizations. There have also been profound differences between these transatlantic believers, particularly in terms of the tactics chosen by British and American groups. The political institutions and structures unique to Britain and America have had a great influence on how religious groups have engaged in politics.

This book compares the political mobilization of evangelical Christians in Britain and America around the issues of temperance a century ago and abortion for the past several decades. Evangelical political activism raises important questions for social scientists about the basis for group mobilization. How does political participation occur through social movement organizations? What role have group ideas played in shaping the political preferences of adherents? To what extent has the ideology of actors contributed to their political involvement, and to what degree has their activism been shaped by exogenous factors beyond their control? This book demonstrates two important points about transatlantic evangelical mobilization. First, a shared religious ideology was the primary impulse for evangelical activism. Second, state institutions shaped the political activism of evangelical groups and influenced the eventual outcome of evangelical politics. Evangelical religious beliefs and cultural values led to the formation of social groups; political institutions unique to Britain and America moulded the way in which those values were translated into practical politics.

1

Drawing on data gathered from group literature and interviews with activists, the book contends that specific religious doctrines and values encouraged the formation of evangelical political groups. The evangelical doctrine that the individual has a part to play in the experience of salvation encouraged believers to be optimistic about the positive social and political role they could assume; the evangelical stress upon the obligation of the converted believer to live a sinless life and to lead others to salvation gave evangelicals the motive for forming groups to bring about social and religious reform; and the evangelical conviction that the Bible is the accurate expression of God's will provided believers with a source for making political choices and helped reinforce cultural values about drinking and human sexuality.

A comparison of evangelical mobilization in Britain and America provides an opportunity to summarize and evaluate the treatment of group ideology in existing social movement theories. The four theories reviewed in the book are status or psychological theory, rational choice, resource mobilization and state structure theory. Psychological theory is flawed because it emphasizes the irrationality of group ideology in social movement formation. Rational choice theory does not account for the way in which an ideology shapes people's basic interests and encourages them to join social groups. Resource mobilization and state structure theory, which examine the importance of political and monetary resources in group formation, do not give sufficient attention to the role of ideological grievances in a social movement.

In contrast, this book outlines a social movement theory which highlights the role of ideology in group formation. Group ideology, the set of values, ideas and beliefs which give meaning to the social experiences of adherents, defines group objectives and legitimates group formation. People who are committed to the norms and values of an ideology feel a responsibility to represent those beliefs in their social and political lives. An ideology provides believers with a sense of obligation necessary to sustain a social group over time. Evangelicals have organized political groups in ways that cannot adequately be explained using the existing social movement theories. Support for evangelical political groups is best explained by looking closely at the shared religious and cultural beliefs of adherents.

These religious norms legitimated the formation of evangelical groups to combat what were perceived to be the social sins of drinking and abortion. In each case, the impetus for group mobilization was religious ideas about salvation and the converted believer's obligation to lead a moral life. Group leaders consciously appealed to these shared religious values in their effort to convince fellow believers to become politically aware and involved on the issues of temperance and abortion. The comparison between America and Britain will help me to isolate the autonomous role of an evangelical ideology in the process of social movement mobilization. I will show that an evangelical ideology led believers of different social classes, different status, and in different political cultures to adopt identical political positions on temperance and abortion. The religious ideology which these trans-atlantic believers shared encouraged them to form political groups to oppose sinful social practices. The comparison will also enable me to reject competing social movement theories which adopt class, status or material incentives as the primary factor in evangelical group mobilization. My analysis of evangelical groups suggests that political science does not have an adequate theory to explain the role of group ideology in the creation of a social movement.

A second objective of the book is to show how evangelical political behaviour has been influenced by the restraints and opportunities provided by the American and British polities. Political structures, particularly con-stitutional norms and electoral party systems, have shaped the political behaviour of evangelical organizations. Britain's unitary polity, strong po-litical parties, and parliamentary sovereignty have limited the places at which evangelical groups could intervene in the policy process and min-imized the political effectiveness of these organizations. Despite their best efforts, British evangelicals did not pass any meaningful restriction on alcohol in the nineteenth century and have had no more success limiting access to abortion services in the twentieth.

In contrast, America's federal polity, weak political parties, and division of political authority at the national level, created multiple points of access for evangelical interest groups which successfully intervened in the policymaking process at the state and federal levels. American evangelicals helped pass a constitutional amendment banning the sale and manufacture of alcohol early in the twentieth century, and have more recently helped to pass restrictions on abortion services at state and local levels. While the preferences, desires and intentions of evangelical organizations were shaped by their religious ideology, the concrete political institutions of Britain and America influenced the political success and behaviour of those groups.

An important aspect of evangelical activism was the conflict between the enthusiasm of leaders who refused to compromise their political objectives and the political need for realism and bargaining. Evangelicals brought to the temperance and abortion cause a religious ideology which legitimated their involvement, made them devoted participants in the cause, and con-tributed to their fervour. However, political realities necessitated a certain degree of accommodation for temperance and abortion organizations to succeed politically. This is a dilemma faced by all social movement organizations where advocacy of a set of values and principles is central to the group's self-understanding.

The difficulty for the student of social movements is to determine when ideology is the predominant factor in the behaviour of a social group and when state structures become paramount. Chapter 2 tries to resolve this issue with the argument that social movements have a two-phase analytically distinct process. Ideology predominates in the phase of group formation. A group's beliefs, values, and norms give the justification necessary for people to form and join a social or political movement. Institutional factors become progressively more important as organized groups attempt to realize their political goals. Group ideology continues to be politically significant in this phase of group activism, but groups have a greater incentive to compromise their ideology as they seek political change. Chapter 2 also outlines and critiques the four competing social movement theories: status, rational choice, resource mobilization and state structure theory.

Chapter 3 provides an extended definition of evangelicalism to show how this religious ideology helps legitimate group formation, define group goals, and influence the behaviour of adherents. Much of the data for this chapter comes from interviews conducted with British evangelicals and group literature from American and British evangelical organizations. The interviews were conducted with the following people: David Coffee, Executive Director, Baptist Union; The Rev. Alan Gibson, Director, British Evangelical Council; Kathryn Ede, Legislative Assistant, CARE (Christian Action Research Education); Dr David Bennett, Director, Christian Alliance; Mr Graham Webster-Gardiner, Chairman, Conservative Family Campaign; Clive Calver, General Director, Evangelical Alliance; the Rev. Malcolm Laver, Executive Director, Fellowship of Independent Evangelical Churches; Dr John Ling, Chairman, Evangelicals for LIFE; the Rev. Duncan White, Director, London City Mission; Martyn Eden, Research and Publications Director, London Institute for Contemporary Christianity; John Roberts, Executive Director, The Lord's Day Observance Society; the Rev. David Winter, Director, Religious Broadcasting for the BBC; Tim Dean, editor of *Third Way*; and Patrick Dearnley, Archbishop's Officer for Urban Priority Areas. Interest group literature was gathered from the following groups: American Life League, California Coalition for Traditional Values, Christian Action Council, Christian Americans for Life, Christian Crusade, Christian Coalition, Christian Life Commission of the Southern Baptist Convention, Christian Voice, Citizens Against Pornography, Eagle Forum, Focus on the Family, Liberty Foundation, Methodists for Life, Morality in Media, National Association of Evangelicals, National Council of Bible Believing Christians in America, National Religious Broadcasters, Operation Rescue, Religious Roundtable, and Traditional Values Coalition. Chapter 3 discusses the findings of this research.

Chapter 4 offers a case study of evangelical activism in the Temperance Movement in Britain and America. The chapter shows how evangelical mobilization occurred because of a religious opposition to drinking. Evangelicals fused a biblical teaching about the Christian obligation to work for a better world with the cultural values of believers about the dangers of alcohol, to justify the formation of religious groups to combat drinking. Once groups were formed, however, American and British state structures determined the political success of each nation's temperance movement. Contemporary work of evangelicals active in the temperance movement in Britain and America provides much of the evidence for this discussion.

Chapters 5 and 6 examine the recent evangelical activism in America and Britain primarily around the issue of abortion, but also includes a discussion of the evangelical involvement around the issues of pornography and religion in state-supported schools. Chapter 5 also shows that evangelicals mobilized because of their religiously-based opposition to specific social practices. Evangelical group leaders used the Bible to reinforce cultural values about human sexuality and to motivate believers to join the moral protest against what were deemed to be sinful social practices.

Chapter 6 demonstrates how governmental structures in Britain and America determined the political success of evangelical organizations. American evangelicals took advantage of a porous political system which gave them multiple opportunities for meaningful political action. British evangelicals, by contrast, inherited a unitary political system which was not as open to the political penetration of social movements and so they were severely restricted in how they could politicize moral issues. The evidence for these chapters comes from the personal interviews conducted with British evangelicals active in the pro-life and anti-pornography movements and group literature of all the major American and British evangelical political organizations. Finally, Chapter 7 assesses the overall strengths and weaknesses of the social movement theory proposed and discusses the future of evangelical politics in Britain and America.

The political activism of American evangelicals has received much attention in recent years.[2] But there have been very few studies which have historically or cross-culturally compared evangelical politics.[3] The comparative and historical analysis of this book provides the basis to judge the ideological and institutional component of group mobilization and activism. Britain and America are good case studies for a number of reasons.

First, evangelical Christianity has been an important aspect of each nation's religious history. Evangelicalism was born in England and quickly spread to America. Evangelicals in each nation have been at the forefront of moral campaigns in the past and present, which allows a test of the hypothesis that ideology has been the dominant factor in mobilization. Secondly, American and British political institutions are different enough to demonstrate the importance of state structures in the political action of ideologically similar organizations. If institutions matter, as I propose they do, a contrast between America's federal and Britain's unitary polity is a good way to test my hypothesis.

The chapters that follow demonstrate how an evangelical ideology shaped the social values and political choices of adherents in Britain and America, and how political institutions, in turn, influenced the political expression of those religious ideas and shaped the political outcome of evangelical politics.

2 Theories of Social Movement Mobilization

Over the past two hundred years, American and British evangelical Christians have been politically active in social movements. In the nineteenth century, evangelicals became convinced that drinking was the root of the religious and social problems in their respective nations and they formed a movement to prohibit the sale and consumption of alcohol. In the past several decades, evangelicals on both sides of the Atlantic have organized a social movement to impose restrictions on abortion services and the publication of pornographic material. Evangelical activism leads to important questions about the study of social movements, particularly about what the cause of social belief and action might be.

Scholars have posited several theories of group formation that become relevant in considering evangelical social movements. The four most prominent are status, rational choice, resource mobilization and state structure theory. While there is some overlapping among these theories, they are nonetheless distinct and important enough alternatives to merit individual consideration. The theories are primarily distinguished by which aspect of a social group they address. Status and rational choice theories are primarily interested in the process of group formation; resource mobilization and state structure theories emphasize the factors that contribute to the political success of a group.

The status or psychological theory of Richard Hofstadter, Neil Smelser, and Joseph Gusfield stresses the relationship among group identity, status discontent, and movement emergence.[1] In this theory, ethnicity, religiosity or language defines a group, and mobilization occurs from groups wanting to raise or maintain their social status. The rational choice accounts of Mancur Olson, Terry Moe, Michael Hechter, and Kenneth Shepsle and Barry Wiengast emphasize the reasons why people join organizations and the strategic behaviour of group leaders.[2] Borrowing the language of utility calculation from economics, a rational choice theory explains organizational formation and activism by examining the costs and benefits of group participation. The focus is on the individual's objectives in joining a group. The resource mobilization theory of William Gamson, Mayer Zald and John McCarthy highlights how organizations raise the resources necessary to institutionalize a social movement.[3] This theory explains how the structures of existing groups are mobilized for a new cause. The state structure model of Theda Skocpol, Charles Tilly and Stephen Krasner accents the ways in which political institutions and elites influence the life of a social group. This theory stresses how governmental institutions condition the objective possibility of a successful protest.[4]

None of the inherited theories gives sufficient attention to the importance of substantive ideas and values in the life of evangelical social groups. These theories focus on material or easily-measurable benefits, but for many organizations, especially religiously-based groups, the incentives which attract members are altruistic or ideological. The theory proposed in this book highlights more explicitly how a shared evangelical ideology contributes to group formation. It builds upon the insights of various analysts who have noted the importance of evangelical cultural values, lifestyles, and world-views in their political mobilization.[5]

This chapter offers a critique of the existing theories of social movements and proposes an outline for an alternative model. First, the four social movement theories are reviewed, with particular attention given to the question of where group ideology might fit into the theories, if at all. Then, a brief definition of ideology is provided followed by a discussion of how group ideology is important for the development of social movements.

The chapter concludes with an alternative theory which divides the study of social movements into the analytically discrete stages of group formation and group activism. An ideology, or shared belief system, is the most important factor which explains how individuals form and join the groups which constitute a social movement. A commitment to enduring values is the primary motivation for the formation of a social movement. Group activism, however, is influenced by the political structures of a given nation. Different political institutions create different opportunities and incentives for activism and shape the ability of groups to achieve their political goals. The process outlined in this book is an interactive one; issues surrounding group formation and activism occur throughout a group's life.[6] In order to understand the political action of the groups which constitute a social movement, it is necessary to know something about the norms of group members and the political structures of the state.

THE ROLE OF STATUS IN GROUP MOBILIZATION

Status theory rests on the claim that if one knows the social status of a group, organized or unorganized, one can determine its proclivity to collective action. The connection between system strain, group discontent, and collective action is highlighted in status theory with the following causal model assumed: system strain causes feelings of anxiety (threatened social status) which leads to group formation and collective political action. In status theory, discontent is felt at a group level in the form of a threatened social status. Social change or system breakdown influences the way in which a group perceives its social status *vis-à-vis* other groups. Collective action occurs in order for a group to protect, maintain or raise its social status.

Richard Hofstadter and Seymour Martin Lipset introduced the concept of status politics in the late 1950s to describe the roots of anti-intellectualism and the sources of McCarthyism. Theorists quickly adapted a status model, however, to explain Progressivism,[7] Prohibition,[8] the New Christian Right in America,[9] and the Pro-Life Movement in Britain.[10] Joseph Gusfield's *Symbolic Crusade*, a theoretical account of temperance activism in the United States, was the most significant of these efforts. Gusfield used the concept of status to explain the history of temperance agitation in America. Gusfield explained the temperance movement as a form of collective action designed 'to raise or maintain the prestige of a group'.[11] Drinking, according to Gusfield, was an indicator of group identity and social status in late-nineteenth and early-twentieth-century America. Groups were demarcated on the basis of their attitude toward alcohol, and drinking and abstinence thereby became symbols of a group's social status. Temperance represented the values of middle-class American Protestants who adhered to an ethic of self-control, sobriety and industriousness. Immigrant cultures threatened the status of native evangelical Protestants by presenting an alternative style of life where drinking alcohol was customary. Evangelicals experienced status discontent in the wake of immigration because 'the prestige accorded to them (evangelical Protestants) was less than that which the group expected'.[12]

Temperance politics emerged in the 1850s as a way for middle-class Protestants to impress upon immigrants 'the central power and dominance of native American Protestant morality'.[13] American evangelical Protestants, who felt that their values and social status were threatened by immigrant groups, responded by trying to raise their status through the temperance movement. Temperance activists turned to political institutions because 'governments affect the distribution of values through symbolic acts'.[14] Success in the Prohibition campaign meant 'the symbolic conferral of respect upon the norms of the victor', while defeat led to the 'disrespect upon the norms of the vanquished'.[15] Victory in temperance politics, in short, was achieved when the state acknowledged the superiority of evangelical, Anglo-Saxon Protestant values over the norms of immigrant cultures. The Prohibition Amendment was the high point of temperance activism. Evangelical Protestant cultural hegemony had been sufficiently threatened by immigrants by the turn of the century that political action through a constitutional amendment was necessary to reconfirm their social status.

Status theory is part of a larger group of psychological models of collective behaviour; the most prominent of these models is that of Neil Smelser.[16] Smelser defines collective behaviour as 'an uninstitutionalized mobilization for action in order to modify one or more kinds of strain'.[17] Strain, according to Smelser, is a necessary condition for collective behaviour: 'For any episode of collective behaviour, we shall always find some kind of structural strain in the background'.[18] There are any number of possible causes of system strain, but Smelser highlights economic deprivation, war, massive immigration, and industrialization as major determinants. Feelings of craze, panic, anxiety or hostility are brought on when there is a disruption in the normal operations of a social system, and collective action occurs among individuals who want to eliminate the cause of their anxiety. Movement participation is intended to resolve the dissonance individuals feel in the light of system strain.

Two major criticisms of status and psychological theory have been that they fail to take account of the role of organizations in a collective movement and that they deprecate the importance of group ideology in collective behaviour.[19] Status and psychological theory assume a one-to-one correspondence between discontent and collective action which is never demonstrated. Smelser asserts that 'some form of strain must be present if an episode of collective behaviour is to occur',[20] but he does not indicate how a grievance becomes institutionalized. Gusfield argues that status discontent created evangelical Protestant mobilization around temperance, but he too neglects to show how those values took organizational form. The reader is led to conclude from both Smelser and Gusfield that organizations will naturally arise to represent the concerns of individuals and groups experiencing social strain or status discontent. Resource mobilization theorists, however, have correctly argued that the existence of grievances is not a sufficient condition for episodes of collective behaviour, because discontent is omnipresent. Feelings of anxiety, threat, or declining social status by some particular group are endemic to political change, but not all affected groups are able or willing to mobilize for political action. What explains the rise of a particular organization is the existence of a set of skilled leaders who can use those grievances to raise resources for organizations.

Status and psychological theory are also deficient in their treatment of group ideology. The metaphors used in status and psychological theory betray a bias against those groups who engage in ideological crusades.

Status movements are posed as an alternative to 'normal' politics where rational individuals and groups pursue self-interested ends. In contrast, the collective action of a status group is a 'politics of backlash . . . and despair';[21] it is impatient and marked by feelings 'of anxiety, fantasy, and hostility'.[22] Since status theory defines 'normal' politics as the pursuit of rational/instrumental goals, it follows that groups interested in symbolic or expressive ends are somehow irrational. Status theory cannot appreciate that political mobilization around 'ideological' or 'cultural' issues can be a rational response by an affected group to social change, because status accounts believe that ideologies themselves are an irrational response to the world.

Both theories attribute adherence to an ideology to feelings of strain, cognitive dissonance, or loss of status and conclude that the ideological component of social movement formation is irrational. What I am arguing is that adherence to an ideology can be intelligible, purposeful and rational; ideologies provide the meaning necessary for social action. While it is true that social movements form when changes in the social world disrupt the beliefs, values and obligations of a group's ideology, it is not the case that this response to change is irrational. If ideologies are viewed as a basic human need and therefore endemic to society, social movements which form in response to a challenge to an ideology can also be understood as purposive. As Roy Wallis notes, 'moral indignation is a normal response to the violation of any deeply cherished norm or value'.[23] Social movement formation occurs as group members try to protect basic norms of their belief system and in so doing maintain their ability to comprehend their social world.

The assumption that ideologies are irrational explains the inability of status theory to take account of the motives given by actors for their social action. Gusfield, for example, showed little interest in the stated claims of temperance activists because their assertions about their own involvement did not fit his status theory. Temperance literature appealed to people in terms of the moral obligations they felt toward the drinker. The assumption was that evangelical Protestants had religious reasons to be concerned about the social and spiritual costs of drinking. It is possible, of course, that temperance activists really were motivated by a desire for status improvement, but that they just didn't want to admit it. Gusfield, however, provides no evidence to prove this claim. Gusfield's mistake, as Wallis correctly argued, is to turn a functional claim into a causal one: 'To identify the consequences of an action as tending to enhance status does not impugn the religious and moral motives of those involved.'[24] Securing temperance legislation may have increased the status of evangelical Christians but that consequence is not proof that status concern was the cause of evangelical mobilization.

In Britain and America, the temperance movement was led by evangelical Protestants who were increasingly concerned about the social, moral and political consequences of alcohol. As is demonstrated in more detail in Chapter 4, drinking and a drink culture disrupted the moral order of an evangelical ideology which taught believers that they had a responsibility for the social and spiritual world of the drinker. Liquor and the saloons and beer-halls symbolized many of the cultural tendencies which threatened an evangelical ideology: drunkenness, broken family-lives and lost sinners. Alcohol and drinking establishments competed with the goals of evangelical religion. As drinking increased in the late nineteenth century, so too did the problems associated with alcohol and the concern of evangelicals for their 'wayward' neighbours who drank. Temperance appealed to evangelicals who wanted to reinvigorate their ideology with meaning in the face of the challenge symbolized by alcohol. The relationship between ideology and social meaning and the manner in which a belief system defines social responsibilities for group members cannot adequately be explained using a broad, ill-defined characteristic like status.[25]

In their failure to take ideas seriously, status and psychological theory are unable to account for the mobilization of groups into a social movement. The ideology which motivates group activism need not be irrational, as these theories claim; instead, an ideology can provide a set of principles which make social action intelligible. Ideological movements are not necessarily a response to status deprivation, cognitive dissonance or any other psychological feelings of anxiety. Social movements form among people who are committed to the tenets of an ideology which is challenged by social change.

Sociological accounts have responded to these criticisms and broadened the concept of status politics into a more encompassing 'politics of lifestyle concern' model.[26] These recent works have greatly improved status theory by focusing on group values instead of group status as the impetus for social mobilization. Page and Clelland argue that status politics should not be viewed as 'the attempt to defend against declining prestige but the attempt to defend a way of life'.[27] The focus in the reformulated status theory is less on group status and more on group values and way of life. The political mobilization of affected groups is explained as a rational and realistic effort to protect and defend the values and institutions which support the group. Louise Lorentzen asserts that 'lifestyle concern is the motivating factor and preservation of a life style is the goal of non-economic movements'.[28]

The politics of lifestyle concern model retains the distinction drawn in status theory between economic and non-economic motivations for political movements, but jettisons virtually everything else from the inherited theory. In fact, orthodox status theory is so changed that it is almost unrecognizable in the more recent accounts. The theory of evangelical mobilization which is offered later in this chapter builds upon the politics of lifestyle approach to social movement formation. Following Lorentzen, Wallis, and Page and Clelland, I show how non-economic factors such as group values, ideology and religious beliefs, rather than group status, can be a motivation for the political mobilization of social groups.

RATIONALITY AND GROUP BEHAVIOUR

A rational choice theory of collective action explains group formation by focusing on the individual's decision to join a group. The theory assumes that individuals act autonomously and with a view to interest or utility maximization in deciding to join a group. People, behaving as rational persons do in market situations, make decisions about joining groups by weighing the costs of participation against the benefits to be derived through membership. The key process is the individual calculus that occurs in the mind of each potential member. Given these assumptions, a rational choice theory highlights the barriers to group formation and collective action.

Mancur Olson introduced a rational choice model to the study of collective action in his seminal work, *The Logic of Collective Action*.[29] Olson wrote primarily about the formation of economic interest groups, but his analysis has been applied to non-economic social groups.[30] Olson rejects the implicit assumption of status theory that group status is the fundamental determinant of political behaviour. Status theory assumes that every group with a discernible social status can have an organization representing it. Olson argues that a common status, by itself, cannot motivate people to join groups. Individuals will not join a social group to work for the interests of their status group unless it is in their individual interest to do so. Olson concludes that 'rational, self-interested individuals will not act to achieve their common or group interests . . . unless there is coercion to force them to do so, or unless some separate incentive, distinct from the achievement of the common or group interest, is offered to members of the group individually on the condition that they help bear the costs or burdens involved in the achievement of the group objectives'.[31] Unless special conditions are met, self-interested individuals will not join groups to achieve their common interests.

Olson arrives at this conclusion by assuming that individuals are rational and economically self-interested, and by applying the logic of collective goods to group formation. When individuals have a collective interest in some political goal it usually takes the form of a collective good. Collective goods are those benefits which cannot be restricted to group members alone. A classic example of a collective good is clean air. Many people would benefit from cleaner air, but the provision of that good cannot be restricted only to those people who pay for it by driving their cars less or by joining environmental groups which lobby for pollution controls. Legalized abortion is also a collective good. A legal abortion cannot be limited to those women who 'pay' for the 'good' by joining a Pro-Choice organization which pursues that common interest. Since anyone can enjoy a collective good without paying for it, there is no reason to join a group which promises to provide the good. A rational, economically self-interested individual has no incentive to join a group when he or she can receive the good without paying for it.

The primary way groups form, according to Olson, is through the provision of selective incentives to group members. Groups can attract members by providing added or selective incentives which benefit only due-paying members. Olson writes that 'the incentive must be selective so that those who do not join the organization working for the group's interest . . . can be treated differently from those who do'.[32] Such incentives can be positive inducements, such as low-cost insurance, or they can be negative ones, for example social sanctions directed against those unwilling to join a group. These incentives give people a 'rational' reason to join a group which is not available to groups which only offer members a collective good. In theory, an incentive can be any social good, including power, status, health or happiness. In his discussion of group behaviour, however, Olson 'suggests' the analogy to a competitive market where firms seek to maximize wealth above all other values.[33]

Rational choice theory focuses primarily on organizations where behaviour is driven by a careful calculation of the costs and the benefits of group participation. The only relevant consideration for an individual, given such an assumption, is determining what he or she will gain by group membership. The reliance on self-interest as the driving force for individual behaviour helps rational choice theory explain why not every interest has a group to represent it, a relationship not explained by status theory. It is not as able, however, to explain those social groups which organize in the absence of a meaningful monetary reward or selective incentive. Olson's rational choice theory has very little to say about group ideology, except to imply that organizations which form on the basis of group norms are irrational events which can best be explained by psychologists.[34]

The primary weakness of a rational choice theory of collective action is that it denies that a group's ideology and values can motivate individuals to join organizations. What I am claiming is that a group's ideology can help organizations overcome the collective action problems outlined by Olson and that social movements can still be explained as meaningful, rational events. Despite Olson's scepticism about the success of collective action, social groups do form and often without 'overcoming' the specific limits to collective action which he outlines. Environmental lobbies organize in America despite the fact that the desired result is for the collective good of a cleaner, healthier world. Abortion mobilizes millions of men and women into competing organizations, a mass behaviour which is difficult to explain if one takes seriously the collective goods problem outlined in rational choice theory. The free-rider problem is largely irrelevant for ideological organizations. Pro-choice groups would happily tolerate billions of people enjoying the collective good of legalized abortions even if few of them ever contributed to achieving it.[35]

There is no reason to accept the claim of rational choice theory that people can only rationally join a collective action group if they receive something of monetary value in return. An alternative explanation is that people join social movement organizations because it provides meaning for them and because they share the goals of the movement. Group members feel compelled to join environmental, abortion and peace organizations because they share the norms of the group. People join a pro-life group, for example, because legal abortion threatens to undermine their religious ideology. Abortion violates particular religious norms that the unborn foetus is a human and that God ought to control reproductivity. Rational choice theory has given no compelling reason to reject out of hand what actors say about their involvement in organizations. The reasons given by actors for their activism refer to the values they hold. While Olson is aware that groups have common interests, goals, and values, he fails to appreciate how those shared convictions are important for group formation independent of rational self-interest.

Terry Moe, Kenneth Shepsle and Barry Weingast have attempted to save the logic of rational choice theory by expanding the notion of selective incentives and focusing on how institutional structures affect the expression of individual and group interests.[36] In so doing, work in the rational choice tradition has responded to critics who claimed that the theory did not account for the non-material interests of actors. These new rational choice theorists elaborate on Olson's account by looking at how group leaders help ensure group formation and maintenance by overcoming the limitations inherent to collective action outlined by Olson. The most important function of a leader in group formation is the creation of 'an administrative apparatus for the production and distribution of valuable incentive packages to members'.[37] A group leader has access not only to material resources but also to the non-material incentives of solidary and purposive interests, defined by Moe as 'various kinds of intangible benefits that accrue to a person by virtue of his support of causes, value systems, or ends that he considers worthwhile'.[38] Rational individuals, therefore, can be appealed to on the basis of the 'intangible rewards' which follow from group participation.

Michael Hechter has also linked rational choice theory to the mobilization of solidary and purposive groups.[39] Hechter contends that actors form such groups 'to attain jointly produced goods that they desire but cannot provide at all, or as efficiently, for themselves'.[40] While the rewards for membership in such groups are such non-economic incentives as fellowship, belonging, or even the promise of salvation, group formation still follows from the production of goods to members. Even a religious sect, therefore, can be understood and explained in terms of the manner in which goods are produced and allocated to members.

The rational choice theory of Moe, Hechter and Shepsle and Weingast does not disparage group ideology in the way that Olson does. In fact, these theorists take great pains to demonstrate that political actors can rationally be guided by purposive considerations such as loyalty to a cause or commitment to a norm. Taking interests as a given, rational choice accounts can explain how individual or group goals might be most efficiently pursued. Group interests, however, ought not to be taken as a given, but should instead be explained. Why do some groups of people come to oppose abortion on demand? How are the preferences of a member of the organization Earth First formed? Aaron Wildavsky warns that it is 'unreasonable to neglect the study of why people want what they want'.[41] Organizations may offer purposive incentives to potential members in the way outlined by Hechter, but these incentives only take on value for people who accept the worth and goals of a particular organization, which leads us back to the question of how people come to value certain ends. As Rogers Smith has noted, however, rational choice theory cannot explain how people come to possess their basic interests.[42]

The revised rational choice theory also gives insufficient attention to the role of ideology in the life of a purposive group. An interpretive grasp of the ideologies that groups possess is necessary to understand their political choices. Randall Terry, founder of the pro-life group Operation Rescue, directly links a religious ideology to a political choice on the issue of abortion:

God has called us to take a public stand against abortion. We are not only standing for the children and mothers but as witnesses of God's righteous laws. We testify to a rebellious generation that they will give an account to God for their actions on the day of judgement. We stand as witnesses before the hosts of hell that God still has a people who uphold His law and stand against wickedness.[43]

Terry's rhetoric has force for those people who share an ideology which teaches them that they have a religious obligation to oppose legalized abortion. Terry's pro-life language appeals to evangelical Christians who come to the abortion debate with a set of beliefs which inform them that they have a moral obligation to the unborn foetus and to God. Believers do not become active in the pro-life cause from a utilitarian calculus of the benefits they will receive from group membership. Instead, they join pro-life organizations because they believe they have a responsibility to mobilize against a social behaviour like abortion which threatens their religious and cultural convictions.

The suggestion that some social groups are more amenable to ideological than material appeals does not dispense with the need for logical scrutiny of ideological or expressive behaviour. Groups which appeal to members on the basis of a shared ideology can still pursue their objectives in a rational manner. Ideological groups can make strategic decisions about the most 'pragmatic' means to achieve their long-term interests. A rational choice model is less helpful, however, as an explanation for organizations where group goals are the major inducement for membership. The language of individual incentives used in this model cannot capture the level of support these groups obtain.

RESOURCES AND COLLECTIVE ACTION

Resource mobilization theories of collective action encompass a variety of disparate analysts who share three major characteristics: a rejection of status or psychological models of group behaviour, an accent on the role of resources in mobilizing groups, and a stress on the organizational structures which link individuals into a social movement.[44] Beginning with the work of Mayer Zald, John McCarthy and William Gamson, resource mobilization has been a revisionist attempt to understand social movement formation, with a heavy emphasis on organizations and institutions.

Resource mobilization theory shares with rational choice theory a scepticism about the likelihood that every social interest will have an organization to represent it. The barrier to mobilization, however, is not self-interest, as with rational choice, but the lack of resources. Without adequate resources there can be no social movement organization. Zald and McCarthy write that 'the transformation of social movement theory rests upon the recognition that the mobilization of resources (labour, materials, and money) for collective action is problematic'.[45] A large number of people may identify with a set of political goals and logically be included as part of that social movement, but not all of them will be members of organizations representing those goals. Collective goods, religious values, political ideology, each can be the basis for mobilization, but only if the necessary resources to ensure organizational formation can be raised. Resource mobilization shifts the emphasis away from incentives, which was so central for a rational choice theory, but it maintains the conviction that there are limitations to collective action.

The major limitation for a social movement is how to translate a shared set of values into an organizational structure. Resource theory highlights the role of a skilled cadre of leaders who are able to capitalize on common values. Since mobilization demands control over resources, the primary task of a leader is to translate an amorphously-held value into political capital. The entrepreneur overcomes the limits to collective action by mobilizing resources for the shared value. A leader accomplishes this task by convincing people who are sympathetic to the goals of a social movement to become mobilized into a social movement organization. The entrepreneurial role is similar in resource mobilization and rational choice theory, though the former highlights politicized social movements while the latter explains collective action of any kind. In both theories there is a cynical undertone which implies that ideas are manipulated by group leaders who are more concerned about raising group resources than the ideology they purport to represent. 'Successful' entrepreneurs are those who use the existence of shared ideals to raise needed resources, thereby overcoming the collective action problem. Ideological identity is understood simply as a potential resource; there is no understanding that group leaders might themselves accept the values of the ideology, nor is there an interest to examine the content of the ideologies to which group leaders appeal.

According to resource mobilization theory, the success of a social movement organization can be explained by looking at the kind of organizational infrastructures that leaders encounter in their mobilization attempt. William Gamson notes that 'successful mobilization depends on recruitment networks in which friends and acquaintances from other organizations are drawn into collective action'.[46] Successful social movements are characterized by a well-established institutional structure from which group leaders draw resources to form new organizations. Jack Walker points out that group leaders can also play an important role in securing 'both start-up funds and reliable sources of continuing financial support from patrons of political action'.[47] These internal networks are initially important for recruitment into social movement organizations. Civil Rights groups recruited members and received resources from religious and educational groups already existing within the black community.[48] Pro-Choice groups similarly took advantage of the existing Catholic and Protestant church organizations.[49] In discussing the outcome of a Billy Graham Crusade, Johnson, Choate and Bunis conclude that 'the major vehicle for the promotion of a Graham crusade is the local church. Local church organizations provide the people and money that make a Crusade possible.'[50] In each case, a pre-existing infrastructure lowered the costs of access to potential members and resources, thereby making movement formation more likely.

The infrastructure of evangelical political organizations has come from a base of existing churches in ways predicted by a resource theory.[51] Group leaders and political entrepreneurs have successfully used religious institutions to form political protest groups. While the stress on institutions is a helpful addition to a theory of collective action, resource mobilization theory emphasizes that role to the detriment of questions about group ideology. The theory, though not wrong, gives insufficient attention to how an ideology can shape a group's political choices.

The 'dense networks' of churches, parochial schools and religious organizations do *more* than just reduce the costs of group mobilization. Their role is not just institutional but also cultural and ideological. Catholic and evangelical institutions pass on to their members an ideological system with a set of beliefs, values and ideals. A social movement has access not simply to the material resources of the Church in mobilizing abortion groups, but also to the shared ideology that a 'good' Catholic or evangelical will think abortion is sinful. The values which religious institutions and believers share make it possible for group leaders to work through existing organizational networks.

What role does a resource theory give to ideology in group-mobilization? A social movement is defined by Zald and McCarthy as 'a set of opinions and beliefs in a population representing preferences for changing some element of the social structure or reward distribution of a society'.[52] Implicit in this definition is an understanding of ideology as a shared set of values and norms on the part of some population of people. In contrast to psychological and status theories, resource mobilization accounts do not assume that these shared ideals are irrational. But the theory does not discuss why and how ideological grievances arise which produce a social movement, nor what role ideology plays in the political choices made by social groups.

Interests are taken for granted, as is evident in the very broad definition of social movements which Zald and McCarthy offer. Resource mobilization theory is less interested in the content of the ideas which are shared by a population than in the institutions which these ideas have in place. Gamson notes that 'the meanings that participants give to their involvement in collective action are made to seem largely irrelevant'.[53] They are 'irrelevant' because resource mobilization theory seems to believe that *any* 'set of opinions which represent preferences for changing some element of the social structure'[54] is sufficient for mobilization given the right kind of resources.

Successful movements are distinguished by the raising of resources, which is highly problematic, and not a shared set of grievances, which is omnipresent. The implication is that different groups would, given the same set of resources, respond in a similar way. But are all ideas the same? Do all ideas have an equal potential to mobilize a population? I say no. Some ideas are held with deeper conviction than others and therefore have a greater capacity for group mobilization. Some values are more central than others to the coherence of an ideology, a fact which any successful group leader recognizes in the effort to form a group. Ideas also influence the choices of organized groups. One cannot explain the unwillingness of many pro-life and pro-choice groups to compromise on the abortion issue without reference to the ideological commitment of group-members to the cause.

Group ideology is important for the study of social movements because shared values can be the energy which drives the process of group formation. Ideology also shapes, and to a certain extent determines, the political choices made by group leaders. Resource mobilization theory effectively analyzes the institutional side of a social movement, but it does not give sufficient weight to the specifics of group ideology which influence both group formation and activism. The theory presented in this book focuses more directly on the influence of ideology in evangelical organizations.

STATE STRUCTURES AND SOCIAL MOBILIZATION

State structure theory places the state, viewed as a social actor and an institution, at the centre of analytical attention.[55] The theory highlights the direct and indirect ways in which state officials and institutions influence social policy. Viewed as a social actor, the state is understood in state structure theory as an internally coherent bureaucratic machinery which has its own set of policy preferences which can be divergent from the most powerful private actors. Stephen Krasner claims that states have 'peculiar drives, compulsions, and aims of their own that are separate and distinct from the interests of any particular societal group'.[56] The degree to which the state is 'autonomous' from social groups determines its capacity to shape public policy. In this 'strong' version of state structure theory, states are viewed as autonomous and active participants in the formation of public policy.

The 'weaker' version of state structure theory emphasizes the ways in which state institutions influence the relationship between social groups and the state. The stress here is less on the capacity of the state to have autonomous interests and power and more on how particular characteristics of a regime, including its constitutional and legal order, structure and therefore influence the context in which social action occurs. Peter Hall refers to the 'organizational factors' of a nation which determine the degree of power that any set of actors has over policy outcomes.[57] The making of political choices is intimately related, in this version of state theory, to the particular political institutions of a regime. Scholars who adopt a state structure theory usually combine these two approaches to the state when explaining a specific political outcome.

Since state structure theory is principally interested in state–society relations, by implication the theory has a lot to say about social movement mobilization and activism. State structure theory has been used by Theda Skocpol to explain revolutionary outcomes in France, China and Russia, by Robert Wuthnow to explain the success of the Protestant Reformation in France and England, by Ira Katznelson to compare working-class consciousness in nineteenth-century England and America, and by Skocpol and Ann Shola Orloff to determine the levels of public spending between Britain and America at the beginning of the twentieth century. These disparate analysts share a focus on how the structure of state power influenced the political behaviour of social actors and contributed to an historical outcome.[58]

State structural theory demonstrates that the political outcome of a social movement is influenced more by objective political conditions than by the subjective feelings of movement activists. Wuthnow convincingly shows that the different results for the Protestant Reformation in England and France are best explained by different levels of state power in the two nations.[59] The fervour, activism or popular support of religious reformers in the two nations is not a factor Wuthnow uses to explain the success of the England Reformation. Instead, he argues that the decisive factor was 'the relative autonomy of the central state bureaucracy from the landowning elite which was closely tied to the established church'.[60] Since the English and French landed ruling-class benefited from the established church, the Reformation could only succeed if state officials introduced policies to threaten the Catholic Church. In order to disrupt the Church, however, state officials needed a high degree of autonomy from the aristocracy, who opposed the Reformation. Henry's autonomy from the aristocracy made it possible for him to initiate policies conducive to the Reformation, while French state officials had no analogous autonomy and power from the aristocracy. Henry's famous divorce case provided an incentive for a state imposition of the Reformation from above but, without 'a favorable arrangement in the structure of power', Henry would have been unable to carry out his policy.[61]

State structure theory is correct to emphasize the importance of state institutions in shaping the political outcome of a social movement. The political institutions and elites most closely related to the making and implementing of political decisions have a greater impact on a nation's policy-choices than do the aspirations of group members. The ability of a social movement to affect policy outcomes depends to a large degree on the institutional structures groups inherit. The representative, administrative, electoral and bureaucratic forms of a government shape the social behaviour of movement organizations and influence their political success.

The claim that institutions have an impact on social action is not, however, new to state structure theory. A stress on the importance of political institutions as exogenous variables has been central to American politics as far back as Madison's contribution to the *Federalist Papers*, and has been highlighted more recently by, among others, Dahl, Wilson and Lowi.[62] State structure theory is, I argue, at its best when it limits itself to this institutional analysis of politics, when it focuses on the formal relationships between organized groups and the state. As I argue below, social movements are influenced at the stage of group activism by the characteristics of a political regime. For many state structure theorists, however, bringing the state back in involves more than a renewed emphasis on political institutions. Bringing the state back in also means, according to Evans, Rueschemeyer and Skocpol 'spelling out the ways in which states influence the *meaning and methods* of politics for all groups and classes' (my emphasis). The authors imply that state structures determine not only the political outcome of a social movement, but also the 'meaning', i.e. the interests and norms, which social actors bring to their political involvement. It is this claim, that state institutions determine the meaning of political action for social actors, that I question in the pages below.[63]

State structural theory is important for my purposes because, in its 'stronger' version, it rejects the claim that group ideology is the decisive factor explaining the norms of a social movement organization. State structural analysis shifts the focus of collective action theory from group ideology to governmental behaviour. Theda Skocpol, in *States and Social Revolutions*, explains the French, Russian and Chinese Revolutions without referring to the ideas of revolutionaries. Skocpol contends that these revolutions occurred because the administrative and military power of the state broke down and *not* 'because of deliberate activities on the part of avowed revolutionaries'.[64] Peter Hall, in a comparison of economic policies in Britain and France, claims that state institutions 'can structure the very logic associated with rational action. . . . Not only does organization alter the power of a social group, it can also affect the interpretation they put on their interests.'[65] In short, state structure theory has a tendency to view group ideology not as an exogenous variable but as a component of a set of social structures.

The principal weakness of state theories of collective action is that they completely ignore the importance of group ideology in explaining the origin, goals and timing of a social movement. While it may be possible to explain the political *outcome* of revolutionary or religious reform movements with reference only to the structural capacity for group activism, it is not possible to understand the *origin* of a social movement without examining the meaning participants give to their political involvement. The ideologies which motivate people to form and join a social movement do not originate because of a favourable arrangement in the structure of state power. A reformation or a revolutionary ideology occurs when the prevailing religious and political ideology is destroyed. The widespread challenge to the principle that Rome had supremacy in spiritual matters made the Reformation possible in the sixteenth century; the loss of belief in the divine right of kings in the seventeenth century allowed for the ideological innovation which called into question the legitimacy of the French state. An analysis of political institutions cannot, by itself, provide the answer to the question of how ideologies arise which lead to the mobilization of social movements. The formation of such an ideology is more important to social movement development than state structure theory allows.

In Chapters 4, 5, and 6 I show how British and American evangelical Christians shared an ideology which led to their political opposition to legalized alcohol in the late nineteenth century and abortion in the twentieth century. These transatlantic believers had nearly identical values *despite* the fact that the structure of state power in the two regimes was different. The different sets of political institutions did influence the outcome of evangelical social movements in the two nations. American believers took advantage of a weak American state to affect policy outcomes in a way not possible for British evangelicals, who inherited a stronger state, which minimized their capacity to influence public policy. Those institutional differences did not, however, structure the content of group norms nor determine the timing of group formation in the way that state structure theory implies that institutions might. In order to understand why evangelicals came to oppose alcohol and abortion it is necessary to look closely at how group ideology was affected by those social practices.

This is not to claim that ideologies, once they are produced, will necessarily gain widespread acceptance. The capacity to institutionalize an ideology depends upon a stable access to resources, and state structures greatly influence the availability of economic and political resources. The alignment of ruling elites no doubt was crucial for raising the resources necessary for the eventual success of the English Reformation and the French Revolution. The production of an ideology to challenge the ruling religious and political elites in Britain and France, however, was not dependent upon resources, but on the breakdown of the prevailing belief system. The ideology of revolutionaries cannot be reduced to the imperatives of particular state institutions. State structure theory is so concerned to explain the political success or failure of a social movement that it fails to take account of why group grievances arise in the first place. Institutional arrangements and the particular interests of state elites can affect an ideology, but they do not determine when ideologies will form to fight for social prominence. The dismissal of ideology in state structural theories as a cause of political outcomes often leads analysts to neglect the important part played by ideologies in determining the timing and the political content of a social movement.[66]

A related problem of a state structure theory is that it narrowly defines the outcome of a social movement in terms of a group's ability to implement its political programme.[67] The outcomes of the English Reformation and French Revolution, for example, are judged by state structure theorists along the single, dichotomous variable of whether or not group norms were institutionalized. It is not clear, however, that such a simple variable can be applied to all social movements. Social movements serve a symbolic and a political function. They do pursue a political agenda, but they also represent the norms, beliefs and values of group members. If participants attach greater value to the meaning they receive from political action than in the pursued goals of the group, then a social movement can succeed symbolically despite political defeat. The very act of participating in the pro-life cause helps evangelicals and Catholics re-establish their moral order despite the political outcome of the abortion debate. State structure theory is not prepared to understand the myriad ways to analyze the outcome of social movement activism.[68]

While a theory of collective action should be aware of how groups respond to state institutions and how political outcomes are determined by state structures, it should also be sensitive to the claim that group ideology and mobilization precede that response. Before adopting a state structural model of social movements, one must understand the grievances that stimulate a social protest. To appreciate how people come to desire social change, why they organize groups to pressure political institutions, and what meaning they attach to their activism, it is essential to understand group ideology as a variable not reducible to state structures. With so great a stress on the role of state structures, in the hands of state structure theory the study of collective action becomes the study of a nation's politics, while the issue of group ideology becomes largely irrelevant.

In each of the case studies cited, the existence of a group with a political agenda is taken for granted. How specific groups legitimated that agenda and how they ensured organizational membership is not systematically explained in any of the analyses. The existence and behaviour of social movement organizations is important despite the powerful role of state structures. For example, it is apparent that Henry VIII had an objective interest in establishing a Protestant state church as opposed to a Catholic one in England and that his political autonomy from the landed classes made such a move possible. It is not clear, however, whether Henry would have been able to establish a Protestant church had there not been a pre-existing religious dispute in England, or if a different religious ideology would have served his political purposes. Henry did not create the ideological division between Catholics and Protestants in England. To understand how Henry used the religious division for his own end, one must understand the source of that division. How, for example, did the ideas of the reformers infiltrate English society? The importance of ideology and meaning can hardly be ignored when trying to explain the origin and attractiveness of a Protestant ideology for millions of people throughout Europe in the sixteenth and seventeenth centuries. The same is true for all organizations which form on the basis of a group ideology. To understand the attractiveness of certain ideas and the timing of group formation it is necessary to appreciate how people come to possess an ideology which leads them to form and join groups.

TOWARDS A DEFINITION OF IDEOLOGY

Ideology will here be defined as a set of values, ideas, and beliefs which give meaning and direction to the social experiences of adherents. Ideologies contain empirical descriptions of how the world is and, explicitly or implicitly, moral claims about how the world ought to be. These descriptive and normative claims provide meaning for actors in a complex social world; they enable adherents to give form and purpose to their disparate social experiences. An ideology is embedded in a group's social life together. As Wildavsky correctly points out, 'preferences come from the most ubiquitous human activity: living with other people'.[69] The salience of a group's ideology is reinforced through the social and cultural practices of its adherents. An ideology is more than just ideas, it is also actions based upon those ideas. The study of group ideology, therefore, is also a study of the culture which reinforces and influences a group's values.

To adherents, an ideology is coherent and comprehensible; believers have the capacity both to make sense of the collection of ideas and values which make up an ideology and, to a certain extent, empirically to test those ideas against their social reality.[70] The importance of ideological intelligibility becomes apparent when an ideology fails to make sense of a believer's experience. Thomas Kuhn's description of scientific revolutions highlights the importance of ideological coherence for science as an ideological system.[71] Kuhn argues that 'normal science' is governed by a set of rules and standards which dictate how scientific inquiry is practised. This scientific 'paradigm', or ideology, provides the foundation for scientists to make claims about the world around them. This paradigm becomes incoherent, however, as scientists discover anomalies in the empirical world which cannot adequately be explained under the practice of normal science. Sometimes the scientific paradigm can be adjusted to explain the anomalies. But there are occasions when anomalies accumulate and become so great that adjustments can no longer be made in the inherited paradigm. When this happens, there is a crisis in the scientific community, a crisis which can only be resolved with the rejection of the old paradigm and the emergence of a new scientific ideology.

Coherence is also an acute problem in religious and political ideologies. In the sixteenth century, Thomas Müntzer preached an ideology which promised that Christ's millennium could be inaugurated by the elect through the force of arms. Müntzer's millenarian ideology faced a crisis of intelligibility, however, when German peasants rallied to his revolutionary teaching only to be defeated by the German princes. When it could no longer render social experience meaningful for adherents, Müntzer's ideology had either to be abandoned or radically altered. Millenarianism as an ideology, however, did not die with Müntzer. New millenarian ideologies arose which retained the promise that Christ would return to bring in a new world order but altered Müntzer's prediction of how and when the millennium would begin.[72] All ideologies make claims about the empirical world which can be challenged by changing social circumstances. When this occurs, the ideology is either discarded, as in the case of an old scientific paradigm, or reinterpreted, as with millenarian ideologies.

In addition to making empirical statements, ideologies make moral claims about how the world ought to be. These propositions, as Robert Wuthnow notes, 'specify how social relations should be conducted and therefore affect how social resources may be distributed'.[73] A feudal ideology taught the mutual obligation between a tenant and his lord. The bonds between them were reciprocal, with the tenant exchanging his service for the lord's protection.[74] The ideology of pre-capitalist peasant societies included a 'moral economy' which bound peasants and landowners to an ethic of reciprocity and subsistence. In these settings, peasants were obliged to pay rent and taxes to landowners, but not when those payments infringed upon what was judged to be their subsistence needs.[75] A liberal political ideology implies a relationship where citizens give allegiance to the state in return for the protection of certain minimal rights. There are also non-political ideologies which share the general framework of the belief systems mentioned. Religious ideologies, for example, have a set of moral values, symbols and propositions which define the relationship among adherents and between the believer and God.

This moral sentiment is the most important and unique property connected to an ideology's ability to inspire people to organize groups to achieve a political objective. Ideologies seek to elicit a response of commitment and obligation on the part of adherents. Clifford Geertz correctly points out that ideologies try to inspire commitment by 'objectifying moral sentiment'.[76] An ideology convinces people that group norms and values are not arbitrary, but rational given their social experience and that adherents have either a right or an obligation to fulfill those ideals. Believers become dedicated to an ideology's universalistic moral claims about how social relations should be conducted and social resources allocated. People make social and political decisions based upon what is normatively reasonable in terms of their ideological commitment.

Social movement mobilization is most likely to occur when the coherence or values of an ideology are undermined by social change. The scientific and millenarian ideologies discussed above are examples of belief systems which were threatened by new empirical data which called into question the coherence of the inherited ideology. In both instances, new movements emerged to reinterpret the old ideology in the light of new findings. Social change can also affect an ideology by altering the moral obligations or norms it proposes. James Scott's work on peasant societies shows how peasant protest movements emerged when elites abandoned their obligation never to violate the subsistence needs of peasants with 'unjust' demands on their goods. Protest groups formed in order to restate the importance and relevance of the inherited ideology which taught what was a just and an unjust demand on peasant property.[77] Changes in the legal code can also lead to group mobilization. Roman Catholics and evangelical Protestants mobilized against abortion once the state legalized what they deemed an immoral, sinful practice. In forming pro-life groups, religious believers were defending a set of preferences which were perfectly reasonable given their ideology and social experience.

An ideology is important for social movement formation because it helps define what values a group wants to institutionalize and, with its stress on commitment and obligation, an ideology provides the impetus necessary for individuals to give their time and talents to a collective political project. An ideology, in short, defines what people value and why they value it and stresses a relationship of dedication without which a social movement could not form. The norms of an ideology and the relationship of active obligation it inspires are the most important properties which contribute to social movement mobilization.

THE IDEOLOGICAL AND INSTITUTIONAL BASIS OF GROUP MOBILIZATION

Social movements are here defined as: (1) a form of organized group action, (2) being directed toward political institutions, (3) trying to change society to conform with group norms and (4) having goals which are not reducible to the material self-interest of group members. (1) above sets the condition of organizational form to a social movement. For a movement to sustain itself over time it must develop institutions to espouse group ideals. As James Q. Wilson notes, organizations provide 'continuity and predictability to social processes that would otherwise be episodic and uncertain'.[78] In America and Britain, the institutionalization of a social movement usually occurs through political pressure groups. The Anti-Saloon League and the United Kingdom Alliance developed in response to evangelical Protestants' growing concern about alcohol abuse in the nineteenth century.

(2) above separates a phenomenon such as the Women's Movement

from an organization such as Alcoholics Anonymous (AA). While both movements strive to affect considerable change, a distinction between them arises because the Women's Movement has goals which can only be attained through political structures, while AA tries to change individual behaviour rather than political institutions. Social movements always have a desire to cause change in the economic or political structures of society. (3) and (4) are the most complex parts of the definition. Each is an effort to distinguish groups which are formed on the basis of the material self-interest of members from those which work explicitly for the benefit of the larger public or society as a whole. The American Chamber of Commerce and the Confederation of British Industry are interest groups which self-consciously represent the material interests of group members. The political preferences of each group are made through a strategic calculation of the benefits of a given policy to group members. Pro-life groups such as Rescue America and the Society for the Protection of Unborn Children, by contrast, are part of a social movement. Group members do not derive material benefit from group membership. Instead, purposive incentives such as the personal satisfaction which members derive from a commitment to the anti-abortion cause are the basis for group membership and maintenance.

The theory of social movements proposed in this book asserts that a group's ideology is an important factor in its mobilization and activism. Social movements tend to emerge and take hold when there is a disruption in the moral order which challenges the coherence, norms or beliefs of an ideology. When social conditions change in such a way as to make the obligations or intelligibility of a belief-system inoperable, social movements will arise to reconstruct the coherence or values of the ideology. An ideology provides the beliefs and values which help structure group objectives, the norms of commitment and obligation which lead people to join organizations, and meaning to legitimate group formation. The protection of group values and way of life is a normal, rational response by people negatively affected by social change.[79]

The fact that social movements arise in periods of disruption does not mean that an irrational psychological strain is the reason for group activism. As Geertz has noted, social actors need an ideology to help them make their way in a complex environment. An ideology enables people to constitute a sense of what they value and why they value it. Social change which calls into question the values or beliefs of an ideology, adherents, culture or way of life, has the capacity to make it more difficult for people to make sense of their lives.[80] In the context of this change, social movements emerge which either call for a new belief-system (revolutionary ideology) or which seek to revitalize an inherited ideology (counter-reform movement).

The women's rights movement emerged in the 1960s and 1970s when the traditional gender ideology failed to provide meaning for millions of American women. Many women rejected the inherited ideology which taught them that they could only be fulfilled if they married, stayed at home and had children. A new ideology of equal rights appeared as women became more aware of their political and economic inequality in America. The women's rights movement made explicit the nexus between beliefs and social behaviour by connecting an ideology of equal rights and opportunities for women to a set of social and political objectives. This new gender ideology led to the creation of a counter-reform movement among women who wanted to invest the traditional ideology with new meaning and power.

British and American evangelical Christians mobilized protest groups in the 1970s because political and cultural changes undermined the religious and cultural beliefs of adherents. Legalized abortion, homosexuality and changing sexual mores called into question the validity of evangelical religious norms. The protest groups which formed on both sides of the Atlantic were intended to represent evangelical religious beliefs and defend deeply-held values.

An ideology is important for social movement formation in at least two ways. First, an ideology legitimates social movement formation by teaching believers that they have a responsibility for influencing particular social outcomes. People need a reason to join groups and to engage in collective action, a justification for spending time and resources pursuing a social or political goal. Ideologies provide the commitment and sense of obligation necessary to convince people that active engagement in the interest of a collective goal is warranted. To borrow the language of rational choice theory, an ideology solves the collective action problem by making committed activism seem like an obligation, not an interest. Second, an ideology helps define group membership and enables organizations to communicate effectively with group members. People sharing a set of symbols and beliefs are, broadly speaking, 'members' of an ideological community. Organizations which have grown out of an ideological community have made explicit reference to shared symbols, beliefs, and rituals when attracting group members. Temperance groups in Britain and America gained valuable members and resources in the late nineteenth century when evangelical Christians interpreted drinking as a social problem which required their attention as religious believers. The proliferation of alcohol and related social problems threatened evangelical religious and family values. An evangelical ideology defined the obligation which believers had to particular social problems and helped organizations communicate those obligations to group members. Religious symbols became commonplace in the temperance movement of both nations in the late nineteenth century.

The ideology of a movement organization can also influence the symbolic strategies groups use in pursuing a political objective. In 1977, the Prolife Nonviolent Action Project was founded to 'promote rescues' at places where abortions were performed. The strategy of being arrested at abortion clinics was intimately related, in the minds of group members, to the religious conviction they shared. Adopting a strategy of non-violence invokes, in the words of one Pro-life pamphlet, 'the same power, the same Spirit, that led Jesus to mount the cross. . . . We can, we should, we must invoke the power that Jesus revealed when, speaking from the cross about those who were killing Him, He said, 'Father, forgive them, for they know not what they are doing.'[81] The symbol of Jesus on the cross invites images of a martyr's death, an image which is a compelling justification for breaking the law.[82] Similarly, driving spikes into the trunks of trees by members of an environmental group serves a practical and an ideological function. Practically speaking, loggers will not cut down these 'affected' trees because it is dangerous do so and because the trees have decreased market value. The action is ideologically appealing because it affirms the group's conviction that a tree has more than monetary value. Members of pro-choice groups share an ideology which claims that the right of women to control their own reproductivity should not be limited by any government. This belief makes powerful the symbol of a bloodied coat-hanger which pro-choice groups sometimes use in protest demonstrations. That symbol implies an argument about what are the consequences of limiting a woman's right to control her own body.

Ideology continues to play an important role as groups engage in political action. Ideological groups frequently have to make a choice between purely expressive action which is ideologically appealing but not politically beneficial, or an instrumental strategy which holds out the promise of some political gain but which often compromises the group's ideology. Wilson perceptively notes that some organizations will choose a political protest as a strategy, not because it is politically effective, but because a protest can be expressive of a lifestyle or is required by the nature of the objective.[83] Virtually all social movements are internally divided between enthusiasts, who refuse to compromise their ideological goals, and 'realists' who believe that it is necessary to be politically accommodating.

The existence of this dilemma makes ideological groups different in kind from organizations in which material interests predominate. Milk producers want public policies which will increase the value of their product. Ideally, they would like subsidies which would increase the price of milk from $15 a hundredweight to $20 or more. However, one cannot imagine that such groups would refuse to sell milk, on principle, with an increase to $17 instead of the desired $20. The group is more than willing to pursue a rational policy and trade off its ultimate goal for a somewhat higher price for its product. Associations that rely on the provision of material incentives to attract group members will not attach much importance to how their objectives are met.

Ideological groups are not as free to make such strategic choices, because interest maximization is not the primary goal of group members. Pro-choice and pro-life groups both have goals which are not easily divisible. The belief that women have a fundamental right to an abortion, or the conviction that all abortion is murder, makes it difficult for both sides of the abortion debate to compromise on their goals. Public opinion polls in America and Britain suggest that a compromise on abortion, which would allow for some but not all elective abortions, is supported by majorities in each nation. If pro-life advocates cared only about maximizing the number of babies 'saved' from abortions each year, support for political compromise would be the rational alternative. The fact that few pro-life groups support such a compromise suggests that these organizations see their interests in a different way. Groups believe that to acknowledge that there are legitimate grounds for aborting unborn babies is to undermine their moral code, which opposes abortion as an act of murder. The same logic determines the political strategy of most pro-choice groups, which often refuse to recognize that there are occasions when women do not have an absolute right to an abortion.[84]

Frequently ideological organizations adapt their campaign over time in order to enhance their political influence. The American temperance movement was marked by a gradual shift, from the radical activism under the leadership of Frances Willard and the Women's Christian Temperance Union (WCTU), to the highly professional, less ideological work of the Anti-Saloon League. Willard was so dissatisfied with the support of the major parties for prohibition that she led the WCTU to support the Prohibition Party. The Prohibition Party was ideologically appealing to many activists because it focused primarily on the liquor question, but it had very little impact on electoral politics. The Anti-Saloon League, by contrast, sought coalitions with every possible organization, compromised on the ultimate goal of prohibition, and worked through both political parties. The recent activism of the Christian Right can be understood in the same way: what began as a highly ideological movement around the issues of abortion, pornography, and religion in public schools emerged into a more professional campaign with a leadership which learned to accommodate its goals to gain political influence.[85]

The dilemma for ideological organizations is that the strategies selected to keep or gain political power are often ones which disenchant group activists. The political need to negotiate compromise to influence the political system creates internal strains for groups formed on the basis of a shared set of beliefs. Ideological organizations are distinctive because they involve an intense attachment to particular issues. Individuals are asked to subordinate their other interests and concentrate on a policy area, such as abortion. If group leaders are seen to be involved in moral and political compromises, however, the unique appeal of the ideological organization is lost. The British Labour Movement has discovered that unions have been more attractive to group activists when they appeal to social justice, class solidarity and public ownership of the means of production. Those policies, however, when adopted by the British Labour Party in the 1980s, proved to be politically debilitating. Labour activists flocked to the party, but rank-and-file voters who were less interested in the ideology of the party and more concerned about the economic costs of party programmes voted Conservative. Ideological groups, in short, are often caught between the Scylla of expressive choices which can fail politically but succeed ideologically and the Charybdis of instrumental strategies which can succeed politically but fail ideologically.[86]

This ideological approach to the study of social movements is not incompatible with the inherited theories, particularly resource mobilization and state structure. In analyzing evangelical activism, one must ask how groups raised the resources necessary to institutionalize a social movement against legalized abortion. The point is not to dispense with the insights of a resource theory, but to give greater weight to the role of group ideology in how resources are raised and groups sustained over time. Nor does this theory jettison the insights of a state structural analysis. Group ideas do not determine a group's ability to achieve its political objectives. A nation's institutional arrangement can facilitate or repress an organization's ability to act on group interests.

Generally speaking, the stronger the state, the weaker the interest groups within that state. In strong states, political change is initiated primarily by state officials and politicians and not by organized interests; interest groups have difficulty creating autonomous means of political action and therefore must rely on the support of key state elites for their political power. Public policy, in strong states, is not primarily a reaction to interested social groups. In weaker states, where political power is decentralized and dispersed, there are more points of access for interest groups to permeate the political process and introduce social change. In weak states, public policy is not made by state officials acting autonomously; instead, policy is formed in response to the pressure of organized groups.[87]

Different political systems present different opportunities and incentives for a social movement organization. The level of democratization, the power accorded to the courts and police, the party structure, the role of the media, all influence the behaviour of groups vying for social and political influence. A federal political system like America's, which divides powers, will create more points of access for an organized group than a more unitary system, like that of Britain. Interest-group lobbying and the use of constituent pressure on elected officials are all common strategies for organized groups in America but are less commonly used by groups in Britain. The American state is so divided, as Polsby has noted, that different interests have the capacity to capture different parts of the state.[88] The unitary nature of the British polity, with the concentration of authority in the hands of the central government, means that pressure groups direct their activities toward the Prime Minister and Parliament. In short, political strategies which are common for groups in one nation will be less common or absent for groups in another nation. The comparison of the mobilization and activism of British and American evangelical Christians in Chapters 4 and 6 demonstrates how the political opportunities afforded by a particular polity affected the political action of these ideological groups.

State elites can more directly facilitate or repress a social movement by supporting or opposing the political goals of organized groups. Orlaff and Skocpol, in an article which contrasts social spending laws in early-twentieth-century Britain and America, show how British interest groups working on behalf of the urban poor benefited from the support of parliamentary elites who favoured social welfare laws. Because the British state had the capacity and interest to pass national welfare legislation, British interest groups realized many of their political goals. The state, acting upon its own interests and preferences, aided interest group efforts.[89] More recently, Presidents Reagan and Bush and the Republican Party helped legitimate evangelical groups through public support for the causes espoused by those organizations. Conversely, Prime Minister Thatcher diffused British evangelical activism by ignoring their groups and issues throughout the 1980s.

CONCLUSION

The theory of evangelical activism presented in this book explains how groups formed on the basis of a shared religious ideology and also attempts to elucidate the effect of political institutions on the success of British and American groups. Group ideology shaped the behaviour of social agents and helped to define group goals. As evangelicals tried to realize their political objectives, however, institutional factors came to assume a prominent role. Chapter 3 reviews an evangelical ideology to show how it has helped to mobilize believers into social movement organizations in Britain and America.

3 Evangelical Ideology and Group Formation

Evangelicals have generated significant social movement development in Britain and America during the past two hundred years. Abolition, Prohibition and numerous broad-based movements designed to promote public education, health and 'morals' developed with the intellectual, political and financial support of evangelical organizations. More recently, abortion, pornography and related 'family' issues have mobilized evangelicals into political organizations. In each instance, an evangelical religious ideology structured believers' views on a specific issue, encouraged their involvement in a social and political campaign, and defined group goals.

Contemporary evangelical activism surprised social scientists who believed that a religious basis for political mobilization would gradually disappear in a modernizing world. These observers reasoned that increased education, scientific discoveries and rapid urbanization undermined traditional religious beliefs and thereby eliminated the nexus between a person's religious ideology and his political behaviour.[1] The resurgence of evangelical politics in the past several decades around such issues as abortion and pornography has called into question the claims of modernization theory. Not only have evangelicals been politically active, but an evangelical religious ideology has been an important part of this activism.

This chapter highlights the first aspect of my social movement theory: the role of group ideology in the life of evangelical social movements. Specific evangelical religious beliefs and cultural values have played a significant role in the formation of political groups. The evangelical doctrine that Jesus is the source of salvation and redemption for individuals, the belief that the Bible is the inspired and infallible Word of God, the commitment to integrating religious convictions into daily living, and the desire to convert others to an evangelical faith have all helped to promote group formation. Group leaders have self-consciously referred to these and other shared values in promoting evangelical group formation. Believers have joined organizations because they share religious beliefs and the cultural values which reinforce them. An evangelical ideology impacts an adherent's political choices.

To demonstrate the importance of an evangelical ideology, the chapter provides an extended definition of evangelicalism, drawing from British and American sources. The chapter uses interest group literature, interviews

36

with activists and the theological statements of faith for the largest evangelical organizations in Britain (the Evangelical Alliance) and in America (the National Association of Evangelicals) to define an evangelical ideology. Public opinion data is also used, but only for American evangelicals where data is available.[2] The chapter concludes that the most important factor shared by these transatlantic believers was an ideological commitment to a set of norms and not a common status or self-interest.

EVANGELICALISM THEOLOGICALLY DEFINED

Evangelicalism began as a reform movement within Protestant denominations in the middle decades of the eighteenth century. Although there was much continuity with earlier Reformed traditions, what became known distinctly as evangelicalism was born with the conversions of George Whitefield, John Wesley and Charles Wesley in England, and the First Great Awakening in America (1730–60). These early evangelicals began a religious revival in the churches of America and England to introduce a more vital religion into what was seen as a sedentary faith. Like many reform efforts within Protestantism, evangelicalism had a schismatic outcome, the formal founding of the Methodist Church after the death of its spiritual founder, John Wesley. More important than this creation of a new church, however, was the impact which evangelicalism had on existing denominations. Baptist, Anglican and Congregational churches were all deeply influenced by the Evangelical Movement in Britain and America. The Second Great Awakening in America (1800–30) solidified the power of evangelicalism within churches, and evangelical thought has been a continuing influence within Protestant denominations in the past two centuries.[3]

Evangelicalism came to be influential in the nineteenth century because its optimistic and affirming theology attracted adherents who were not served by the Calvinist orthodoxy of their day. Calvinists had taught that no one could be assured of his salvation; evangelicals, led initially by Wesley, emphasized that the individual was free to accept salvation through personal conversion at any time. Conversionism concluded in a doctrine of assurance which was unique in Protestant theology. Implied in the evangelical understanding of conversion were the ideas that the individual had the ability to save himself by his own free choice, that lives could radically be changed by accepting salvation, and that humans had the ability to do good by bringing others to the means of salvation. Each of these ideas was consistent with popular Enlightenment assumptions of the day and stood in stark contrast to the Calvinist notions that humans were innately depraved and incapable of good works, and that God elects, or saves, individuals without any act on the part of the chosen. The simplicity and power of evangelical theology attracted the most numerous class of people in Britain and America – members of the middle and lower middle class who lived in the country and small towns.[4]

Evangelicals are Protestant Christians who emphasize salvation by faith in the atoning death of Jesus Christ through personal conversion and the authority of scripture in matters of faith and Christian practice.[5] The denominations most closely associated with Evangelicalism are various Baptist churches, the Assemblies of God, the Church of Christ, the Pentecostal Church, and the Church of the Nazarene. Evangelicalism, however, exists within and across denominations, including the Presbyterian Church, the Methodist Church, the Anglican Church and the Evangelical Lutheran Church. Table 3.1 lists the statements of faith for the largest evangelical organizations in the United Kingdom and the United States: the Evangelical Alliance and the National Association of Evangelicals (NAE). These transatlantic 'mainstream' evangelical organizations share a nearly identical statement of faith.[6]

The three most distinctive and characteristic evangelical doctrines which can be derived from the statements of faith are: a belief in the sacrificial nature of Christ's death on the cross (the third point in both statements), a deep respect for the authority of the Bible as the infallible Word of God (the first point), and an emphasis on integrating religious beliefs and social conduct, what is described as living a 'Christian' or 'godly' life (point 7, EA; point 5, NAE). Also important is the emphasis placed upon the 'resurrection of damnation' or 'eternal consequences' for those who do not accept Christ's sacrificial death (point 7, NAE; point 3, EA). The doctrines of the Trinity (point 2), the Holy Spirit (point 4), and the priesthood of all believers (point 6) are shared by virtually all Protestant denominations and are therefore not distinctly evangelical.

Many of the distinctions between evangelical and non-evangelical Christianity arise from the form of belief rather than its content. The doctrine of the Fall is one example. The Roman Catholic and most Protestant churches teach that humans are separated from the love of God because of sin. Sin is defined in Protestant and Catholic theology as the purposeful disobedience of a person to the known will of God. The consequence of human sin is a life lived outside of God's forgiveness, the only thing which can guarantee the believer salvation or eternal life. Most churches have not actively rejected the doctrine of the Fall, but the notion of human sin has been altered among many Catholic and Protestant religious organizations. Non-

Table 3.1   Evangelical statements of faith

Evangelical Alliance	NAE
1. The divine inspiration of the Holy Scriptures and its consequent entire trustworthiness and supreme authority in all matters of faith and conduct.	1. We believe the Bible to be the inspired, only infallible, authoritative Word of God.
2. The sovereignty and grace of God the Father, God the Son, and God the Holy Spirit in creation, providence, revelation, redemption, and final judgement.	2. We believe that there is one God, eternally existent in three persons: Father, Son, and Holy Spirit.
3. The universal sinfulness and guilt of fallen man, making him subject to God's wrath and condemnation. The substitutionary sacrifice of the incarnate Son of God as the sole and all-sufficient ground of redemption from the guilt and power of sin, and its eternal consequences.	3. We believe in the deity of our Lord Jesus Christ, in His virgin birth, in His vicarious and atoning death through His shed blood, in His ascension to the right hand of the Father and in His personal return in power and Glory.
4. The illuminating, regenerating, indwelling, sanctifying work of God the Holy Spirit.	4. We believe that for the salvation of lost and sinful man, regeneration by the Holy Spirit is absolutely essential.
5. The expectation of the personal, visible, return of the Lord Jesus Christ in power and glory.	5. We believe in the present ministry of the Holy Spirit by whose indwelling the Christian is enabled to lead a godly life.
6. The priesthood of all believers, who form the universal church, the Body of which Christ is Head, and which is committed to the proclamation of the Gospel throughout the world.	6. We believe in the spiritual unity of all believers in our Lord Christ.
7. We here assert doctrines which are crucial to the understanding of faith, and which should issue in mutual love, practical Christian service and evangelical concern.	7. We believe in the resurrection of both the saved and the lost; they that are saved unto resurrection of life and they that are lost unto the resurrection of damnation.

evangelical churches have shifted the emphasis from the sin of the individual to social sins. The Prophetic Justice Unit of the National Council of the Churches of Christ in the USA (NCC), the largest American ecumenical organization, talks about sin in precisely these terms: 'We advance the idea that society and its systems are in need of reform just as individual persons are.'[7] Evangelicals contend, by contrast, that liberal churches have effectively neglected the doctrine of original sin. The Rev. Alan Gibson, General Secretary of the British Evangelical Council, claimed that 'mainstream' Protestant churches 'have lost their sense of authority. They no longer teach that man is separated from God by his sin.'[8]

The conviction that Jesus is the sole source of salvation for individuals makes a doctrine of the Fall especially important for evangelicals. The only way to overcome the consequences of sin ('the resurrection of damnation') is for the sinner to turn to Christ in faith for forgiveness. The cross represents the death which Christ suffered for human sin. Christ's death atones for human sin, but salvation is still dependent on a personal act of faith. Sermons preached in evangelical congregations frequently refer to the need for the listener to 'accept' the salvation offered by Christ. The Rev. David McKinnis of St Aldates, Oxford, made precisely that point to his congregation: 'The Lord Jesus Christ died for us and despite our sin we can have our names enrolled in heaven if we accept his sacrifice.'[9]

Evangelicals are distinctive among Christian believers because of their emphasis upon a personal faith in Jesus as the only way to salvation. A person can only be 'saved', according to evangelicals, by understanding and believing that Christ died on the cross for his or her sins. Malcolm Laver concluded in an interview, 'we (evangelicals) believe in the justification of the sinner solely by faith in our Lord and Savior Jesus Christ and any church which does not preach that is not evangelical'.[10]

Evangelicals also emphasize the need for the conversion of sinners to faith in Jesus Christ. The major theological conviction of evangelicalism, salvation through faith in Christ, serves as the content for the conversion. People are urged to be converted to a faith in that doctrine. A stress on the act of conversion makes religious experience radically individualistic. Eternal life becomes a 'good' which an individual accepts. The individual is adopted as a child of God, is forgiven and becomes a new creation. In the words of the British Evangelical Council, a group linking 1200 local churches together, evangelical Christians are people 'who have experienced the life-changing reality of Jesus Christ'.[11] From religious revivals to Sunday-morning services, evangelical worship often includes an invitation for a personal acceptance of this life-changing faith.

This emphasis on human agency in the process of conversion has continued to be a central notion in evangelical thought and practice. The Rev. McKinnis asked his listeners in a sermon if they wanted to 'come to Jesus? All you have to do is want to come', McKinnis told them, 'the moment you come Jesus welcomes you with open arms.'[12] One can only understand the dynamism of the evangelical movement in the context of the personal assurance adherents receive because of their faith. Not only salvation, but assurance can be attained through personal choice. D. W. Bebbington argues that the assurance which comes from the evangelical doctrine of conversion also helps legitimate group formation. Evangelicals, who *know* that their sins are forgiven, are freed from anxiety for Christian witness.[13] Clive Calver, the Executive Director of the Evangelical Alliance, writes, 'to those who ask his forgiveness and receive his life in them by the Holy Spirit come the *certainties* of rebirth'[14] (my emphasis). The theological ideas that humans have a free will, that they can discern the will of God, and that they can be assured of the life-changing reality of salvation encourage evangelicals to perceive their social world as dynamic and subject to change by their efforts. Because the individual is certain of salvation, he or she can help others to be saved as well. What follows for evangelical social movement mobilization is a confidence on the part of activists that their involvement can be efficacious. British evangelical John Stott assures his readers that 'the world can be won for Christ'.[15]

The evangelical emphasis on conversion also creates a boundary between those who have experienced this life-changing event and those who have not. What is structurally important for this theological doctrine, in the words of James Barr, is that 'the differentiation between true and nominal Christians . . . is allowed to become the paramount governing element in all judgments about the churches and their members'.[16] Barr overstates the argument but the point is well taken. Conversion becomes an act which marks a boundary between the saved and unsaved. In writing about nineteenth-century Evangelicalism, Bebbington states that 'the line between those who had undergone the experience and those who had not was the sharpest in the world'.[17] In our day, the distinction still means a great deal. In the words of Jerry Falwell, it means that 'the unredeemed person never sees things from God's point of view . . . . We who have known Christ are seated with Him in the heavenlies. We can have God's perspective.'[18] Not all evangelicals share Falwell's political agenda, but all would agree that conversion marks a distinction between the evangelical and non-evangelical. The Rev. David Johnson of St Ebbe's, Oxford, urged his congregation not to be troubled by the decline of worship in the United Kingdom because 'the point is that you are saved, the rest are not. You alone are right, the rest are wrong.'[19]

A second essential characteristic of Evangelicalism is biblicism, the belief that all religious truths are contained in the Bible. British evangelical Michael Saward describes this position as 'a deep respect for the Bible as God's word, the supreme authority, if you want to know the truth about what to believe and how to express it'.[20] Evangelicals invariably focus on the Bible as the final test of whatever claims to be the voice of God. This appropriation of the Bible clearly distinguishes evangelical from non-evangelical Christians. For Roman Catholics, religious knowledge comes not only from scripture, but also from church leaders and from church tradition, while liberal Protestants place greater emphasis on theology, history and human experience to make religious claims. Few evangelicals believe that it is possible to rely on the Bible to the exclusion of tradition or reason, but they do distinguish themselves from Catholics and liberal Protestants in their claim that scripture is the ultimate source of religious authority.[21]

This generalization is supported by a poll conducted by George Gallup in 1981 on religious attitudes in America.[22] Sixty-two per cent of the evangelicals in the poll cited the Bible as the most important authority for testing their religious beliefs, another 31 per cent claimed that direct revelation from the Holy Spirit was their most important source. Only 25 per cent of the Catholics in the poll placed the Bible first, while 27 per cent relied primarily on 'What the church says'. Among non-evangelical Protestants, 52 per cent put the Bible first, only slightly lower than among evangelicals. In terms of the Bible and religious practice, however, the difference between evangelicals and non-evangelicals is much more apparent. According to a 1979 survey conducted by *Christianity Today*, 44 per cent of evangelicals read the Bible daily and 38.2 per cent read it weekly; this compares to 10.7 per cent of non-evangelicals who read the Bible daily and 18.5 per cent who read it weekly.[23]

Evangelicalism is also distinctive in its claim that the Bible is 'infallible' or 'inerrant'. Infallibility means that what scripture says may be taken as reliable and true. As Tony Baker says, 'we (evangelicals) need to assert vigorously that all scripture is true'.[24] Evangelicals tend to read the biblical text ahistorically; neither history nor culture can change the essential message received in the Bible. The biblical accounts, from the history of God's revelation to ethical prescriptions, are not accepted as probabilities, but as unchanging truths. In the words of British evangelical J. I. Packer, 'Christianity is built on truth: that is to say, on the content of divine revelation.'[25] For evangelicals, faith in God and confidence in the biblical account are about certainty, and doubt is implicitly an assault upon those convictions. It does not matter if evangelicals are 'correct' in claiming that the Bible can be read with enough clarity to provide a single basis for truth claims. What matters is that evangelicals believe that such a biblical reading is possible and they form their doctrine and organizations on that assumption.

A clear difference emerges in the poll data on evangelical and non-evangelical attitudes toward the Bible. One hundred per cent of the evangelicals in the Gallup poll affirmed the following statement on biblical infallibility: 'the Bible is the word of God and is *not* mistaken in its statements and teachings'. Only 41 per cent of the Catholics and 38 per cent of the non-evangelical Protestants accepted an infallible position. Thirty-six per cent of the Catholics and 30 per cent of the Protestants believed a milder claim that the Bible 'is the word of God but is sometimes mistaken in its statements and teachings', while 20 per cent of the Catholics and 18 per cent of the Protestants were of the non-orthodox opinion that the Bible 'is a collection of writings representing some of the religious philosophies of ancient man'.[26]

Interviews and group literature confirm the importance of scripture for evangelicals. Tim Dean, editor of the British evangelical journal *Third Way*, claims simply that 'we cannot know Christ without knowing scripture'.[27] Since knowing Christ is necessary for salvation, it is apparent how important knowing scripture is for evangelicals. St Ebbe's distributes a welcoming brochure to all visitors which says 'as ordinary Christians we have found the Bible to be true'.[28] This use of the Bible distinguishes evangelicals from non-evangelical Christians. The Rev. Alan Gibson claimed in an interview that many Protestant churches had lost their authority 'because they gave up the word of God to rationalism'.[29]

Liberal Protestants have certainly not discarded or overlooked the Bible in the way suggested by some evangelicals. The NCC talks in its constitution about being a 'community of communions, which in response to the gospel as revealed in the Scriptures, confesses Jesus Christ'.[30] Liberal Protestant organizations do not, however, speak of the Bible, or religious truths in general, as infallible. Instead, they take a more flexible view of the Bible, make a theological argument for God's progressive revelation in human history, and are generally more tolerant of theological and religious differences of opinion. Liberal churches and organizations believe that members ought to exercise freedom of thought on religious questions.[31]

A third evangelical characteristic is an emphasis on integrating religious beliefs and personal conduct. Evangelicals are noteworthy for their attempt, as James Hunter remarks, 'to know and to live Christianity in its authentic and divinely intended manner'.[32] Evangelicalism introduced into Protestant thought the radical idea that individuals were responsible for their own salvation. Calvin taught that God was solely responsible for the conversion of the sinner; Wesley, while never denying God's activity, gave primacy to the part which individuals played in accepting God's invitation to faith. As John Hammond notes about evangelicals, 'since conversion only required a change of heart, it was an act of will upon the part of man and fully within his power'.[33] This doctrine of free will gave new import to the idea that the converted sinner had the capacity to lead a good life. If the sinner could choose to be saved, evangelicals reasoned, he or she could also choose to lead a moral life. For evangelicals, it was unfathomable that a true believer would continue living a sinful life after accepting God's salvation. Evangelicalism introduced a radical notion of human agency and free will to Protestant theology and thereby encouraged the belief that individuals could help transform the world spiritually and politically. Believers had an obligation to live a moral life, a conviction which is retained by contemporary evangelical organizations, as is evident in the fifth doctrine of the NAE statement of faith which refers to the 'godly life' which the converted Christian is expected to live.[34]

There is ample evidence to show that evangelicals translate their religious beliefs into organizational membership and activism. According to a poll conducted by *Christianity Today* in 1979, 62.5 per cent of evangelicals responded that they contributed ten or more per cent of their income to their church or other religious organizations, compared to 29.9 per cent of non-evangelicals.[35] A 1980 Gallup poll indicated that 80 per cent of evangelicals reported that they did voluntary work for the church or some other religious organization. Only 48 and 36 per cent of non-evangelical Protestants and Catholics respectively said they did voluntary work for the church.[36] Evangelicals are also more likely to attend church than non-evangelicals. According to data from the 1984 presidential election study conducted by the Center for Political Studies at the University of Michigan, 50.3 per cent of evangelicals attended church weekly compared to 23.4 per cent of non-evangelicals.[37]

Even more important for evangelical mobilization is the obligation believers feel to 'serve' the God who saved them. Evangelicals are unique among Christian groups in joining an assurance of salvation with an attempt to forge what Weber called 'an ethic of vocation in the world'.[38] Activism in the world assumes a religious significance for evangelicals, who believe that they have an obligation to pattern their lives according to the will of God. While the Christian knows that he cannot earn salvation through acts of benevolence, he seeks, nevertheless, as one evangelical said, 'to serve God in gratitude for grace'.[39] Implied in an evangelical faith is an obligation to do what is pleasing in God's eyes, to try to act 'morally'. The statement of faith for the Evangelical Alliance assumes a correspondence between belief in salvation and an ethic of activism when it claims that understanding the doctrines of the organization 'should issue in . . . practical Christian service and evangelical concern' (point 7). The quest for salvation, in short, has consequences for the believer who accepts that his or her life must reflect religious faith in God.

The importance of theological doctrines for evangelical group formation is underscored in virtually all group literature. Joining an evangelical organization is similar to joining an evangelical church. In order to be accepted as a member, a potential recruit must pledge her intellectual assent to a set of beliefs. The membership form for the National Association of Evangelicals is typical of this pattern, as it asks applicants to check a box indicating 'I subscribe to the NAE statement of faith.'[40] Groups expect a doctrinal as well as a financial commitment from group members. Member churches of the more liberal National Council of Churches of Christ, by contrast, do not have a statement of faith to which they must subscribe.

THE SOCIAL AND HISTORICAL CHARACTERISTICS OF EVANGELICALISM

In addition to an adherence to theological beliefs, evangelicals can be defined as a socio-religious group found in Britain and America in the past two centuries. As Corwin Smidt notes, to view evangelicals as a social group 'places emphasis upon the fact that the religious beliefs, experiences, and practices of evangelicals tend to be expressed within a particular social or subcultural context'.[41] This stress upon the cultural context in which evangelical beliefs are expressed in turn makes it necessary to look closely at the historical and sociological characteristics which evangelicals share. Although it is difficult to generalize about evangelical social characteristics in the absence of public opinion data, the argument can be made that British and American evangelicalism were both denominationally and class-diverse throughout the nineteenth century. The evangelical revival that swept across England in the late eighteenth and early nineteenth centuries broke out among three distinct religious groups: the working-class and lower middle-class Methodist followers of Wesley, the skilled working-class and middle-class members of older dissenting churches (i.e. Baptist, Presbyterian and Congregational), and upper-class members of the Church of England. Evangelical influence was pervasive in the Methodist Church, strong in dissenting churches, and important, although not dominant, in the Church of England. The close association of nonconformists with the Liberal Party, which opposed the established church, made it difficult, however, for Anglican evangelicals comfortably to cooperate politically with their evangelical peers.[42]

Evangelical religion became more middle-class as the century progressed. By the end of the century, the British evangelical Congregational, Methodist and Baptist churches were almost entirely middle-class in composition. Evangelical theology attracted significant working-class support in the early decades of the century, especially among the Primitive Methodists, but many of the converted rose out of the lower ranks of society into middle-class communities and occupations. Bebbington and Harrison have noted that evangelicalism was itself an avenue for upward social mobility for the working-class poor.[43] As Bebbington concludes, 'this process meant that the gospel abstracted individuals from their original setting rather than mingling with the lifestyle of the poor'.[44] The middle-class composition of evangelicalism continued throughout the nineteenth and into the early part of the twentieth century.

In America, evangelicalism became the dominant religious perspective by the middle decades of the nineteenth century. Sydney Ahlstrom concludes that evangelical doctrine was so pervasive by that time that a *de facto* 'common-core Protestantism' had emerged which was nearly synonymous with evangelical theology.[45] Hunter simply claims that nineteenth-century evangelicalism was 'unquestionably predominant'.[46] In the early decades of the nineteenth century, the evangelical revival fuelled the Second Great Awakening, which suffused most Protestant churches, including the once-powerful Congregational and Presbyterian Churches and the newly-prominent Methodist, Baptist and Disciples of Christ denominations. The class and social composition of American evangelicals in the nineteenth century was as diverse as the denominations which supported the theology: upper-class Congregationalists joined with middle-class Methodists and working-class Baptists in support of an evangelical theology. This evangelical hegemony lasted into the twentieth century.[47]

Evangelical Protestantism was not politically or religiously conservative in nineteenth-century Britain or America. As was noted above, the evangelical stress upon individual conversion and social responsibility marked a decisive break with the Puritan orthodoxy in America and the Anglican orthodoxy in Britain. In Britain, evangelicals were opposed by the Conservative Party and the Anglican hierarchy. Evangelicals supported what they deemed vital and progressive legislation for the moral reformation of their respective societies, including the prohibition of alcohol, the building of public schools, and closing shops on Sunday. These various 'progressive' causes united believers of numerous denominations and social classes who were otherwise politically divided.

In due time, social forces challenged evangelical doctrine, hegemony and appeal in Britain and America. Evangelical unity broke apart in each nation in the early decades of the twentieth century as the secularizing forces of modernity (urbanization, industrialization, science, education) divided evangelicals between those who chose to hold firm to their religious convictions despite the questions raised by modernity (conservatives), and those who consciously accommodated their religious beliefs to meet changing social conditions (liberals). Liberal Protestants gradually abandoned the evangelical stress on the Bible as the inspired and infallible Word of God and the evangelical emphasis on individual conversion and morality. In its place, liberals, wanting to make Christianity compatible with a modern, industrializing world, stressed a social and non-literal biblical interpretation. As Hunter notes, the distinguishing characteristic of liberal Protestantism was 'a shift in emphasis from the spiritual to the social and practical'.[48]

Conservative evangelicals, by contrast, came predominantly from the lower-middle social class and were less affected by modernity. Evangelicals formed subcultures which insulated believers from the 'corrupting' effects of modernity. This cultural isolation allowed conservative believers to maintain their inherited beliefs in the face of intellectual and cultural challenges. In order to defend traditional beliefs and cultural values, evangelicals formed their own religious organizations which placed an even greater stress on the unqualified truth of the Bible and the absolute need for personal conversion.[49]

The acrimony between the two groups of evangelicals created a cleavage within most Protestant denominations in Britain and America. The opposition to modernity among American conservative evangelicals was so great that the fundamentalist movement was born. Fundamentalism became a pervasive social force in America, leading eventually to the formation of new churches and the creation of lasting divisions within existing denominations. British conservative evangelicals also opposed modernity, but fundamentalism, and the rift within denominations, was not as pervasive as in America.[50] The divergence between liberals and conservatives destroyed the intra-class appeal of evangelicalism. By the second decade of the twentieth century, those who retained traditional evangelical doctrine, now simply called evangelicals, were increasingly concentrated in the lower middle classes. Liberal Protestantism, by contrast, represented the middle and upper-middle classes. As the twentieth century progressed, the theological differences between evangelicals and non-evangelicals were increasingly also reflected in cultural, social and political differences.[51]

Public opinion data suggests that contemporary American evangelicals are still more widely represented among the working and lower classes than are liberal Protestants and Catholics. A poll conducted by the Gallup organization in 1979 and used by James Davison Hunter in his *American Evangelicalism*, and Corwin Smidt's analysis of the data drawn from the 1980 and 1984 presidential election studies conducted by the Center for Political Studies at the University of Michigan, show an income and educational discrepancy in America between evangelicals and non-evangelicals.[52] The Gallup poll found that over one-third of the evangelical population, 37 per cent, had not completed high school, compared to 25 per cent for liberal Protestants and 24 per cent for Catholics. Less than one-quarter of evangelicals, 24 per cent, had some university training, while 31 per cent of liberal Protestants and 33 per cent of Catholics had some college education. The data drawn from the Michigan study shows a similar pattern: in 1980, 29.5 per cent of the evangelicals were not high-school graduates, compared to only 21.8 per cent of non-evangelicals. In 1984 the figures had changed slightly, with 26.6 per cent of evangelicals having no high-school diploma, compared to 17.8 per cent of non-evangelicals.

Evangelicals also have a slightly lower income than the non-evangelical population. Of those evangelicals surveyed in the Gallup poll, 25.3 per cent were in the lowest income bracket ($6999 and under), compared to 23.9 per cent of liberal Protestants and 20.4 per cent of Catholics. By contrast, only 7.1 per cent of the evangelicals polled were in the highest income group (over $25 000), while 16.2 per cent of liberal Protestants and 18.1 per cent of the Catholics were in the highest income bracket. Hunter's conclusion that 'evangelicals are more widely represented among the moderately educated, lower and lower-middle-income occupations' seems inescapable.[53]

Various analysts have concluded that evangelicals have retained conservative theological and political views because these believers have not been introduced in large numbers to the liberalizing effect of higher education.[54] The data suggests that increased education, and related wealth and influence, make individuals more liberal in religious and political terms. The data fail to show, however, that American evangelicals have been gradually moving into a more middle-class position without completely abandoning their conservative views. There is no data from the early part of the century to compare with the figures from the 1980s, but all of the historical evidence suggests that evangelicals have been becoming more middle-class. Certainly, nowhere near one-quarter of evangelicals went to college in the early and mid-twentieth-century. The dramatic growth of evangelical colleges, seminaries, and institutes during the 1960s and 1970s led Robert Wuthnow to conclude that evangelicals were educationally and economically, 'coming to resemble the broader society'.[55] What has been unique, however, is that for many believers higher education has come at evangelical institutions, making it possible for evangelicals to retain some isolation from secular society and thereby pass on religious and cultural values.

The picture is further complicated when British evangelicals are considered. There is no public opinion data specifically on British evangelicals, but the evidence suggests that British evangelicals are *not* predominantly lower-class. The most dramatic fact of British religious life in the past several decades has been the precipitous fall in church-membership, down to below 15 per cent of the total population in 1985.[56] Working- and lower-class segments of the population have been particularly disenfranchised from the churches; British church-members are drawn disproportionately from the middle-class. Evangelicals, according to one estimate, are now one-half Anglican, the denomination most obviously middle- and upper-middle class. The remainder of evangelicals come from a variety of denominations, including Methodists, Baptists, and various Pentecostal bodies, which are middle- and lower-middle-class in composition.[57]

British and American evangelicals have, as a rule, been more isolated, by choice and circumstance, from the secularizing effects of modernity than their liberal counterparts. Liberal Protestantism embraced modernity and generally supported religious and cultural pluralism and diversity. This commitment to diversity and pluralism has eroded the shared moral, political and cultural values of liberal churches. Evangelicals are not as culturally isolated as they were fifty years ago, but they are still less receptive to diversity and pluralism and have, as a consequence, been better able to retain common religious, cultural and moral viewpoints.[58] These shared religious and cultural values have become particularly relevant as evangelicals entered politics.

The history of evangelicalism is evidence for the theory that religious ideas and groups are powerful sources of commitment and motivation. While the doctrinal and sociological characteristics discussed help define evangelicalism, what needs still to be clarified is how these particular features become linked to an inclination to join organizations. How, specifically, does a teaching about salvation and the biblical text, coupled with a desire to convert others, incline evangelicals to act differently from people who do not share those beliefs?

PREACHING THE FAITH: CONVERTING THE NON-BELIEVER

The logical place to start to examine how an evangelical ideology has led to group formation is with their central doctrine that a person is justified, 'saved' by faith alone. The primary reason for evangelical group formation was and is to bear witness to the claim that salvation by faith in Christ is the fundamental fact about the religious life. The creed of the Fellowship of Independent Evangelical Churches of Britain could be applied to hundreds of other evangelical organizations: 'The Fellowship's objective is to pre-serve the purity of the Gospel of our Lord Jesus Christ and to advance the evangelical faith.'[59] Evangelical social involvement most often takes the form of membership in organizations which teach the evangelical doctrine of salvation by faith in Christ alone.

Evangelical organizations in the United States and Great Britain were initially created because of theological conflicts within denominations. Evangelicals had a unique and powerful religious understanding which was not shared by non-evangelicals. English Methodism, the denomination most influenced by evangelical theology, was different from Anglicanism in the belief in how a person was saved. Anglicans stressed the centrality of tradition and church-membership, while Methodists claimed that faith alone was the criterion for salvation. The Methodists eventually broke away from the Anglican Church because of this theological dispute. Evangelicals also formed ecumenical organizations to do their religious work. The London City Mission (1838) was the first of many pan-evangelical organizations in England which united believers of numerous denominations.[60]

Evangelicals continue to be more likely than non-evangelicals to join organizations whose primary goal is the promotion of the Christian faith. The Gallup poll data indicates that evangelicals are more committed to proselytizing than other Christian groups. Fifty-one per cent of American evangelicals polled said that 'helping to win the world for Jesus Christ' should be the most important priority for Christians; for Catholics and Protestants the highest priority was placed on 'concentrating on the spiritual growth of one's self and one's family'.[61] The data suggests that liberal Protestants are more open to theological diversity and tolerant of different social groups and faiths than are evangelicals.[62] The National Council of Churches, by contrast to the Evangelical Alliance and the National Associ-ation of Evangelicals, is very open to religious diversity and pluralism: 'The unit's work on Interfaith Relations promotes the mutual respect between Christians and people of other living faiths.'[63]

The strictness of evangelical doctrines has helped them sustain distinct social groups and religious cultures in the past two centuries, as the distance between evangelicals and non-evangelicals has grown.[64] Some of this 'dis-tance' is a consequence of an ideology which defines a necessary difference between believer and non-believer. Harold Lindsell, an American evangel-ical, writes, 'fellowship . . . indicates a common bond which believers have with believers because of their common faith. Their common faith has content so that their fellowship is based upon this common content.'[65]

The missionary impulse inherent in evangelical theology has also at times led believers to the conviction that they have the duty socially and politically to serve God in the world. Conversion is understood as a life-changing event which structures not simply the beliefs of the convert but also his behaviour. Internal spirituality may be the ultimate measure of a Christian, but outward, upright behaviour is implicitly expected of the converted believer. The National Evangelical Anglican Association affirms that, 'The one God not only demands our exclusive allegiance but also impels us to go out to bring others to the same allegiance.'[66]

The evangelical obligation to serve God came to imply the duty to oppose specific social practices which believers considered sinful. As Wesley noted, 'I have never heard or read of any considerable revival of religion which was not attended with a spirit of reproving . . . . All subjects of revival are reprovers of outward sin.'[67] The same spirit which led the converted believer to perceive the sin in his own life led him also to reprove the sin in society at large. Even if it meant coercion, evangelicals have been willing to use political means to eradicate sinful social practices. The minutes of the New England Annual Conference of the Methodist Episcopal Church in 1868 stated about alcohol, 'we argue that it is the duty of the state to pass a prohibitory law . . . to suppress vice and immorality'.[68] Evangelicals have seen it as a duty to use the political process as a way of realizing the religious goals which they believe are consistent with God's will. A pamphlet of the Christian Life Commission of the Southern Baptist Convention makes the case for the political involvement of believers: 'Christians should be working to elect good officials and also working for good laws through our state, local, and national governments. Each Christian should base his or her views and votes upon the values of the revealed Word of God.'[69]

Max Weber's work on religion can help shed light on the relationship between a religious ideology and individual behaviour. In his *Protestant Ethic and the Spirit of Capitalism*, Weber argues that individual Protestant ascetics, trying to incorporate faith into their daily lives, created an economic ethos which was essential for the development of capitalism. A Calvinist religious ideology encouraged believers to work hard and save their money, a religious belief system which supported capitalist enterprise. Weber may not be correct to connect the growth of modern capitalism so tightly with this Protestant ethic, but he is right to assert that religious ideas influenced the behaviour of individual adherents. In all of his work on religion, Weber contends that religious doctrines function as a motivational element in individual activism.[70]

Evangelical activism can also interpreted in Weberian terms. The religious values of believers have influenced their political conduct because evangelicals believe that they have a sacred obligation to live a Christian life and to pass on the faith to non-believers. In this way, the ethical imperatives of evangelical doctrines serve as a motivational guide to group formation. Weber also recognized that a religious ideology which teaches adherents that they have the responsibility for their own salvation will create a high degree of uncertainty in individuals about that salvation. What Weber wrote about the Protestant ascetic can also be applied to evangelicals: 'the ascetic's assurance of grace is achieved when he is conscious that he has succeeded in becoming a tool of his God, through rationalized, ethical action completely oriented to God'.[71] Evangelical groups form, in part, as an outlet for group members who want some assurance, from themselves and others, that they are saved, and find a confirmation of their status through membership in a religious organization. Membership in an evangelical organization does not proffer salvation to the individual, but an opportunity to manifest the fact that he or she is saved. The Christian Life Commission of the Southern Baptist Convention legitimates evangelical political involvement precisely in these terms: 'Our good works should glorify our heavenly Father and should be convincing to the non-Christian world. Good works should so naturally evolve from our union with Christ that they serve as *proof* of the grace of God in our lives.'[72]

Evangelicalism is not, however, inherently a political ideology. Evangelical doctrine does not explicitly call for the use of political means to bring about social reform. Evangelicals have, however, often concluded that their moral values ought to become public law and they have enlisted the aid of the state for the abolition of slavery, the prohibition of alcohol and the re-criminalization of abortion. They have become politically involved when a social practice conflicts with their religious and cultural values. Groups have formed around biblically-defined 'sins'. As will become apparent, however, the Bible is an elastic document which can and has been used by evangelicals to justify a variety of political positions. It is still an open question if the Bible is important as an independent variable in evangelical political choices, or if group leaders simply use the Bible to support positions that have come from other sources.

WITNESSING TO THE FAITH: THE BIBLE AND GROUP FORMATION

The 'biblical' justification for political involvement is the most interesting and complex way in which an evangelical ideology leads to group-formation. At first glance it would seem self-evident how the transition is made from a biblical norm to the formation of a social group: what the Bible 'taught' on a particular issue would result in the formation of a group to promote that cause. The relationship is, however, more complex and assumes a number of things about the Bible. Two implied claims are made when an evangelical group moves from a biblical teaching to a political principle. First is the assumption that the Bible is the significant source for making 'moral' or political choices, and second is the claim that the scriptures can be made to speak with clarity on a particular issue.

Evangelicals bring to their political involvement the conviction that as Christians they have a 'distinctive understanding' to introduce into the political arena.[73] Evangelicals believe that the Bible is authoritative, that its message is unchanging, and that they have an insight into God's teaching which no 'non-biblical' group, secular or religious, can claim. Carl Henry, a contemporary American evangelical, refers to the Judeo-Christian scriptures as 'the revealed will of God . . . where the principles of social ethics are divinely revealed'.[74] While non-evangelical Christians also appropriate the Bible for their use, evangelicals more seriously cull scriptures for ethical and social guidelines. Evangelicals are deeply committed to discovering the meaning of scripture and in directly applying its message to their lives. As the National Evangelical Anglican group recently asserted, 'What scripture says God says, and what God says we must believe and obey. . . . We have no liberty to disagree with scripture.'[75]

Interviews with evangelical leaders underscore the relationship between the Bible and the social views of believers. Kathryn Ede, of CARE, said that her organization 'wanted Christians involved in every level of politics; people who know the mind and heart of God as revealed in the scriptures'.[76] When evangelicals form political organizations they do so in the belief that no lesser authorities than God and the Bible are on their side. Liberal Protestants, in abandoning a belief in the absolute and clear authority of the Bible, cannot so easily mobilize members into organizations based on biblical exegesis alone. As Steve Bruce has argued, among Christian groups only evangelicals rely so heavily on the content of biblical revelation to recruit group members.[77]

How do the evangelical biblical assumptions influence the extent of group solidarity and the process of consensus formation? Kenneth Tucker, in his analysis of the role of ideology in group-formation, argues that an ideology 'provides a type of knowledge and reasoning by which members understand social life . . . which can contribute to group solidarity'.[78] The evangelical assumption that the Bible is God's unchanging and accurate word contributes to group formation by providing believers with a source for making epistemological claims about social realities. Evangelical group solidarity is enhanced because members believe that their perspective is accurate and, since no other religious groups rely so extensively on the Bible to discern God's will, evangelicals can assert that their perspective is unique. The Evangelical Alliance describes itself as an organization which 'brings together Bible-believing Christians to be a united voice to the nation and an encouraging and initiating force in the churches'.[79] The literature assumes that the distinguishing characteristic between members and non-members is the extent to which one is a Bible-believing Christian.

Are there, in fact, political differences between evangelical and non-evangelical Christians? Polls conducted in 1980 by George Gallup, Stuart Rothenberg and Frank Newport, and the Center for Political Studies at the University of Michigan, found that evangelicalism had a great impact on those political issues which had a moral or religious character.[80] Each of the polls discovered a strong relationship between an evangelical religious ideology and conservative views on matters such as abortion, pre-marital sex, and school prayer. In looking at all of the survey data on American evangelicals, Smidt and Kellstedt conclude that on questions 'related to the role of women in society, prayer in public school, and abortion . . . evangelicals were significantly more conservative in their positions than non-evangelicals'.[81]

Evangelicals do have distinctive political views. The question remains, however, to what extent is an evangelical moral conservatism a function of their biblicism and to what degree can those views be explained by exogenous factors? It is impossible to assert that the Bible, by itself, is the only factor which explains evangelical viewpoints. In fact, historically evangelicals have been divided on a 'moral' issue such as slavery, and profound political differences exist between the contemporary British groups the Evangelical Coalition for Urban Mission and CARE, and American groups such as Sojourners and the Christian Coalition. To claim that evangelicals will mobilize to represent a biblical teaching begs the question of what the Bible says, who decides, and how people are convinced that those definitions are accurate.[82]

The Bible is important for evangelical politics, but so too are the cultural values which evangelicals bring to their reading of the scriptures. Evangelicals in Britain and America have, as a whole, been more isolated from the secularizing effects of urbanization, modernization and education than have liberal Christians. Chapter 5 explains how evangelicals in Britain and America have successfully created distinct cultures with schools, churches and other organizations which have helped believers to retain their values in the face of secularization. As a result, the evangelical culture has more effectively maintained support for conservative or traditional moral values than their liberal co-religionists. This moral traditionalism, supported by biblical interpretations, has helped foment evangelical grievances with particular social practices.

This is not to say that evangelicals have invented *ad hoc* biblical justifications for socially conservative political views. Evangelicals have historically provided a plausible reading of the Bible on slavery, drinking, abortion and pornography. Those who have shared that interpretation and the culture out of which those views have arisen have become active against the sale of alcohol, and against legalized slavery and abortion, and widespread pornography. In this way, the Bible and evangelical culture have reinforced each other.

Evangelical groups have consciously used the Bible to justify their social and political views. Evangelical organizations have had the opportunity to appeal to group members through scripture because evangelicals are receptive to claims made on the Bible's behalf.[83] Evangelicals accept the relevance and accuracy of the Bible, which makes it possible for groups to form on the basis of a biblical claim. Evangelical statements about specific social issues involve an explicit reference to a transcendental set of values, norms which exist independently of the political community and can be used to judge the virtue of that order. The Bible provides that authoritative source to judge the merit of a particular social issue.

Interpreting the Bible to condemn a social practice is a necessary condition for evangelical activism, but it is not a sufficient condition. Human society is full of 'sins' which evangelical Christians deplore, but not all of them serve as conduits for political mobilization. Moral issues are not necessarily political ones. Adultery is a moral issue which evangelicals would unanimously agree is 'sinful' conduct, but this agreement has not led to the formation of political groups to combat extra-marital affairs. British and American evangelicals mobilized around abortion and gay rights, but not adultery and the liberalization of divorce laws. Why are some moral issues better able to mobilize evangelicals than others?

Evangelical leaders have an important role to play in helping to form groups. Leaders need to convince evangelicals that a social practice is sinful and that the consequences of that particular sin are grave enough to demand their political involvement. Leaders in the early temperance movement in America and Britain had the intractable problem of convincing sceptical evangelicals that there was a biblical warrant and a political necessity for temperance societies. As is recorded in the minutes of the Virginia Society for the Promotion of Temperance in 1829, 'It is reported by members of the

Church that there is no warrant in the Bible for temperance societies.'[84] The minutes show that evangelicals had agreed that temperance as a personal practice was scripturally mandated, but most did not concur on the biblical justification for temperance societies or national prohibition. Temperance did not become a political passion until evangelicals were convinced that drinking threatened their religious goals of the conversion of the sinner and the reformation of his social world.

Evangelical group leaders have to persuade potential followers that the dangers of specific social sins are so great that a political remedy is the only answer to the problem. Christian Voice writes to its evangelical constituency that 'America is now facing a grave crisis. Unless we, God's faithful, stand up and are counted, we could see our entire nation destroyed from moral decay.'[85] The extent to which Christian Voice can convince its evangelical audience that 'the breakdown of the family unit, humanist brainwashing of our children in public schools, pornography, and sexual perversion'[86] are genuine threats to evangelical religious and cultural values determines the group's ability to attract members.

This does not mean that any issue, given the right set of leaders, has an equal capacity to mobilize evangelicals. Evangelical theology, with its stress on personal faith and practice, leads believers to be more concerned with political issues which can be interpreted in terms of an individual's lifestyle, behaviour and morality than those issues which are corporate in nature. This stress upon personal behaviour and salvation has led evangelicals to highlight issues such as drinking, gambling and sexual practices while largely ignoring matters of economic justice or foreign policy where the connection between individual choice and social outcome is far less certain. This distinction is reinforced in contemporary public-opinion data which show that evangelicals share conservative positions on moral issues but are diverse on economic and foreign policy questions.[87]

Evangelical organizations and group members derive their social and political values from a shared religious belief system. The evangelical outlook, especially its emphasis on conversion and living a life according to God's will, has led evangelicals to perceive an obligation to translate their religious ideas to their social and political practice. These values have been reinforced in evangelical cultures which have self-consciously maintained a distance from the secularizing effects of modernity. Evangelical cultures have supported a common religious and cultural worldview which has enabled mobilization around particularly potent moral issues. Evangelicals have formed social groups to pass on their faith to non-believers, to witness to biblical doctrines dealing with political issues, and to oppose what they believe to be dangerous social sins. The content of their ideology and the social values of the culture which support that worldview, have been the decisive factors in evangelical mobilization.

ALTERNATIVE THEORIES

Rational choice and status theories of collective action offer competing hypotheses about evangelical mobilization. According to the logic of a rational choice account, salvation could be viewed as a 'good' which is implicitly offered to people who join evangelical organizations. It is possible that evangelical groups overcome the collective action problem by convincing potential recruits that salvation is a valued good and that the only way to attain it is to join an evangelical group. Once evangelical groups had formed on the basis of rational choice, resources could, as Michael Hechter notes, be used to pursue social and political causes.[88]

Membership in evangelical organizations is not, however, rationally produced through an incentives package. Evangelicals join groups because they believe that their membership is consistent with their religious obligation to serve God and not because they expect to receive salvation as a reward for joining evangelical groups. Since evangelical doctrine teaches that organizational membership is inconsequential for salvation, it is impossible for group leaders to use the promise of salvation as an incentive to attract group members. Salvation can only be attained, evangelicals claim, by believing in 'the substitutionary sacrifice of the incarnate Son of God'. (point 3 of the EA Statement of Faith). In order to treat salvation as a selective incentive, rational choice has to ignore what evangelical churches assert in their statements of faith and attribute to actors interests and motives which adherents explicitly say they do not have.

More likely is that evangelicals have formed organizations because their ideology teaches that believers have an obligation to make every aspect of their life a witness to a set of religious values. Evangelicals have pursued their social and religious agenda through collective action groups because of the theological convictions group members share. Evangelicalism has historically been an ideology which has demanded a great commitment on the part of the adherent. British evangelical John Stott writes, 'A Christian is somebody who not only confesses with his lips that Jesus is Lord, but brings every aspect of his life under the sovereign lordship of Jesus – his opinions, his beliefs, his standards, his values, his ambitions, everything.'[89] Membership in political and social organizations naturally follows for believers who are encouraged to make their religious faith tangible in their lives. A rational choice account gives insufficient focus to the importance of group ideology.

A similar problem plagues a status theory of evangelical mobilization: it ignores the independent role played by a religious ideology in group formation.[90] According to this theory, evangelicals have mobilized groups in order to raise or maintain their social prestige or status; movement-formation is tied to the status discontent of evangelical groups. In the temperance movement, for example, American evangelicals were motivated to impose alcohol prohibitions on an entire nation because of threats they were facing from an immigrant population which did not share their cultural values about drinking and sobriety. The doctrinal attachments of evangelicals, status theory claims, acted as a surrogate for a conflict over a group's social status. A group's ideology acted as a justification masking the real issue of some existent strain.

The principal problems with a status theory are that it implies that evangelicals can be demarcated into a single status group and it too ignores the role which an evangelical ideology and cultural values play in mobilizing believers. Evangelicals have historically based their mobilization on shared religious doctrine and cultural values, and not on a common status. Evangelicals have formed religious organizations to pass on their distinct faith to non-believers and political groups to oppose a sinful social practice. In both cases, evangelicals have wanted to pursue the religious goals of the conversion of the sinner and the reformation of his social world. The principal motive of evangelical mobilization revolves around what believers consider to be universal values relating to how a person can be saved or how he or she ought to behave. These shared values led believers to oppose drinking in the nineteenth century and they continue to shape the evangelical political response to issues such as pornography and abortion.

CONCLUSION

This definition of evangelicalism has provided an insight into the ways in which an evangelical ideology has led to group formation. Evangelical religious and cultural values have been the primary motivation for group mobilization. These values have helped shape the evangelical response to a variety of moral, social, and political issues. Social movements do not, however, occur in a vacuum; they are necessarily created within a political environment which shapes their behaviour. In order to show how evangelicalism is affected by its political institutions, the next chapter reviews the temperance movements in America and Britain. An analysis of those movements will show the importance of an evangelical ideology in legitimating group mobilization. A comparison between the two countries will also demonstrate the importance of political structures in determining the forms of group mobilization and the ultimate political success of the two movements.

4 Temperance Politics in Britain and America

In a 1905 speech before the Baptist World Congress, George White, a Liberal member of the British Parliament, expressed an opinion about alcohol which was widely shared by evangelicals on both sides of the Atlantic: 'The centre of operation against this monster evil should undoubtedly be the Christian churches. We exist to fight the devil in all his works, and this drink evil is undoubtedly his greatest masterpiece.'[1] By 1905, most evangelicals had become convinced that the only solution to the 'alcohol evil' was the total prohibition of its sale and consumption. How was it that these transatlantic Christians came to share a religious condemnation of drinking and why did they conclude that they had a religious obligation to impose their temperance ethic on an entire nation?

This chapter reviews the political mobilization of evangelical Christians in the British and American temperance movements. The chapter highlights the role of evangelical religious ideas and values in the formation of organizations to prohibit drinking. Evangelicals in Britain and America gradually came to the conclusion that they had a religious obligation to address the social, moral, and spiritual problems associated with drinking. With a faith that emphasized evangelism, social activism, and the idea that individual moral reform could take place through legislative action, evangelicals were naturally drawn to the temperance cause which promised the reformation of the sinner's world.

Evangelicals translated their enthusiasm for moral reform into politically powerful temperance organizations from the mid-nineteenth century and into the twentieth. Evangelicals in each country provided moral enthusiasm for reform, intellectual and material resources for a leadership anxious to end the traffic in alcohol, and a religious justification for social action based on a religious understanding about the sinfulness and danger of alcohol abuse.

Once groups were formed, however, political structures unique to each nation shaped the political success of the respective movements. American groups used their resources and political influence to pass state and local prohibition laws and eventually a national amendment to the constitution prohibiting the sale and manufacture of alcohol. British organizations, by contrast, were unable to effect any meaningful change in drinking laws despite almost a century of political agitation. This chapter shows how the different political outcomes can be explained by examining the state institutions with which American and British temperance groups interacted. The most significant institutional differences between Britain and America which structured temperance politics were the presence or absence of an established church and the relative strength of the two states. The fact that Britain had a stronger state than America in the late nineteenth century had very different consequences for temperance politics.

The political success of temperance required the unification of British evangelicals, but the presence of the Established Anglican Church, and the subsequent polarization of religious groups along partisan lines which it created, restricted any pan-evangelical mobilization. The Conservative Party worked to preserve the social, religious and political privileges of the Established Church, while the Liberals fought for social equality for nonconformists. Evangelicals, who were most likely to support temperance, were denominationally and politically divided between Anglican and nonconformist churches. The established Church of England, which divided Anglicans (members of the state church) and Nonconformists (all dissenters from the Church of England) into the competing Liberal and Conservative political parties, strongly influenced strategic relations between British religious groups. The cross-cutting effect of the party cleavage restricted the political unity of evangelical Christians.

Britain's unitary polity also limited the efforts of temperance organizations. Temperance leaders tried to overcome the evangelical cleavage in a non-partisan movement, but since they were seeking change that could only be brought about by an act of Parliament, they could not help but become involved in the party-political process. Interest groups did not have the use of a political referendum to overcome partisan divisions, nor could they take advantage of their power in local regions to pass local drinking restrictions. Ideally, temperance groups wanted to put the drink question to a direct vote of the people, but Parliament was the only institution which could grant them that power. Temperance, as a result, became inexorably bound to the Liberal Party, which seemed most sympathetic to the cause.

In America, there was no state church and no special political privileges for a particular denomination to divide evangelicals into competing political parties. America's federal polity weakened the state and provided myriad opportunities for temperance activists to use their political influence at state and local levels. Restrictions on drinking were introduced into towns, counties and states well before the drive for national prohibition. Activists used the political referendum, initiative, and state-constitutional amendment to bring votes on drinking directly before the people. These non-party appeals allowed group leaders to overcome evangelical partisan divisions, as believers successfully translated their moral enthusiasm into political proposals.

EVANGELICAL IDEOLOGY AND DRINKING IN BRITAIN AND AMERICA

Evangelicals had a well-formulated opposition to drunkenness prior to the formation of the first temperance organizations in America and Britain in the 1820s and 1830s, but not to moderate drinking. There is no explicit condemnation of drinking in the Bible; in fact, Old and New Testament biblical figures are frequently portrayed enjoying wine. The first recorded miracle of Jesus in the Gospel of John in the New Testament is his turning water into wine at the wedding in Cana (John 2:1–11). The Bible, however, could easily be interpreted to oppose drunkenness. In the New Testament book 1 Corinthians, there is a clear condemnation of drunkenness: 'Do you not know that the unrighteous will not inherit the Kingdom of God. . . . Neither the immoral, nor idolaters, nor adulterers . . . nor drunkards.'[2] John Wesley had referred to drunkards as 'a public enemy',[3] expressing an attitude which was shared by most evangelicals.

The original temperance organizations, following what seemed to be the biblical teaching, wanted to reform people's drinking habits, but they did not have in mind the legal prohibition of alcohol. The intent of these initial groups was to moderate the habits of the heavy drinker. The minutes of the First Temperance Society in Cherryfield, Maine show that the concern was about abusive drinking: 'The volume of scripture has plainly taught that the practice of intemperance is incompatible with religious duty.'[4] British temperance organizations also initially sought to reduce the volume of drinking in their country; they did not oppose the moderate use of alcohol. The Blackburn Temperance Society in 1831 passed a resolution which stated: 'that the *excessive* (my emphasis) use of intoxicating liquors now so prevalent is productive of much poverty, disease, and crime . . . and it is the duty of the philanthropist to seek means to change the habits of the community'.[5] In these early years, temperance organizations believed that the best way to change drinking patterns was to use moral suasion rather than legal proscription. Temperance, consequently, was not initially viewed as a political issue.

Evangelical churches did not initially embrace the new temperance cause in Britain or America in the 1830s. Individual evangelicals were at the forefront of the Movement, but the churches as a whole took no stand on the alcohol question beyond a condemnation of drunkenness. Temperance and teetotalism were actually opposed by some religious bodies in America and Britain in the 1830s. Evangelicals were members of cultures in which the consumption of alcohol was an accepted social practice and, for most believers, most notably the Anglicans, drinking sacramental wine was part of a weekly religious ceremony. There seemed to be no religious obligation or social imperative to legitimate evangelical involvement in temperance organizations.[6]

By the 1860s and 1870s in Britain, and the 1870s and 1880s in America, however, evangelical Christians and churches had become prominent advocates for alcohol reform. For the next several decades, evangelicals mobilized an opposition to drinking with the goal of prohibiting the manufacture and sale of alcohol. What happened to justify this new evangelical political involvement? Why was drinking seized upon as a threat by evangelicals? The conversion of evangelicals to the prohibition cause occurred because believers came to view alcohol as the principal enemy to social reform. The evangelical principles of conversionism and social activism became relevant to the question of alcohol as believers became convinced that the best way to reform their world was to end the blight of drinking. By the end of the nineteenth century, evangelicals in large numbers believed that alcohol lay at the root of American and British social problems.

Jack Blocker and Norman Clark argue convincingly that the case for alcohol reform in America and Britain was not overstated; drinking was causing severe social problems in the late nineteenth century.[7] The per capita consumption of alcohol rose dramatically throughout the nineteenth century, reaching the highest levels to date in Britain and America by the 1870s. Brian Harrison noted that there was a constant increase in wine and spirits consumption and in the number of liquor licences granted in Britain between 1800 and 1870. The rate of growth for both was more rapid than population increase.[8] Consumption and liquor licences also increased rapidly in America in the first three-quarters of the nineteenth century. Blocker shows that beer-production in America rose from 158 million gallons in 1866 to 298 million gallons in 1873. During the same period, per capita consumption rose from 4.4 gallons to 7.0 gallons, the highest level of consumption to that point in American history.[9]

It is certainly arguable that with per capita consumption on the rise in Britain and America, the problems associated with drinking, including violence against women, broken homes, alcohol-related deaths, and crime would also have increased throughout the nineteenth century. What is apparent is that evangelicals increasingly blamed alcohol for social problems, and they used their religious ideology to justify political support for temperance and prohibition. Alcohol reform became, in the minds of evangelicals, social reform, and social reform was religious reform. By striving to reform society through purifying and uplifting it, evangelicals believed that they were performing a religious duty. White spoke for many evangelicals in 1905 when he said: 'The temperance reformation is at the bottom of all social reform. . . . No great social problem can be solved without it.'[10]

Evangelicals united a spiritual and material argument about alcohol because they saw only an artificial distinction between these types of concerns. Evangelicals wanted the reformation of the drinker and the creation of a culture in which religion, and religious values, could flourish. As reborn sinners, evangelicals felt obliged to demonstrate their commitment to God through a battle against social evils. The Third Annual Report of the Virginia Society for the Promotion of Temperance made the connection between social action and religious witness as early as 1829: 'When vice is to be put down, and virtue promoted, the Christian is called by a voice which he cannot disregard, by the voice of religion and God, to take an active and zealous part.'[11]

The most obvious way in which alcohol came to be viewed as inimical to evangelical social and religious values was the growing conviction of believers that drinking stood in the way of the conversion of the sinner to faith in Jesus Christ. Drinking, evangelicals came to believe, was a primary obstacle to the reception of the gospel message. A British temperance tract of 1854 stated the matter succinctly: 'We believe that drinking is a prodigious barrier thrown up in the sinner's way which makes his conversion more difficult and lessens the likelihood of his turning to God.'[12] In 1905, Mr White lamented before the World Baptist Congress that drinkers were unreceptive to the good news of Jesus Christ: 'We know the rock upon which they (drinkers) could be most securely planted is the Rock Jesus Christ, but the message does not reach them, and though it is the best news they could ever hear they will not come to listen'.[13]

The church was urged to support prohibition because it would help the drinker to be saved from his sin. Colonel Wright, of the Salvation Army, argued in 1897, 'he (the drinker) has a soul to save and it is the special business of the church to endeavour to bring him into such circumstances as will be most likely to contribute to that end'.[14] This was not an empty platitude which evangelical activists manipulated to mask a simple conservatism. Evangelicals placed the highest possible value on their personal conversion and their obligation to convert their neighbour; they had always seen it as a special duty of theirs to convert sinners to the Christian faith.

Evangelicals believed that the ultimate goal of life was salvation and that they could and should help bring that message to non-believers. When it became apparent to evangelicals that drinking inhibited their religious witness, they concluded that prohibition had to be supported. Drinking was not simply a social practice they rejected, it was a sin which made salvation impossible to obtain. Temperance organizations used the authoritative witness of reformed drinkers who preached to audiences that they personally had been lost to the sin of alcohol but had been saved by sobriety and God.

Evangelicals came to believe that drinking, and a drink culture, were a threat to the corporate work of Christian churches. In 1876, the New England branch of the Methodist Episcopal Church claimed that 'we unhesitatingly assert that the most powerful evil that confronts the Christian church today, in her onward march to the conquest of the world, is intemperance and the consequent accursed traffic in intoxicating beverages'.[15] In Britain, the notion that drink customs were an alternative form of worship to Christianity became popular in religious circles. The British evangelical clergyman Dean Close asked in 1862, 'is it not drink above all things which . . . keeps back numbers from the house of God, which degrades the masses of society, and mars almost every effort to win souls for Christ?'[16]

Evangelical activists became convinced that a culture which allowed drinking to take place was one which was antagonistic to the pursuit of religion. Evangelicals saw themselves as called by God to oppose social sins, especially a sin such as drinking, which limited the appeal of evangelical religion. Alcohol was particularly singled out by evangelicals because it was perceived as the greatest of sins. A tract from the Edinburgh Temperance Society asserted in 1854, 'when one particular sin rises to a towering height among us, may we not single it out as the object of special attack. . . . We single out this sin because it is rampant in the midst of us.'[17]

As evangelicals came to accept that there was a connection between drinking and religion, temperance-group leaders legitimated evangelical involvement through an explicit appeal to believers' religious conscience: 'Every Christian ought to look upon Temperance societies as a valuable auxiliary to the grand and ultimate object – the salvation of the soul.'[18] Evangelicals concluded that the political goal of a dry nation was a necessary adjunct to the spiritual goal of the churches to convert non-believers. The New England Methodist Episcopal Church Conference of 1906 claimed, 'the whole church must line up against the liquor power. We want our consciences quickened, nerves strengthened, wills emboldened, and a determination not only to vote and work as we pray but to do all these things until complete victory is achieved.'[19]

Temperance reformers coupled an evangelical awareness of the problem of alcohol with the conviction that something could and should be done about it. Evangelicalism contributed to the prohibition movement in the late nineteenth century an ideology which justified a close relationship between religion and politics. In America and Britain, evangelical Christians legit-imated the transition from private morality to public policy on the ground that the alcohol evil was so great that it called for extraordinary measures. God had called them as Christian believers to promote virtue and put down vice and to spread the saving message of Jesus Christ, which is precisely how evangelical activists viewed the prohibition 'reformation'. At the pro-ceedings of the Seventh Annual Session of the Baptist Congress in 1888, the Reverend H. A. Delano of South Norwalk, Connecticut argued that 'the Church of God should kneel with fixed bayonets, ready and set and resolute forever against the mad incursion of this monster crime'.[20]

Evangelical support for temperance organizations in Britain and America also occurred because believers accepted the argument that there were tremendous social costs associated with drinking. Group leaders enlisted the aid of doctors, lawyers and social scientists to demonstrate a link between drinking and poor health, crime, poverty, violence and the dis-integration of the family. These experts used their 'objective' viewpoint to catalogue the host of social ills caused by drinking, and thereby granted legitimacy to the temperance cause. According to a paper delivered by Emory Aldrich before the American Social Science Association in 1881, the question of the harmful effects of alcohol was 'a question of facts which can be determined only by an appeal to the evidence in the case'. The 'evidence' which Aldrich cited indicated that 'the relation of cause and effect between the common use of intoxicating liquors and crime and poverty has been repeatedly demonstrated by legislative and other invest-igations in our country'.[21]

'Evidence' about the consequences of alcohol was also produced from justices, doctors, legislators and ministers. Chief Justice Noah Davis of New York argued that 'intoxicating drinks enable men to commit crimes, by firing the passions and quenching conscience'.[22] At the English National Prohibition convention in 1897, a Mr Charles Roberts used charts and a statistical analysis to show a correlation between drinking and crime. Roberts concluded, 'you will see by following the lines that drunkenness as meas-ured by the police apprehensions tends to vary in the same proportion as crimes of violence and sexual crimes'.[23] John Ellis, a medical doctor from New York City, asserted in 1887 that 'intoxicating drink has hurt and killed more of the human family than all other poisons or evil uses pertaining to food and drink together'.[24] Finally, drinking, because it led to crime, vio-lence, and poor health, came to be seen as dangerous to the fabric of family life. Canon Hicks of the Anglican Church argued, 'the drink demon is always and everywhere the corrupter and breaker-up of homes'.[25]

Evangelical activists were happy to use the evidence of 'expert' scientists, but they frequently added their own apocalyptic language to demonstrate colourfully the dangers of alcohol. The Reverend J. M. Stearns asserted that alcohol produced 'a hundred thousand victims every year, and a vast army of criminals, paupers, and drunkards, and endless misery and death'. Drinking, Stearns concluded, 'is the mother of all abominations'.[26] Lyman Beecher, the great nineteenth-century Congregational minister, reported in his autobiography that he opposed drinking because of its 'deadly effect on health, intellect, the family, society, civil and religious institutions, and especially in nullifying the means of grace and destroying souls'.[27] Beecher nicely fused what to him were self-evident propositions: drinking threatened the physical health of the body, the institutions of a nation and the spiritual health of the soul.

A final argument justifying evangelical activism, and one which would become popular a century later in the abortion controversy, was that by allowing the sin of alcohol within their nation, Christians were somehow responsible for participating in that sin. Beecher argued, 'If we countenance establishments in extending and perpetuating a national calamity, are we not partakers in other men's sins?'[28] George White claimed that 'if we do not as Christian citizens use the power He (God) has placed in our hands and dethrone this juggernaut, we shall as nations and people reap our reward in decadence, sin, and ruin'.[29] In the case of alcohol, it seemed, the sin of omission was as great as the sin of commission.

It did not occur to temperance activists to question why people drank in late-nineteenth-century Britain and America; temperance literature did not address the social and cultural function of alcohol. Evangelicals were members of societies experiencing tremendous social problems associated with industrialization and urbanization. Temperance activists claimed that drinking was the primary cause of the poverty, disease, crime and poor health which seemed rampant in the urban slums of New York and London. They never entertained the idea that drinking might have been a response to those social problems, rather than their cause. Prohibition attracted evangelicals who wanted to do something positive to reform their social world and who believed that the drinking problem could be rectified by statute. Prohibition was not, however, perfectly consistent with an evangelical ideology which traditionally focused attention on the regeneration of the individual by divine love and not by human laws. If drinking were a moral defect, as some evangelicals implicitly argued, it is hard to imagine how public laws could be made to reform the immoral drinker.

Brian Harrison and Jack Blocker correctly argue that evangelical activism had the effect of secularizing religion by supplanting religious principles with a political cause.[30] Almost imperceptibly, the evangelical focus on alcohol shifted from a claim about the need to convert the individual who drank, to an argument about the social consequences of drinking as a whole. Temperance activists, evangelicals included, began to rely more and more heavily on secular and 'scientific' justifications for their activism, rather than on religious principles. Irving Fisher, professor of political economy at Yale University, proudly claimed in a document from the early twentieth century that 'the movement for prohibition is not today primarily an emotional movement. It rests rather on the cold-blooded calculations of the scientist, the statistitian, the economist, the public health officer, and the industrial manager.'[31] The claims of the statistitian and the health officer may have helped to objectify the temperance movement but, in so doing, removed the religious undergirding which provided the initial impulse for evangelical concern and activism. Evangelicals succumbed to a consequentialist fallacy of implying that if the indirect results of an action (drinking) were sinful, than the action itself must also be sinful. The American activist E. J. Wheeler openly admitted this bias when he wrote, 'It is wrong to drink because of the consequences, not because of the inherent sinfulness of the action. . . . The sin of such an act lies in its harmfulness, in its consequences.'[32]

Evangelicals began to emphasize the social dangers of alcohol and the potential benefits of a prohibition law to such an extent that they were often guilty of asserting the non-orthodox view that sin could be eradicated from the human heart by legislation, rather than by faith. The American activist Rev. A. M. Richardson claimed that 'prohibition is in the line of God's Providences, and an important factor in the Christian and reformatory work of the age.'[33] Some Christian thinkers raised the objection that religionists who supported prohibition were guilty of replacing the biblical story of God's salvation with an account of a human-driven salvation. As one minister angrily asserted about temperance organizations, 'let no syren voice, under the garb of religion, draw you away from the Word of God which declares that the only way to save a man is by the Cross of Christ'.[34] Evangelicals who supported prohibition did not, however, believe that their social activism in any way obscured the religious message of Christ. Prohibition was, for them, the cause of God and therefore perfectly consistent with their religious obligation to save sinners. A British evangelical tract, responding directly to the religious critics of prohibition, asserted 'we have never attempted to substitute abstinence for conversion to God. We have never sought to mislead the poor sinner so as to make him suppose that he may enter the Kingdom of heaven without being born again.'[35]

The confusion between the social and religious arguments in favour of temperance underscored the extent to which group leaders used religious and secular appeals to increase the scope of the temperance movement. Group leaders needed to marshal as many political and monetary resources as possible. To do that, religious appeals had to be combined with secular arguments which would attract non-religious resources. To raise resources and have political success, the British and American temperance movements had to move beyond a simple appeal to evangelical Christians.

What happened to the evangelical reliance on the Bible in all of this new-found excitement for prohibition? How did evangelicals justify a prohibition ethic in the light of the apparent scriptural legitimation for moderate drinking? Some Christian leaders argued that there was no scriptural justification for prohibition. A Reverend W. H. Ten Eyck concluded from his study of the Old and New Testament scriptures that there was 'never an intimation that the remedy for drunkenness is total abstinence; nor a single command that Christians must abstain because some men use wine to excess'.[36] Most evangelicals, however, argued that Christians had an obligation to abstain from drinking alcohol *despite* the fact that abstinence was not explicitly biblically-mandated. These evangelicals argued that the example of believers living a sober life could help drinkers whose lives needed radically to be reformed. The Reverend Herrick Johnson acknowledged in 1872 that he did *not* believe that 'the drinking of wine is a sin per se'. He asserted, nonetheless, that Christians ought to abstain from drinking and even agitate for temperance laws: 'Do not those who love Jesus Christ, and who profess to be actuated by his love, owe a duty to them that are weak? Are we not bound to help them abstain both by our precept and our example?'[37] Temperance reform was considered so vital for the spiritual and physical reformation of Britain and America that evangelicals came to the conclusion that they had a special obligation to go beyond the biblical mandate against drunkenness to include all forms of drinking. The Reverend Edward Jewett argued that 'it should be the duty of every Christian body to remove a deadly temptation from the weak'.[38]

Evangelicals also engaged in creative biblical exegesis and historical study to prove that much of the wine mentioned in the Bible was not, in fact, alcoholic. Evangelical activists claimed that there were two classes of wine referred to in the Bible, one which was fermented and alcoholic and the other which was unfermented and non-alcoholic. The wine which Jesus drank at the Last Supper, evangelicals argued, was non-alcoholic. A rigorous debate ensued in Christian tracts and periodicals around this so-called 'wine question', and many churches began to use grape juice rather than wine in their communion services. A Dr John Ellis claimed that 'it may clearly be seen that the Sacred Scriptures distinctly recognize two kinds of wine: one kind is ripened and sweetened by the Lord, a good, healthy, nourishing fluid; the other is the product of leaven and will intoxicate'.[39] Temperance evangelicals were so concerned to give biblical legitimacy to this two-wine theory that they annually published *The Temperance Bible Commentary*, which gave an extended exegesis of every biblical verse which referred in any way to 'wine and strong drink'.[40]

The biblical exegesis used by evangelicals was creative, to put it mildly. This does not mean, however, that the religious and biblical rhetoric was simply a smoke-screen masking some other motivation for evangelical activism. Evangelicals felt a religious obligation to reform their neighbour's social world; that is why they went to the trouble of finding biblical evidence for a social practice which they concluded lay at the root of society's problems.

Evangelicals also incorporated their religious ideology into the strategies of temperance organizations. In Britain and America, temperance campaigns consciously adopted the form of a religious meeting. Temperance hymns were sung, personal testimonies were given by reformed drinkers, and the audience was invited to pledge themselves to the moral campaign. The symbols and moral discourse were similar to those of a Sunday morning worship service. One of the most popular activities of temperance groups, especially in England, was the signing of a pledge on the part of the drinker promising personal abstinence. In many instances, as Lilian Shiman notes, the taking of a pledge for a reformed drinker was 'like being baptized'.[41] Evangelical leaders imagined that the temperance cause would be 'a Christian movement not merely for bettering men's bodies, but for saving their souls'.[42]

Evangelical activists eventually succeeded in attracting widespread religious support for the political goal of prohibition. In 1862, the Church of England founded a temperance organization, the Church of England Temperance Society (CETS), which had the support of the large evangelical wing of the church. Nonconformist evangelicals, meanwhile, were active through the United Kingdom Alliance founded in 1853. Brian Harrison noted that in 1848 only 566 ministers were listed as prominent teetotallers in Britain; by 1866 the figure rose to 2760.[43] Evangelical churches were also at the forefront of the Temperance Movement in America by 1870, providing resources first for the Women's Christian Temperance Union (1874) and then for the Anti-Saloon League (1893).[44] In both nations, nearly all evangelical leaders publicly supported the temperance cause by the late 1870s.

Temperance activists never passed a prohibition law in Britain. American groups, by contrast, used the political opportunities at their disposal to pass a prohibition amendment to the Constitution. Prohibition failed in Britain because evangelicals were politically, socially and culturally divided by the Established Church and because reform groups inherited a unitary political system which limited the ability of groups to pressure for political change. American temperance activists, who were free of establishment constrictions, took advantage of a weak polity which was remarkably open to a wide variety of democratic pressure at local levels.

TEMPERANCE POLITICS AND THE CHURCHES IN BRITAIN

The nineteenth-century temperance movement in Britain originated in the 1830s with the founding of the British and Foreign Temperance Society and the British Teetotal Society. Moderation, not prohibition, was the goal of these early groups. In 1853 the United Kingdom Alliance (UKA) was founded and for the first time English temperance reformers suggested legislating the prohibition of traffic in alcohol.[45] The founders of the Alliance were Protestant nonconformists who, out of a religious concern for the poor in England, believed that only the total and immediate prohibition of liquor would improve the spiritual and material lives of working-class families. According to the UKA, the preaching of moderation and simple licensing of drinking places had 'utterly failed to reduce the evil consequences of alcohol'.[46]

The Alliance believed that the most effective way to reform drinking habits was to introduce local prohibition into England. This goal, however, was complicated by Britain's unitary political structures, which curtailed the autonomy of local political authorities such as borough and county councils. Regional bodies did exist in Britain in the late nineteenth century and they did enjoy significant political authority. Local authorities were responsible for the provision of a variety of services, including education, police, and water and sewage, but they did not have the power to prohibit alcohol. The political change which the Alliance wanted (local prohibition), however, could only be brought about by Parliament. Temperance activists could not initiate direct local votes on the alcohol question through a Referendum or an Initiative, which limited their ability to take advantage of their electoral support in certain areas.[47]

Ira Katznelson, in an article which contrasts working-class formation in nineteenth-century Britain and America, has argued convincingly that the British state gradually expanded its power during the nineteenth century at the expense of local regions. Katznelson cites the passage of such acts as the Poor Law of 1834; the Public Health Acts of 1848, 1866, and 1875; the Police Acts of 1839 and 1856; and the Food and Drug Acts of 1860 and 1872 as evidence that Parliament took on responsibility for social policy in Britain. The consequence of this gradual expansion of state power for political reform groups, including temperance organizations, was that they had to direct their political pressure to the centre, to Parliament, which increasingly dictated the pace and form of social reform.[48]

The Alliance had no choice but to pressure Parliament for democratic political reform at the national level in order to have the right to legislate restrictions against alcohol in local areas. The Alliance struggle for alcohol reform quickly became enmeshed in the question of how much democratic control voters would enjoy over local political affairs and, by implication, how strong the national state would become. Ironically, the Alliance wanted at one and the same time to curb the power of the national state and give local regions and voters some autonomy, while at the same time the group wanted to expand the reach of state power to limit the sale and consumption of alcohol. John Kempster, Chairman of the London Auxiliary of the UKA, recognized the close connection between questions of alcohol reform and political self-government when he argued that 'the most approved method of attaining to Prohibition is to apply the process of Local Self Government. And we must not forget that all forms of Local Government are invariably and of necessity prescribed and regulated by the state.'[49] The practical reality was that the path to any form of prohibition led by necessity through Parliament which, as the nineteenth century progressed, dominated issues of social reform.

For the Alliance to succeed in Parliament, it had to attract the support of evangelical voters from all the denominations. A minister active in the UKA asserted that prohibition could easily be secured if the churches united: 'If all Christian communions would unite in denouncing the liquor traffic, in twelve months there would be no liquor traffic to denounce.'[50] Evangelicals seemed well placed in the late nineteenth century to pursue a political programme; they dominated the Nonconformist, Congregational, Baptist, and Methodist churches by middle of the century and were influential in the established Church of England and Ireland and the Church of Scotland. As the 1851 religious census demonstrated, over one-half of the British population were church members, and evangelicals outnumbered non-evangelicals. Evangelicals were powerful enough to command the attention of both political parties.[51]

In theory, the theological convictions of Anglican and Nonconformist evangelicals could have mobilized them together for the cause of temperance reform. Despite their denominational cleavage, evangelicals shared a theology which stressed personal salvation and a religious view that politics was an arena to be used to bring about the eradication of sin. Evangelicals wanting to save the sinner's soul might also have been united in the cause of the reformation of his or her social world. Some organizations had already been formed to fulfill the dream of pan-evangelical unity. The London Missionary Society (1795), The Religious Tract Society (1799), The British and Foreign Bible Society (1804), and the London City Mission (1835) were all endeavours in which Anglican and Nonconformist evangelicals cooperated. But the unity which these organizations achieved was nominal; believers were brought together for the non-political goals of foreign and domestic missionary work and Bible translations, and even these organizations had limited success overcoming the cleavage between Anglicans and Nonconformists. It would prove to be even more difficult to sustain evangelical unity on the political issue of temperance.[52]

The social and political cleavages between Anglican and Nonconformist believers caused by the Established Church hampered evangelical unity. Members of the Church of England had rights not shared by believers in all other denominations. Anglican churches and clergy were supported by taxation, Bishops of the Church of England sat in the House of Lords, and the tie remained close between membership in the Church of England and the franchise, political office, university membership and landownership. The political questions of disestablishment and religious equality were vital ones in late-nineteenth-century England as Nonconformists tried to abolish religious tests for university admission, gain the freedom to hold burial services in parish churchyards, and establish an undenominational system of education.[53]

The Church of England had its own reasons to fear Nonconformist churches. Anglicans had been converting in large numbers to Nonconformist denominations for well over a century. The 1851 religious census, which showed that total membership in Nonconformist churches was greater than that of the Church of England, concerned Anglicans who read into the figures a mounting political protest against the religious establishment.[54] Anglicans adopted a strict interpretation of their duty to give full obedience to the established church and frowned upon official contact with evangelical churches and organizations outside the Church of England, such as the United Kingdom Alliance. Anglican evangelicals came to believe that the preservation of the Establishment was essential for the religious conversion of England. Church leaders increasingly restated the traditional teaching that it was the duty of the state to support the religious education of its citizenry and that the Church of England was essential for the preservation of social order.[55]

Anglican evangelicals found themselves in the most awkward situation of all. Having shared a religious experience of conversion, Anglican evangelicals often had more in common with their Nonconformist peers than with their High Church Colleagues. Some individual Anglicans supported a pan-evangelical approach to social issues which crossed the Anglican–Nonconformist divide.[56] William Wilberforce and Lord Shaftesbury are the best-known among scores of Anglican evangelicals who cooperated with Nonconformists on a variety of social issues. Anglican evangelicals, in the words of the sociologist David Martin, 'experienced a conflict of mind and heart'.[57] In their hearts they knew themselves to be evangelicals sharing with other 'true' believers a common faith which transcended denominational loyalties. In their minds, however, they were defenders of the Establishment and opposed to Nonconformist politics and movements.

The denominational cleavage between Anglicans and Nonconformists was mirrored in a rigid party-division. The Conservative Party, supported by the majority of Anglicans, fought for the preservation of the privileges of the Established Church, while the Liberal Party sympathized with the Nonconformist goal of religious and political equality for all believers, including Catholics. By 1850 this cleavage in both religious and political life produced 'highly homogeneous and mutually hostile Nonconformist – Liberal and Anglican–Conservative groupings'.[58] Kenneth Wald, in an exhaustive study of voting patterns in the late-nineteenth and early-twentieth centuries, concludes that Protestant Nonconformity was the best predictor of support for the Liberal Party.[59]

The UKA concluded that the best way to maximize its political support would be to develop a non-partisan campaign which would remain independent of the major parties. The Alliance believed, correctly, that such a strategy was the only way to avoid the political cleavage among its evangelical constituency. In a manifesto from 1859 the Alliance appealed to its members to focus solely on the alcohol question: 'Rising above class, sectarian, and party considerations, all good citizens should combine to procure the enactment prohibiting the sale of intoxicating beverages.'[60]

The Alliance focused its political efforts on electing MPs who were likely to support the Permissive Bill, a law which would have given voters at local levels the right to control the sale and consumption of alcohol. The Permissive Bill proposed that a vote on prohibition would be taken in a borough, parish, or district if ten per cent of the electors signed a petition requesting such a vote. If a two-thirds majority of the persons voting on the question supported Prohibition it would become law. The Alliance lobbied for the Permissive Bill from its founding in 1853 until 1895, but it was never passed. With local option, the Alliance believed that they would be able to pass prohibition laws in those regions where their support was strongest, leading eventually to a momentum for a national law prohibiting alcohol. John Hilton, parliamentary agent for the UKA, confidently predicted that public opinion so favoured prohibition that 'the local veto would be widely exercised by the voters'.[61]

Local temperance leaders sought pledges from voters to vote only for the candidate, regardless of party, who supported the Permissive Bill, or to abstain from voting if no suitable candidate could be found. The *London Alliance Review* reported on a by-election in 1899, for example, in which one candidate, Mr Costolloe, 'gave a hearty adherence to the principle of the popular control of the liquor traffic by a Direct Veto', while the other candidate, Mr Wrightson, 'was not willing to entrust to the persons primarily concerned with such a voting power'. Not surprisingly, the *Review* concluded that the 'friends of Temperance should give their hearty support to Mr Costolloe'.[62] The Alliance hoped that the threat of pulling pledged voters away from a party candidate would lead Conservative and Liberal parties to compete with one another for the temperance vote and speed up the process of reform.[63]

The Alliance's non-partisan campaign was aided in the early and middle decades of the nineteenth century by the size of the electorate and weakness of political parties. The electorate had been expanded in the First Reform Act of 1832 from 409 000 to 814 000 registered voters, a large enough number to remove aristocratic dominance of the Commons, yet small enough to ensure that well-organized pressure groups with small blocks of dedicated voters had a genuine prospect of holding the balance of power in particular elections.[64] The Alliance also benefited from the weakness of political parties throughout the middle decades of the century. Samuel Beer has described the period between the First and Second Reform Acts (in 1832 and 1867), as 'the golden age of the private MP' because political parties were not yet strong enough to impose party discipline on their members.[65] Without strong political parties, candidates had to respond sympathetically to organized interests within their constituency. Pressure groups such as the Alliance took advantage of a political system which, for a short time, encouraged interest-group activism, and flourished in mid-nineteenth-century Britain.

The political neutrality of the Alliance during this period allowed it to capitalize on Anglican and Nonconformist evangelical discontent with the drink trade, and evidence suggests that their political efforts succeeded.

There were prominent Conservatives in the Alliance in the 1850s and by the late 1860s Anglican leadership in the organization was at an all-time high of 22 per cent. Although Liberals had dominated the Alliance since its founding, no temperance activist had tried to link the alcohol question with the Liberal Party until the 1870s.[66]

The utility of a non-partisan electoral strategy fell following the Second and Third Reform Acts, however, as the electorate was increased from 1.3 to 2.5 million voters in 1867, and 3.1 to 5.7 million voters in 1886. With more voters within a constituency, the value of a small number of voters pledged to vote only for Alliance candidates decreased substantially. In order to have the balance of power in a particular election, the Alliance, with the larger electorate, had to pledge a much larger number of voters.

The extended franchise and formation of new constituencies brought about by the Reform Acts also led to the creation of well-financed party organizations which registered voters, mobilized widespread electoral support, and competed with pressure groups.[67] Party organizations flourished in each constituency and began to dominate the electoral process. Pressure groups like the Alliance gradually discovered that there was very little that they could accomplish independent of party support. By all indications, party structures became more important after 1867; individual MPs now took their cues from party elites and not a small number of dedicated voters within a constituency. In 1850 and 1860, respectively, a mere 16 per cent and 6 per cent of all votes in the Commons were party votes. By 1871 party votes had risen to 35 per cent of the total and subsequently increased to 47 per cent in 1881 and 76 per cent in 1894.[68]

As political parties began to dominate the electoral process, the strategy of the Alliance had to be to persuade one of the parties which had a chance of forming a majority in Parliament to take up reform. The only way for issue-based groups such as the UKA to succeed in the new electoral environment was to win the active support of the party in power. In the early 1870s, the Alliance cautiously aligned itself with the Liberal Party.[69] It seemed logical for the Alliance to support the Liberal Party, which had always been more sympathetic to temperance than the Conservative Party. A delegate to the 1877 Conference of Temperance Electors realistically argued about the new partisan strategy, 'after all, temperance people have more to hope and expect from Liberal members of Parliament than from Conservatives'.[70] The Alliance continued to give rhetorical support to the notion that they were a genuinely non-party movement, but for all practical purposes they became a section within the Liberal Party.

The Alliance, in choosing a partisan strategy, responded rationally to the political opportunities at its disposal after the Second Reform Act but, in so doing, it fractured the delicate balance between its Anglican and Non-conformist supporters. The identification of the Alliance with the Liberal Party threatened Anglican evangelicals who believed, quite correctly, that the party supported a wide variety of political and religious reforms, including the disestablishment of the Church of England, which conservative Anglicans could not countenance. One Anglican vehemently responded to the Alliance's new electoral policy with the claim that temperance was now 'identified with the curse of socialism, infidelity and many secret organizations, whose object is to change all our political and religious institutions'.[71]

The alliance of Anglican and Nonconformist evangelicals which the Alliance desperately needed to maintain, officially broke apart when Anglicans formed their own temperance society, the Church of England Temperance Society (CETS), in 1873. Anglicans, who formed the CETS in direct response to the close association of the UKA with the Liberal Party in the 1870s, hoped that their new organization would serve as a conduit for Church of England believers concerned about temperance but who no longer wanted to associate with the Alliance. The political struggles between the Alliance and the CETS and their inability to unite behind a common platform was a major limitation to any successful temperance reform.[72]

It was unrealistic for the Alliance to expect that the temperance vote of evangelical Anglicans and Nonconformists could survive the cross-cutting effect of other political and religious issues. Conservative voters found it more and more difficult to vote for Liberal candidates for the sake of temperance because of the close association of temperance with Liberalism. At a temperance conference in Manchester in 1881, one brave Conservative speaker put the difficulty directly before the delegates: 'at any ordinary time they (Conservative temperance voters) might sacrifice all to their love of temperance, but hardly now when such questions as those of disestablishment and religious education are in the front'.[73]

As temperance became a party issue, the partisan votes on the Permissive Bill in the Commons became readily apparent. In 1875, only 11 out of 266 conservatives voted in favour of the Bill.[74] The CETS did not help the Alliance pressure Tories to vote for the Bill. Conservatives concluded that the Permissive Bill was dangerous because it had more to do with political than alcohol reform. With its emphasis on democratic decision-making at the local level, the Bill was the kind of political reform which naturally attracted the support of the Radical wing of the Liberal Party and the scorn of the Tories. The CETS, conscious of the Conservative critics of the Permissive Bill, never joined the Alliance in calling for the passage of the Bill. Instead, it supported a stricter licensing system for drinking places, a moderate goal which the Alliance angrily denounced.[75]

By late in the century, the leadership of the Alliance did not even try to hide its partisan sympathies. John Kempster noted in 1897, 'just as the Liberal Party depends so largely upon the votes of the Temperance electors, to the same extent the Conservative Party depends upon the votes of brewers, distillers, wine merchants, publicans, and the host of their share-holders'.[76] Kempster also assailed Anglican clergy who 'claim sympathy' for the prohibition cause but who refused to 'vote sympathy'. In Kempster's mind, the Anglican clergy voted Conservative because 'they rely upon that party to buttress the church'.[77] Kempster spoke aloud the beliefs of most Nonconformists: the Tory party was inexorably bound to the Estab-lished church and to liquor interests. His public pronouncement, however, did nothing to overcome the inherent division between Anglican and Nonconformist temperance voters.

The Alliance also did not hide its antipathy toward the CETS. In 1899, the *London Alliance Review* noted that the Church of England Diocesan Temperance Branches did not 'find it convenient at present to hold Tem-perance Sunday on one particular Lord's Day'. By contrast, 'The Non-conformist Temperance Association, some years ago, chose for this purpose the last Sunday in each November.'[78] The implication could not have been made clearer: Nonconformist churches were helping the temper-ance cause, the Church of England was not. The angry rhetoric of the UKA leadership did little to bridge the gap between Anglican and Nonconformist sympathizers.

While the identification of the Alliance with the Liberal Party was unavoidable, it did not prove to be beneficial. As has already been noted, it divided temperance voters into competing political parties. The Alliance also lost the independence and political leverage it desperately needed and which it enjoyed when it was genuinely a non-partisan organization. What threat could the Alliance use to persuade the Liberal Party to push temper-ance reform now that the group had disassociated itself entirely from the Tory Party? The Liberal Party, wanting to attract the votes of evangelical Nonconformists, rhetorically supported the electoral aim of the Alliance, but Gladstone's Liberal Governments of 1868–74 and 1880–86 showed that the Party, once in power, would do very little for the temperance cause.

The Liberal Party supported a wide range of causes, including Home Rule for Ireland, the disestablishment of the Church of England and educa-tion reform. The Party could not attend to all these reforms in a single

Parliament, and the Alliance could not expect that temperance would be placed at the top of the party's agenda. The Alliance tried to pressure the party to push the Permissive Bill through Parliament by threatening to withhold its support from the party, but it quickly recognized that it could not expect temperance voters to abandon Liberalism on the temperance issue alone. As D. A. Hamer has noted, 'it was naive in the extreme to imagine that there was a temperance vote which could be preserved completely uncontaminated by the uses to which it was put'.[79]

The Alliance did successfully pressure the Liberal Party officially to endorse the ideas behind the Permissive Bill in its 1891 Newcastle Programme, but its 'victory' proved to be Pyrrhic. The Liberals' election defeat of 1895 seemed to prove that public opinion was not ready for national prohibition along the lines advocated by the Alliance. The prohibition issue was seen by many contemporary pundits as a primary reason for the Liberal Party defeat.[80] The Alliance, not surprisingly, rejected this interpretation of the Liberal defeat. The temperance politician W. S. Caine argued that the Liberal support for the Permissive Bill did not contribute 'one jot or tittle to the defeat of any Liberal Candidate who was not afraid of it'.[81] The damage, however, had been done and the momentum for the Permissive Bill and prohibition quickly evaporated.

The Alliance never compromised on the goal of a local veto law, which they believed to be morally and politically superior to licensing laws and restrictions in opening hours. Local option was morally attractive to prohibitionists because it did not allow concessions with what was considered an evil and dangerous practice: 'We do not license smallpox, infection, or sewer disease – why this?'[82] An editorial in the *London Alliance*, the magazine for the United Kingdom Alliance, stated the matter succinctly when it said: 'we are not an organization of licence reformers. We are Prohibitionists – and we hope to secure Prohibition by means of a local veto.'[83] Local option also attracted prohibitionists because it seemed consistent with the idea of democratic decision-making: 'Our proposal is to enable the people by a vote on the one issue distinctly and definitely to say whether they want the Trade or not.'[84] Compromise on the question of local prohibition was rejected by the Alliance with the same fervour which these evangelical Christians exhibited in theological debates.

A recurring theme in evangelical political action has been a conflict between the enthusiasm of leaders who refused to compromise their political goal, and the political need for realism and accommodation. Evangelicals brought to the temperance cause a religious ideology which legitimated their activism, made them devoted participants in the cause, and contributed to their fervour. The problem was that political realities necessitated a certain degree of accommodation and compromise for temperance organizations to succeed. The Alliance leadership never resolved the tension between these extremes.[85]

In 1899, the Government published the Peel report, which suggested reform along the lines of reducing the number of liquor licences granted, but rejected the idea of the Local Veto. The Alliance mobilized opposition to Peel's plan on the argument that it was not stringent enough. The temperance politician T. P. Whitaker defiantly proclaimed, 'Lord Peel can come into the running . . . but we will never give up on the Direct Veto.'[86] The Alliance, however, was no longer powerful enough to advocate a more radical set of reforms within the Liberal Party and it was apparent by the turn of the century that any alcohol reform would come at the behest of the national state. Prohibition was never introduced into England. The political structure of the British state never allowed local votes on the prohibition of alcohol, and the national strength of temperance activists continued to decline into the twentieth century.

Prohibitionists continued to believe that the public favoured their cause, but that non-democratic structures and an intransigent Parliament limited their capacity to realize an alcohol-free Britain. John Kempster bitterly complained about the lack of receptiveness shown by Parliament: 'How on earth are we to extract beneficent legislation from that Parliament of ours? We are tempted to vituperate, when we contemplate our Parliamentary system of legislative strangulation, by which all salutary enactments are delayed and obstructed almost beyond human endurance.'[87] The criticism of the UKA was not unfounded; it is likely that had Parliament passed the Permissive Bill, some areas would have experimented with local prohibition. It is not apparent, however, that prohibition would have attracted the nationwide support that Alliance activists claimed it would.

British evangelicals engaged in temperance activism because they had a moral vision of a better world order. The established Church of England, strong party structures after the 1870s, and a strong national government, however, frustrated evangelical efforts to bring about reform. Evangelicals were unable to mobilize behind the common goal of the control of alcohol because they were socially and politically divided by the Established Church. The political goals of the United Kingdom Alliance could only be reached if evangelicals of all denominations joined together for the cause of prohibition. The United Kingdom Alliance, however, was unable to keep temperance a non-partisan issue and prohibitionists lost any hope they had of legislating the traffic of alcohol in England.

TEMPERANCE POLITICS AND THE CHURCHES IN THE UNITED STATES

American evangelicals shared with their British peers a religious ideology which justified an opposition to the drink traffic in the late nineteenth century. The Prohibition Movement succeeded in America where it failed in Britain, however, because the American state was weak, which in turn allowed temperance activists effectively to pursue a single-issue campaign by introducing local prohibition laws that eventually produced the Eighteenth Amendment. The weakness of American political parties also made it easier for groups to pressure elected officials. The Anti-Saloon League (ASL), the most important temperance organization in the late-nineteenth and earlier-twentieth centuries, took advantage of America's federal and open political system to create an organizational alliance among evangelicals to pass prohibition legislation. The non-partisan pressure of the ASL eventually led to the ratification of the Eighteenth Amendment in 1919, prohibiting the traffic in alcohol in America.

The ratification of the Eighteenth Amendment culminated a century-long mobilization against alcohol in America. The first of these movements, in the middle of the nineteenth century, was led by Neal Dow, an evangelical Christian from Maine. Dow and his supporters, mostly Quakers and other evangelicals, successfully pressured thirteen states to pass the Maine Law, or the prohibition of alcohol at the state level, by 1855. By the end of the Civil War, however, most of these state prohibition laws had been repealed. Individual evangelicals were active in this first phase of the American Temperance Movement, but the churches as a whole took no stand on the alcohol question.[88]

The second period of activism came in the 1870s and 1880s, largely as a result of the pioneering efforts of the Woman's Christian Temperance Union (WCTU), led by Frances Willard. Under Willard's leadership, the WCTU became the largest women's organization to that point in American history with local chapters in every state and territory. Willard brought to the WCTU an evangelical faith and a political agenda which included a wide range of social issues, including workers' rights, women's suffrage, and a progressive tax on wealth. The WCTU adopted this 'Do Everything' policy when Willard came to power, in order to broaden the vision and appeal of temperance legislation. The Prohibition Party, the political party favoured by WCTU activists, reflected this multifaceted programme of reform in its party platforms of 1888 and 1892.[89]

The attitude of evangelicals to the WCTU was diverse, ranging from unqualified support to active opposition. A number of evangelical organizations and churches passed resolutions endorsing the movement. These evangelicals combined a religious and material argument about the danger of alcohol, arguing that temperance reform was indispensable to social welfare and personal salvation. Most evangelicals, however, sympathized with the goal of prohibition, but opposed the WCTU's social and political agenda. The WCTU leadership was deeply divided between those who, like Willard, wanted to address a wide variety of social reforms and those who thought that the focus should be limited to the alcohol issue. Willard, the WCTU and the Prohibition Party were eventually undone because they could not survive the cross-cutting effects of other issues in local politics.[90]

The WCTU discovered the same problem that plagued the United Kingdom Alliance: the unity of evangelicals on the temperance issue demanded a non-partisan campaign. Evangelical Christians were overwhelmingly prohibitionist in principle, but most of them were not willing to abandon the Democratic or Republican parties solely on the alcohol issue and they would not give unified support to an organization which advocated radical social reform. A perceptive pamphlet published by the National Temperance Society correctly gauged the political necessity of abandoning the idea of a Prohibition Party: 'We can agitate on this better without a party than with one; for as soon as a party is organized, those are alienated who belong to other parties and are arrayed against the very cause we wish to promote.'[91] Not all evangelical reformers of alcohol left the Prohibition Party, which remained quite important into the late nineteenth century, but the bulk of evangelicals were more comfortable pursuing prohibition through the established Democratic and Republican parties.

In some respects, American evangelicals were as divided as their English counterparts. Believers in America were not divided by an officially Established church, but America was the most religiously pluralistic nation in the world, as was expressed in the myriad denominations which flourished in the late nineteenth century. H. Richard Niebuhr argued in his classic work of 1929, *The Social Sources of Denominationalism*, that this pluralism underscored social and religious divisions among believers. The Baptist, Methodist, and Presbyterian churches experienced an ecclesiastical South–North separation because of the Civil War, and in the post-bellum period this division was reflected in the evangelical voting pattern. Northern evangelicals were primarily Republicans, while white Southerner believers were overwhelmingly Democrats.[92] Prohibition activist E. J. Wheeler recognized the problem of this partisan cleavage of evangelical sympathizers: 'the temperance sentiment that is in the Republican party is in the North and that in the Democratic party is in the South. . . . The very element that is most attached to the cause of Prohibition, is the one most inimical to Republican ascendancy.'[93]

Evangelicals were also divided by social class, a fact which was reflected in the different set of issues believers associated with alcohol reform. Walter Rauschenbusch, the most prominent voice for the Social Gospel Movement in the early twentieth century, supported the ASL, but he also championed labour causes, minority rights and government activism on behalf of the urban poor. Rauschenbusch, and many other upper-middle and upper-class evangelical Christians, supported prohibition because they viewed it as progressive reform which was justified in scientific, social and religious terms. These evangelicals believed that alcohol reform would improve the lives of the urban poor in the same way that health care and worker rights would help them. Almost all of the upper class were members of the Episcopal, Congregational and Presbyterian churches; the latter two officially supported the ASL.[94]

Most American evangelicals did not share the political views or social class of Rauschenbusch, as the WCTU and the Prohibition Party discovered. Conservative southern evangelicals were not interested in alcohol reform as part of a campaign to improve the rights and lives of minorities and women, nor did they vote in large numbers for the Prohibition Party. They did, however, believe in the value of temperance as a form of self-improvement and social control. The editor of the *Christian Advocate*, the voice for the Southern Methodist Church at the turn of the century, wrote in 1890: 'During a residence of nearly twelve years in Nashville we have seen nothing that could truthfully be called a race trouble in this thriving city. But we have seen no end of whiskey troubles for both races. The politicians who are now having spasms over national peril are as blind as bats as to where the chief danger lies.'[95] Political success on prohibition required an alliance between evangelicals as socially and politically divided as Walter Raushenbusch and the editor of the *Christian Advocate*.

The final wave of prohibition activism, resulting in the ratification of the Eighteenth Amendment in 1919, began in 1893 with the founding of the Anti-Saloon League (ASL) by the Congregational minister Howard Hyde Russell. The founders of the ASL were evangelical Christians who were convinced that the radical political agenda of the WCTU and the Prohibition Party would never be accepted by the vast majority of American evangelicals and so they consciously designed an organization which would attack the liquor traffic but which would not disturb evangelical unity. In an address at the National Convention of the ASL in 1911, John Woolley spoke for a new generation of activists when he said, 'cooperation is the key note of the future. The right hand of fellowship among ourselves is the best formation we can use against the enemy'.[96] The ASL became a highly-effective single-issue pressure group which focused its attention solely on the passage of prohibitory legislation at the county, state, and national levels.[97]

The ASL realized that an effective political campaign against alcohol necessitated the unification of evangelical Christians who, in 1890, represented 80 per cent of American Protestantism and 55 per cent of the nation's religious population.[98] The Reverend A. M. Richardson correctly predicted that a mobilization of Christians against alcohol would result in political victories for prohibition forces: 'when Christian people vote only for men who are heartily in sympathy with our Prohibition policy, then will come the downfall of the liquor traffic'.[99] Conscious of the partisan and denominational cleavages among its evangelical constituency, the League appointed members from all of the major denominations and both political parties to its board of directors. The League appealed to America's Protestant churches to spread the message of salvation from the sin of alcohol; the United Presbyterian, Methodist–Episcopal, American and Southern Baptist, Disciples, and Congregational Churches responded with official declarations supporting the aims of the ASL. The League formed grass-roots contacts with local pastors who provided lists of church members willing to vote for politicians sympathetic to the League. Each cooperating church was asked to give up its pulpit on a yearly basis to an ASL speaker. The resources of evangelical churches proved to be essential for the success of the Anti-Saloon League.[100]

In order to maximize its political support, the ASL disassociated itself from all other types of political reform. The League realized what the WCTU and the Prohibition Party never understood and what the United Kingdom Alliance was unable to achieve: to secure the support of all evangelical Christians, the ASL had to become a single-issue pressure group. In its annual *Yearbook*, the League explained its non-partisan purpose in this way: 'The Anti-Saloon League is omnipartisan because it does not believe that a distinctively moral issue should be entrusted to the varying fortunes of a political party. It is not the province of a political party to inaugurate and assume the guardianship of moral issues. That belongs to the church.'[101] Anti-Saloon League activists followed a strategy which would become familiar in special-interest campaigns in America; they cut across partisan, regional, and denominational lines by focusing attention on the single goal of prohibition. The ASL accepted whatever allies it could find. In California and Colorado, for example, the League joined forces with Progressives while in Oklahoma and most of the South it cooperated with conservative Democrats.[102]

The Alliance in Britain recognized the need to develop a single-issue focus on the alcohol question, but British political structures limited their capacity to do so. American political structures, by contrast, enabled the ASL to sustain a non-partisan political campaign.[103] America's federal political system allowed the League to focus attention on local prohibition where temperance sentiment was strongest, without disrupting evangelical unity. Activists centred their electoral pressure on towns and even sub-sections of towns via the 'four-mile laws' which restricted how close saloons could be to schools and churches. By making prohibition a local affair, the ASL leadership could term the debate in ways most appealing to the religious constituents of that particular region and avoid the partisan division of evangelicals nationally. Middle-class, Democratic Baptists in Mississippi did not have to cooperate with upper-class, Republican Congregationalists in Maine to pass statewide prohibition laws. Each group could maintain its class, denominational and partisan bias while the progress on prohibition marched on.

Stephen Skowronek has shown how American constitutional federalism was the most important factor which inhibited the centralization of political authority and the strength of the American state in the nineteenth century. Federalism, which 'ensured the integrity of these states, each with its own institutional organization, legal code, and law enforcement apparatus', encouraged the mobilization of reform groups, including prohibition organizations, which might not be capable of securing national reform but which could capture the control of local political regions.[104]

America's federalism allowed the ASL to experiment with statewide prohibition before turning its attention to a national campaign. Cities, counties and states became laboratories for the ASL as it tried to establish which political tactics worked best and what laws were the most successful in reducing drinking. The League explicitly compared the disparate experiences of states to show the purported benefits which accrued to those states which had passed restrictive prohibition laws. Noah McFarland, Commissioner of the United States Land Office in Topeka and President of the Kansas State Temperance Union, cited various statistics on health, morals and material prosperity to show how beneficial statewide prohibition had been in Kansas. McFarland concluded by claiming that prohibition in Kansas had 'enlarged our wealth, and powerfully advanced the material, educational and moral interests of our people'.[105] McFarland's document was read and signed in agreement by the Governor, Secretary of State and Chief Justice of the State Supreme Court.

As an organization, the ASL benefited from a federal system which gave voters the capacity to affect political outcomes within their own community. Votes taken on town, city, county, and statewide prohibition generated membership and interest in the ASL, which was situated to provide the expertise necessary to organize a successful campaign. The strength of the ASL lay in its decentralized structure which gave local branches the freedom to direct their own organizations. John Woolley described this strategy when he said that 'local option means progressively – town democracy, county democracy, state democracy, and federal sovereignty'.[106] The Alliance never got to the point of having the power to legislate drinking restrictions in local areas. People were more likely to support an organization such as the ASL, which was situated to affect change in local affairs, than a group like the Alliance, which did not have the opportunity to initiate votes on local prohibition.

Political changes which were taking place in late-nineteenth and early-twentieth-century America created expanding opportunities for ASL activism. The Alliance used the relatively new political initiative and popular referendum, in those states which allowed them, to introduce direct votes on the alcohol question. The Initiative, Referendum, and state-constitutional amendment enabled the ASL to bypass party cleavages by introducing votes on alcohol directly to the people. E. J. Wheeler noted the obvious advantages of being able to introduce popular statewide votes on prohibition: 'it is in the adoption of a prohibitory amendment that the non-partisan organizations come into play. The question is then submitted to a direct vote of the people. They vote on the question, not directly through candidates, but directly, yes or no, on the amendment itself.'[107] National prohibition organizations published and distributed literature to local activists on how best to run pressure groups and amend state constitutions.[108]

The American and British states were developing in divergent ways during the late nineteenth century, and this had a direct impact on temperance groups in each nation. Katznelson and Skowronek both note that the relative strength of the British and American states were different in the late nineteenth century. America was doing its best to preserve and, in some cases, expand the autonomy and power of individual states. Great Britain, by contrast, experienced a progressive centralization of authority in Parliament. For political pressure groups such as the Alliance and the ASL, the political changes had profound consequences. The weakness of the American national state and the absence of a coherent alcohol policy opened up myriad opportunities for meaningful local activism. The relative strength of the British state meant that local regions had very little political autonomy, which, in turn, discouraged local activism.[109]

This is not to say that the ASL ignored electoral politics. In fact, the ASL lobbied candidates for most political offices, supporting the one, regardless of party, who was most sympathetic to prohibition legislation. The myriad elected offices in America created ample opportunities for interest-group activism. American voters chose the President, senators (after 1913), representatives, governors, state senators and representatives, county commissioners, and, in some cases, judges. The direct primary, which was introduced in many states in the early twentieth century, also increased the importance of local prohibition activism. The rise of the political primary as the means of selecting a party candidate took candidate-selection out of the hands of party conventions and elites and put it before the voting public; this in turn gave the ASL another election to influence the views of party candidates on prohibition. The Anti-Saloon League was perfectly placed to take advantage of these political changes.[110]

The first and most spectacular success of the ASL in local politics occurred in the Ohio gubernatorial race in 1905. Myron Herrick, the incumbent Republican, opposed a local option law advocated by the League. The Democrats, with the support and pressure of the ASL, nominated John Pattison, who supported local option. The race was an obvious choice between a wet incumbent Republican and a dry Democratic challenger. The ASL urged its many followers to support the Democrat Pattison even though most of the League's leadership was Republican. Pattison won the race despite the fact that the rest of the Republican state ticket swept to victory. The ASL established for itself the power of a single-issue, non-partisan focus. The pledge of support from the ASL became important in state races beyond Ohio, thereby forcing both major political parties into a situation where they were vying for the votes of temperance forces while speeding up the process of reform.[111]

The weakness of national party organizations during the late nineteenth and early twentieth centuries worked to the benefit of prohibition groups. Leonard White, Stephen Skowronek and Richard Jenson have noted that American political parties were powerful in the late nineteenth century – but at the state, not the national, level. The national Democratic and Republican parties had neither the interest nor the capacity to impose a coherent policy on state party organizations on the alcohol question. The fact that neither of the national parties became intimately associated with support for prohibition did not, however, hurt the ASL. What was more important for the Prohibition Movement was the support of local party leaders, Democrat and Republican, who had significant power within their own constituencies. The permeable nature of American parties created more opportunities for issue-based groups like the ASL to have a political impact.[112]

In 1913, eight states, Georgia, Kansas, Maine, Mississippi, North Carolina, North Dakota, Oklahoma, and Tennessee, had absolute prohibition of intoxicating liquor. The remaining 40 states had more or less dry territory under the operation of some kind of local option law or legislative prohibition. Michigan in 1913, for example, had 30 counties which had voted for prohibition under local option laws and 53 counties where alcohol was still legally sold. The basic pattern from state to state had essentially been the same for the past decade: the number of dry counties increased to a certain point and then stabilized. Local option laws allowed the ASL to pass prohibition in those areas where evangelicals were most powerful, but they were less able to pass statewide prohibition amendments.

Convinced that only an amendment to the Constitution would forever rid the nation of the drink evil, the ASL began to push vigorously the national debate on prohibition in 1913. Success at the state level had not peaked by 1913, but the ASL believed that statewide laws were not sufficient, because the liquor interests 'warred upon the dry states, so as to make dry laws ineffective'.[113] The ASL abandoned its decentralized structure for a more centrally-directed national organization which pressured elected representatives to pass a national prohibition amendment.

The ASL had benefited from America's federal polity in passing state and local prohibition laws in the early twentieth century. In order to pass a constitutional amendment, however, the ASL needed to coordinate disparate elements of the polity. At a minimum, it appeared that success would be much harder to achieve. Prohibition proved to be electorally appealing to national politicians, however, who submitted to local pressure, and in 1917 Congress voted to submit the proposed constitutional amendment to the states. A little more than one year later, in 1919, Nebraska became the thirty-sixth and last state needed to approve the Eighteenth Amendment to the Constitution.[114]

The success of the American Prohibition Movement is in marked contrast to the failure of the British campaign. Evangelicals in both countries were at the forefront in the effort to prohibit drinking, and group leaders knew that the respective movements would only succeed if evangelicals mobilized together. Temperance activism, however, was caught up in the larger political world, which dictated how successful the respective movements would be. In America, the political institutions inherited by prohibition advocates created the conditions necessary for the successful mobilization of evangelicals. In Britain, political institutions limited the capacity of the United Kingdom Alliance to pass prohibition laws.

The Alliance inherited political structures which made it difficult for them to maintain the non-partisan approach necessary for evangelical unity. Britain's unitary political structure did not allow the Alliance to introduce direct votes on local prohibition. When prohibition became a party issue, it was caught up in the partisan cleavage between Anglican and Nonconformist evangelicals. Without local option, the Alliance was forced into a national debate on the Permissive Bill where evangelical cleavages were exposed. Votes on prohibition at local political levels allowed the Anti-Saloon League to avoid the partisan cleavage of American evangelicals. The League was able to do this only because America's federal political system provided opportunities for meaningful local activism.

ALTERNATIVE THEORIES

Alternative explanations for the temperance movement have highlighted different causes for the formation of groups and contrary reasons for their political success or failure. The most noteworthy account of temperance activism is that of Joseph Gusfield.[115]

Gusfield's status theory relies on the claim that evangelicals were motivated to act on alcohol because they perceived a threat to their social status with the influx of immigrants at the turn of the century. This threatened social status provided the grass-roots evangelical support for a movement which wanted to impose prohibition laws in order to codify evangelical status.

At first glance, there is much to commend Gusfield's theory. There was a mass immigration of non-evangelical believers into America throughout the nineteenth century. Total immigration into the United States climbed from 2.8 million in the 1870s to 5.2 million in the 1880s, 3.6 million in the 1890s, and, in the largest number of immigrants in any single decade, 8.8 million between 1901 and 1910. Sydney Ahlstrom concludes that it was during the post-Civil War period that the American people 'felt the full impact of the country's ethnic and religious pluralism'.[116] This mass immigration may well have threatened evangelicals who had never before perceived non-evangelicals as a potent political foe.

The charged rhetoric of some prohibition supporters also lends support to Gusfield's argument. The Rev. Frank Ellis, of the Eutaw Place Baptist Church in Baltimore, Maryland, spoke for many evangelicals when he asked in 1888, 'who are the saloon keepers? Ninety-one per cent in New England a few years ago were foreigners. The American saloon is sustained by foreigners.'[117] Quotations such as that lead one to suspect that evangelicals wanted to control immigrants as much as they wanted to decrease drinking. Paul Kleppner has described the political expression of religious alliances in late-nineteenth-century America as a Pietist–Liturgical split.[118] Kleppner correctly notes that there was a political cleavage between

Pietist denominations (Baptist, Methodist, Congregational, Disciples and Presbyterians) and Liturgical churches (primarily Lutheran and Roman Catholic). The division noted by Kleppner certainly holds true for prohibition support: evangelical pietists supported it while liturgical, non-evangelicals opposed it.

There are two principal problems with Gusfield's theory. First, American evangelicals did not share a single social status, which calls into question Gusfield's claim that a shared status led to their mobilization. Support for prohibition in America came from evangelicals with different social statuses. The denominations which passed prohibition resolutions crossed class and status distinctions. Upper-class and higher-status Congregational and Presbyterian churches joined with the middle-status and lower-class Northern and Southern Methodists, American and Southern Baptists, Disciples of Christ and Seventh-Day Adventists in support of the ASL.

While Gusfield is correct to point to the unity of evangelicals for prohibition and the opposition of the Roman Catholic, Episcopal and Reformed churches, he is wrong to contend that the reason for evangelical unity was their threatened social status. Evangelicals mobilized against alcohol because their ideology taught them to be concerned about the physical and spiritual dangers of drinking. Evangelicals opposed Catholics and Lutherans because they believed that their cultural and religious values, especially in regard to the drinking, were dangerous and sinful.

The second problem with Gusfield's theory arises in the comparison of American and British evangelicals. Evangelical Christians in the two countries did not share the same social status, however measured. In England, temperance attracted the support of middle-class evangelicals who were, by all indications, rising in status and engaging the ruling elite in a political battle to further their social rights. Gusfield claims that the status of American evangelicals was falling in the wake of massive immigration. Even if we assume that Gusfield is correct, why is it that evangelicals, occupying different social positions in the two nations, similarly mobilized against alcohol? It is possible to claim that both sets of believers were engaging in status politics and that they were simply at different status positions in their society. However, it is more instructive to look at what these transatlantic evangelicals shared: an ideology which legitimated involvement on the question of alcohol. Moreover, there was no significant immigration into England in the late nineteenth century to threaten the social status of evangelical Christians.

A cursory glance at where temperance succeeded further undermines Gusfield's claim. Statewide prohibition laws were passed in those areas least affected by immigration: the south and the far west. Presumably, evangelical Christians in those regions should not have felt a threat to their social status since immigrants had not settled in large numbers there. In England, the temperance movement was an urban phenomenon. The Alliance enjoyed its greatest political success in Britain's industrial heartland where evangelical nonconformity was strongest. The common denominator explaining temperance activism in Britain and America is not status, but religion. Temperance, not surprisingly, prospered in areas where evangelical Christians were the predominant religious culture. In those places, evangelicals had the greatest opportunity to translate their religious values into politics.

A second set of theories which explain evangelical mobilization against alcohol without regard to activists' religious ideology is the modernization and class analysis put forward by Charles Foster, Paul Johnson, Lilian Shiman and A. E. Dingle.[119] These theorists have linked the timing of the temperance movement to the emergence of industrialization and rapid urbanization in the nineteenth century. According to a class analysis, industrialization introduced a new economy which required a work force which was disciplined, responsible and sober. Temperance helped inculcate an emerging working class in the values necessary for industrial production. Massive urbanization accelerated the need for a new set of social values as millions of workers were displaced by capitalist expansion and had increasing difficulty adapting their 'traditional modes of behaviour to their existing circumstances'.[120]

Britain and America were transformed in the nineteenth century from predominantly agricultural, rural nations to manufacturing, urban countries. Most historians date Britain's industrial revolution to the end of the eighteenth and beginning of the nineteenth century, several decades before the rise of temperance societies, but industrialization and urbanization were social processes which continued throughout the nineteenth century. In America, the timing between temperance as a social movement and industrialization and urbanization as social realities is even closer. By 1893, when the Anti-Saloon League was founded, the factory had outdistanced the farm as the country's chief producer of wealth and, by 1919, when the Prohibition Amendment was passed, the population had shifted decidedly to the cities.

The temperance values of thrift, sobriety and responsibility were consistent with the interests of industrial production. Drinking, as Shiman correctly notes, 'caused absence and instability among the working classes',[121] and therefore decreased worker efficiency. Individual entrepreneurs in Britain and America were active in the temperance campaign, and it is possible that their intent was to control working-class behaviour. Dingle contends that temperance attracted businessmen for precisely this reason: 'nonconformist businessmen expected that prohibition would benefit them economically. Sober workmen would be more disciplined and productive and, once drink expenditure had been eliminated from their budget, they could purchase more consumer goods.'[122] A temperance ethic could have served as a form of social control for those members of the working class who were attracted to it. Paul Johnson argues that this temperance propaganda 'provided masters social peace, a disciplined and docile work force, and an opportunity to assert moral authority over their men'.[123] According to a class analysis, evangelicals used temperance and religion as a solution to the 'problems of class, legitimacy, and order' generated by capitalist production and urbanization.[124]

The most glaring problem with a class and modernization analysis is that it ignores the fact that the British temperance movement originated among the working class and not the middle or ruling class. Brian Harrison has argued convincingly that temperance was initially a movement to gain social respect and self-reliance for those making the transition from working to middle class. Support for the Alliance came from groups who had mounting political and economic importance. As Harrison notes, the Alliance 'attracted quite precise groups in British society – groups hitherto largely excluded from political power'.[125] In Britain, the class which ought to have benefited most, the ruling elite, had little interest in the movement.

It is difficult to test a class hypothesis with voting data since there were so few votes directly on the issue of prohibition in England, but a comparison with America is instructive. In America, the places where temperance succeeded were those areas *least* likely to be affected by industrial growth. Statewide prohibition at the end of 1916 came primarily from western and southern rural states and not the industrial centres of the midwest and the east. If temperance and prohibition were simply a response to the problems generated by industrialization and urbanization, why did evangelicals in rural areas respond so enthusiastically to the movement? What did they have to gain, from a class perspective, from temperance?

Status, class and modernization theories argue that the evangelical motive for temperance activism cannot be read off directly from the religious ideology of adherents. The reasons given by these theories for evangelical mobilization, however, cannot account for the cross-class and cross-status support for temperance in Britain and America. More importantly, these theories ignore the stated reasons given by evangelicals for their mobilization: a desire to save the sinner from the effects of drinking. Temperance was a moral crusade on the part of evangelical Christians who wanted to end the blight of drinking. Evangelicals had a religious motive to prohibit drinking: they believed it was their sacred obligation to oppose such a sin which stood in the way of the conversion of the drinker and caused so many social problems.

The second aspect of my theory of group mobilization is that, once organizations are formed, their success is largely determined by the political structures they inherited. In the case of temperance, America's federal and open political structures allowed temperance groups to flourish, while in Britain the unitary system discouraged group activism. Austin Kerr has offered the competing resource mobilization theory to explain prohibition politics.[126] According to Kerr, the political success of the Anti-Saloon League had to do with its ability to raise political resources, recruit group members, and form local organizations devoted to passing prohibition legislation. Evangelical churches were important to the ASL because they provided the institutional resources necessary for efficient and effective group mobilization.

There is no question but that part of the success of temperance groups was tied to their ability to raise resources, principally from churches, for a political cause. Temperance groups in Britain and America became more effective, from a resource perspective, as the nineteenth century progressed. The ability to raise political resources did correlate, to some extent, to the political success and failure of temperance organizations. It is not so much that resource mobilization theory is wrong, but that it is insufficient as an explanation for the temperance movement.

Kerr does not compare the American and British movements, but it is possible to argue using a resource perspective that the divergent political outcomes had to do with the different levels of resources which temperance groups raised. It is true that evangelical Christians, the constituency most likely to support temperance groups, were more numerous in America than in Britain in the late nineteenth century, and it therefore follows that American groups had access to greater monetary, political and electoral resources than their British counterparts. A case could be made that British groups failed politically because they were not large enough nor well enough equipped to bring significant pressure to bear on political parties and leaders.

Several problems emerge in a closer examination of a resource mobilization argument. In the first place, the Anti-Saloon League and the United Kingdom Alliance were both large organizations which raised considerable resources for political purposes. While it is true that evangelical Christians were more numerous in America, they were also the predominant religious group in Britain. Evangelicals had been at the forefront of successful protest movements earlier in the century, including the anti-slavery campaign from 1790 to the 1830s and the Anti-Corn-Law League in the 1830s and 1840s. The political success of these movements calls into question a resource claim that evangelicals were not a large enough group to have a political impact. My claim is not that the numerical difference between these trans-atlantic believers was politically insignificant, but that this alone does not explain the success and the failure of American and British temperance organizations. Had British evangelicals been as numerous as their American counterparts, the Alliance would still have been unable to pressure the government to introduce alcohol reform.

The most significant difference between the two nations was in how state structures influenced the political activism of the UKA and the ASL. The British state began to dominate social policy in late-nineteenth-century Britain. The expansion of the power of political parties after the Second Reform Act of 1867, coupled with the increasing centralization of political authority in Parliament, minimized the opportunities for meaningful inter-est group activism which was autonomous from the state or the major political parties. The pressure of interested social groups such as the Alli-ance, however intense it might have been, could not force state officials to push for reform which they did not want to support. Earlier in the century, British groups had greater latitude directly to pressure individual MPs, which in turn enabled groups such as the Anti-Corn-Law League to become politically powerful. The Alliance, which recognized that only a non-partisan campaign such as that adopted by the Anti-Corn-Law League would enable temperance voters of all parties to come together for the cause, came to fruition too late to be able successfully to use such a strategy. By the end of the century, the state and the major political parties had become the dominant players in the formation of public policy. This forced the Alliance to seek the support of the Liberal Party, which divided evangelicals along partisan lines. Temperance alone could not survive the cross-cutting effects of other partisan issues, and the temperance movement slowly faded away.

The success of the Anti-Saloon League in America followed directly from the decentralized, fragmented polity which the group inherited. Amer-ica's federal polity allowed groups to initiate votes on prohibition at state and local levels. This allowed group leaders to term the debate in the way most appealing to particular constituencies and avoid the partisan cleavages of its evangelical constituency. The ASL took advantage of a polity which gave them multiple opportunities to capitalize on evangelical discontent with the drink trade. The Initiative, Referendum and state-constitutional amendment allowed groups to force a direct vote on the alcohol question in local areas in the late nineteenth and early twentieth centuries.

The weakness of the American state and political parties gave the ASL the opportunity to pursue an effective and politically potent single-issue campaign. It was not the resources alone which explain the political success of the ASL and the failure of the UKA. Instead, it was the political context in which those resources could be used, particularly the power of the state and political parties, which determined whether or not temperance groups in America and Britain would be able independently to introduce social policy on alcohol.

CONCLUSION

This chapter has highlighted how an evangelical ideology led to the formation of a temperance movement in Britain and America. This ideology caused believers to become concerned about the social and spiritual dangers of alcohol abuse and to support the political efforts of the United Kingdom Alliance and the Anti-Saloon League. The chapter has also demonstrated how state structures shaped the political success of each nation's Temperance Movement. Temperance has served as a model for a theory of social movement mobilization which highlights the importance of ideology in the process of group formation and the role of political structures in the outcome of a movement.

5 The Political Mobilization of Evangelicals from 1960 to the Present

Evangelical Christians in Britain and America mobilized political protest groups in the 1970s and 1980s around the issues of abortion, pornography, and religion in state-supported schools. In contrast to the evangelical mobilization against alcohol discussed in the previous chapter, evangelical activism of the past few decades has not focused on a single social issue. Instead, believers in each nation organized groups in response to a series of social and political changes. The reason for evangelical involvement now and a century ago, however, is essentially the same: social change conflicted with evangelical religious and cultural values. This chapter demonstrates how an evangelical ideology led believers to form social and political groups against abortion and pornography and in favour of religion in state-supported schools.

Evangelicals opposed legalized abortion, the proliferation of pornographic material and the removal of religious themes from public schools because of their beliefs about sexuality, the sanctity of the 'traditional' family and the place of religion in public life. Evangelicals justified their views through scripture, the most significant source of moral legitimation for evangelical political positions. This biblical teaching became politically important with the legalization of abortion, the liberalization of pornography laws and the removal of religious themes from the schools during the 1960s and 1970s. Evangelicals coupled a personal opposition to the changing morality with a belief that they had an obligation to do something about it. As their religious values and personal lifestyle were threatened by the social change around them, evangelicals argued that that they had a religious duty to join protest groups to oppose the new morality. The evangelical norms of social activism and public witness against social sins helped legitimate the formation of political protest groups which pressured elected representatives and publicized the evangelical cause nationwide in the hope of affecting public policy. Together these groups formed the core of a movement whose common denominators were evangelical religious and cultural values.

The formation of evangelical protest groups came at a time when evangelical churches and institutions were growing rapidly and liberal church organizations were losing members. Evangelicals formed religious and political organizations to fill the void left by liberal churches and institutions which gradually abandoned their commitment to 'orthodox' religious doctrine and conservative moral views in the 1960s. The evangelical opposition to liberal theology was not, of course, new. What was novel by the 1970s was the overwhelming sense that liberalism had been a theological and social disaster and the growing distance in terms of moral and cultural attitudes between evangelicals and non-evangelicals. Evangelicals no longer saw themselves as a beleaguered minority protecting their faith by retreating into religious enclaves. Instead, they returned to social and ecclesiastical involvement confident that they could fill the social and religious void left by the liberals. This chapter opens with a discussion of the growth of these American and British evangelical institutions.

LIBERAL DECLINE AND EVANGELICAL GROWTH

The political involvement of evangelicals in the 1970s can only be understood in the context of the perceived failure of liberal theology to respond forcefully to the religious and social challenges of the 1960s. The liberal/evangelical divide created in the 1920s on the issue of biblical inspiration became acute after the Second World War as the polity and leadership of the major denominations became decidedly more liberal, even radical. In the 1960s especially, church leaders and structures adopted existential, liberationist, pluralist and secular intellectual models. In America in the 1960s, the death-of-God theology, an attempt to demythologize Christianity by doing away with the supernatural features of orthodox belief, attracted attention in intellectual religious circles. Although the announcement of God's death by a small group of liberal theologians was hardly translated into the practice of most local churches, it was, nonetheless, symptomatic of a concerted effort on the part of most mainline churches to reconceptualize Christianity in a more pluralist, accommodationist way. Liberal seminaries and churches began accepting the idea that Protestant Christianity was but one of many ways to appropriate 'truth'. Evangelicals responded by recommitting themselves to the non-accommodationist position that Jesus Christ was the *only* way to discover truth or, more to the point, salvation.[1]

In England, the new pluralism of the Churches was best expressed in the debate surrounding the publication of J. A. T. Robinson's 1963 book, *Honest To God*. Robinson, who was the Bishop of Woolwich in the Church of England when he wrote the book, created a tremendous controversy with his work, which reinterpreted Christian doctrine within an existential frame-work. According to Robinson, the traditional orthodox Christian doctrines needed to be reconceptualized because most lay people found those teachings meaningless and irrelevant. Evangelicals criticized Robinson's book because they believed that it departed from Christian orthodoxy. For better or worse, the major denominations in England altered their outlook to keep up with the latest secular intellectual models. Both the Church of England and the historic nonconformist denominations adopted an increasingly pluralist theology for their churches.[2]

The liberal/evangelical theological divide in the 1960s coincided with the precipitous decline in church membership in both Britain and America. Membership in British churches fell throughout the twentieth century but it became especially pronounced in the 1960s. Table 5.1 shows the membership totals for selected Protestant churches from 1960 to 1990. Of the denominations listed, the Assemblies of God, House Churches, and Fellowship of Independent Evangelical Churches could be described as evangelical. House Churches are groups of evangelical or pentecostalist Christians who have formed sectarian churches outside traditional denominations. Two different sources were used in gathering these figures; the first source, which covers 1960–70, uses a less rigid membership definition than the second, which explains the rise in membership between 1970 and 1980 for the Anglican Church (see Table 5.1).

Religious practice in Britain in the 1960s and 1970s was as low as it had been for centuries and there was no indication that there would be a widespread change in the future. By 1980, only 15 per cent of the total population of the UK were church members; of those church members, just over half were Protestants. Church membership had reached a high of 5.8 million in 1930 but fell to 4.3 million in 1970. When measured against population growth during the same time, declining membership becomes even more significant. Between 1900 and 1970, the British population rose from 37 to 53 million. In 1900, one out of every six persons was a member of a Protestant church; by 1970 the ratio had fallen to less than one out of ten.[3]

The decline in membership nationwide was especially pronounced in the largest denominations, which were, coincidentally, most closely associated with a liberal theology. Evangelical denominations fared better throughout the 1960s. As Table 5.2 shows, the only denominations which experienced a real growth in the 1970s were those most likely to embrace an evangelical theology. The Baptist Church, the major denomination most closely associated with evangelicalism, lost members at a slower rate than any other large denomination.

Table 5.1   Church membership, selected UK denominations

	1960	1970	1980	1985	1990
Anglican	2 398 000	1 804 000	2 135 000	1 984 000	1 838 659
Scottish Presb.	1 332 000	1 197 000	935 564	901 975	832 120
Methodist	728 589	617 018	541 773	503 822	483 387
Baptist	311 778	261 521	239 874	243 736	241 842
Cong. (1)	355 120	282 018	189 546	131 213	117 900
House Churches	n.a.	n.a.	20 000	75 000	120 000
Fell. of Ind. Evang. Ch.	n.a.	n.a.	21 923	30 150	33 000
Assemblies of God	n.a.	n.a.	n.a.	40 000	45 000

Note   Figures include those churches which united into the United Reformed Church on 26 September 1981.

Sources: Robert Gilbert, Alan Currie and Lee Horsley, *Churches and Church-goers* (Oxford: Clarendon Press, 1977), pp. 32, and 147–58; Peter Brierley (ed.), *The United Kingdom Christian Handbook 1987/88* (London, 1986), pp. 132–47; and Peter Brierley (ed.), *The United Kingdom Christian Handbook, 1992/93* (London, 1991), pp. 210–38.

Membership also declined in American churches, but more selectively and less gradually than in Britain. There was no membership decline following the Second World War in most churches; in fact the major denominations grew consistently throughout the 1950s. However, in the latter years of the 1960s most denominations stopped growing for the first time in the nation's history. With the noticeable exception of the Southern Baptist Convention, the mainline churches began losing members in an unparalleled manner. Smaller Pentecostal and evangelical churches such as the Assemblies of God and Churches of God grew rapidly (see Table 5.3).

Membership decline was especially pronounced in liberal churches; the more conservative denominations, the Southern Baptists, Church of God, Assemblies of God and other smaller evangelical bodies grew throughout the 1960s and 1970s (see Table 5.4). Church membership nationwide was

Table 5.2   Percentage change in British church membership

	1970–75 %	1975–80 %	1980–85 %	1985–90 %
Anglican	–5.5	–8.0	–9.0	–8.0
Presbyterian	–8.5	–8.0	–11.0	–7.0
Methodist	–10.0	–14.5	–13.5	–3.0
Baptist	–12.0	–2.0	+2.0	–1.0
House Churches	n.a.	n.a.	+200.0	+60.0
Fell. of Independent Evangelical Churches	n.a.	n.a.	+37.0	+9.4

Source: *The United Kingdom Christian Handbook, 1987/88 and 1992/93* (London, 1986), p. 132; and (London, 1991) pp. 214–15.

Table 5.3   Church membership, 1960–85, selected US denominations

	1960	1970	1975	1980	1985
Methodist	10 641 310	10 509 198	9 861 028	9 591 407	9 291 936
Presb. (USA)	4 161 860	4 045 408	3 535 825	3 362 086	3 092 151
Episcopal	3 269 325	3 285 826	2 857 513	2 786 004	2 775 424
Cong. (UCC)	2 241 134	1 960 608	1 818 762	1 736 244	1 696 107
Southern Baptist	9 731 591	11 628 032	12 733 124	13 600 126	14 341 821
Assemblies of God	508 602	625 027	785 347	1 064 490	2 135 104
Church of God Cleve., Tn.	313 057	422 476	509 506	505 775	582 203

Source: Constant H. Jacquet (ed.), *Yearbook of American and Canadian Churches*, various editions (Nashville: Abingdon Press).

Table 5.4   Percentage change in American church membership

	1960–70 %	1970–80 %	1980–85 %
Methodist	–7.3	–8.7	–3.1
Presb. (USA)	–2.8	–16.8	–8.0
Episcopal	+0.5	–15.2	–0.3
Cong. (UCC)	–12.5	–11.4	–2.3
Southern Baptist	+19	+17	+5
Assemblies of God	+22.8	+70.3	+100
Church of God (Cleveland, Tn.)	+34.9	+19.7	+15.1

Source: Constant H. Jacquet (ed.), *Yearbook of American and Canadian Churches*, various editions (Nashville: Abingdon Press).

still high by the English standard. In the early and mid sixties, approximately three-quarters of the American population reported they were church or synagogue members. By 1982, 67 per cent of Americans claimed to be church members, a remarkably high percentage when compared to Britain. The decline in active church membership was, however, pronounced among young people who left the church altogether or turned to alternative religious movements. It was clear to religionists in both nations that the churches were not successfully recruiting as many active and faithful supporters as they once had.[4]

British and American evangelicals concluded that the decline in church membership vindicated their long-held view that liberalism was a danger to Christianity. British evangelical Michael Saward asserted that 'the undermining voice of liberal Christianity has had its chance and we are seeing the consequences of its failure'.[5] Evangelicals believed that religious values and commitments no longer had sustaining power, because of the willingness of liberal churches and institutions to alter their message to meet changing social norms and values. Evangelicals asserted, by contrast, that their organizations, which were not as open to theological diversity and were less willing to accommodate their values, had been more effective in keeping old members and attracting new ones. The National Association of Evangelicals claimed in its literature that 'the ongoing strength and vitality of NAE is explained by its seven-point statement of faith descriptive of the true evangelical'.[6] John Ling, Executive Director of Evangelicals for LIFE in Britain, concluded in a personal interview, 'I cannot see why anyone would want to attend a non-evangelical church. Evangelical churches have and know the truth; liberal churches have succumbed to relativism.'[7] There are reasons to be sceptical about statements by group leaders concerning the causes of evangelical growth, but the fact remains that evangelical churches grew while liberal churches declined in the 1960s and 1970s.[8]

There have been no nationwide polls on religion in Britain to sustain the argument that evangelicals have retained a higher degree of religious participation than liberals, but all of the accounts of resident experts agree that evangelical churches and organizations have flourished while those that are more liberal have declined. Evangelicalism enjoyed a renaissance beginning in the late 1950s. Billy Graham, the American evangelist, helped provide impetus for a British evangelical revival with his watershed crusade to Britain in 1954. Graham drew enormous crowds to his crusade which was reviewed in all of the daily newspapers. Graham's ministry had the important effect of bringing Anglican and nonconformist evangelicals into a closer relationship. The resolution of church/state conflicts in the early twentieth century had eliminated the political separation of believers, and Graham showed evangelicals just how much they had in common. The crusade encouraged evangelicals to abandon their pietistic enclaves and return to their churches confident that they had something important to offer.[9]

During the next two decades, evangelicalism became a vital force in British Christianity. In addition to the numerical growth of evangelical churches, evangelicals became more a prominent force within the mainline denominations. The polity of the Baptist church became more conservative and evangelical than it had been since the early part of the century. The Church of England, by far the largest Protestant church, experienced a renewed evangelicalism. Evangelical parishes within the Anglican church – St Aldates, Oxford, St Michael-Le-Belfry in York, and All Souls Langham Place, London, to name a few – were the most visible and vibrant within the denomination. Ordained Anglican ministers were decidedly more evangelical in the 1970s and 1980s than they had been in the 1950s and 1960s. In 1950 only 10 per cent of ordained clergy in the Church of England came from evangelical seminaries; by 1969 this figure rose to 31 per cent and to an all-time high of 51 per cent in 1986. Evangelicals also formed organizations within specific churches, such as Conservative Evangelicals in Methodism (1970), the Anglican Evangelical Assembly (AEA, 1982), and the Baptist Evangelism Office (1985).[10]

There was also a proliferation in the number of evangelical organizations formed after 1960. The number of congregations affiliated with the Fellowship of Independent Evangelical churches rose from 244 in 1953 to 434 in 1980. The Evangelical Alliance, founded in 1846, has been an umbrella organization which currently represents over one million British Christians. The Alliance brings together into a single organization the myriad evangelical groups throughout England. In 1986, 220 groups were officially affiliated with the Alliance; over half of those groups, 111, were formed after 1960. By 1990 the number of groups affiliated with the Alliance had grown to 510.[11]

In many instances the growth of evangelical groups came at the expense of established liberal organizations. Evangelicals formed groups to minister to college students, the Universities and Colleges Christian Fellowship (UCCF), doctors, the Christian Medical Fellowship (CMF), and groups which focused on political action, CARE Trust, the London Institute for Contemporary Christianity, and the Jubilee Centre. These groups challenged the existing liberal church groups which purported to represent the same religious constituency. The UCCF is especially interesting in this regard. It was founded as an evangelical alternative to the liberal Student Christian Movement (SCM) which mainline denominations supported. For decades the two organizations competed with one another for the support of university students. By 1970, however, the SCM had all but folded, while the UCCF continued to grow.[12]

Evangelical vitality is even easier to measure in America. By 1970 the Southern Baptist Convention, the most evangelical of the mainline denominations, was the largest single church in America. The fastest-growing American churches in the 1960s and 1970s were the Churches of God in Christ, the Church of the Nazarene and various independent evangelical or fundamentalist bodies. While these churches have been surprisingly diverse theologically, they can all nonetheless be described as evangelical. Nationwide polls also indicated an evangelical vitality. In 1976, a Gallup poll reported that one out of every three people in America claimed to have been 'born again'. Using a more rigorous definition of evangelicalism, Gallup still estimated that 35 million American adults were evangelical Christians.[13]

Evangelical organizations also grew in number and strength after the Second World War. In 1943, Evangelicalism gained a national focus with the formation of the National Association of Evangelicals (NAE). Describing itself as a 'movement for Bible-believing Christians', the NAE was self-consciously an evangelical alternative to the increasingly liberal Federal Council of Churches, later renamed the National Council of Churches.[14] The NAE provided a platform for a variety of special-purpose evangelical organizations. Chief among them were the Evangelical Foreign Missions Association, the largest missions organization in the world, and the Evangelicalism and Home Missions Association. Evangelicals began to dominate in the foreign missions field, an area which Liberal churches gradually abandoned; by 1960, evangelical missions groups provided 65 per cent of the total number of foreign missionaries; today the figure is over 90 per cent.[15]

The NAE was also instrumental in the founding of the National Religious Broadcasters, a group formed to lobby for the right of churches to purchase radio and television air-time. Evangelical radio and television ministries grew rapidly and overtook the efforts of liberal churches. Evangelical mobilization also occurred within liberal denominations; Presbyterians for Biblical Concerns (1965), Forum for Scriptural Christianity in the Methodist Church (1966), and the Biblical Witness Fellowship in the United Church of Christ (1980) were all founded to represent a wide variety of evangelical concerns within those churches. More important, however, were the parachurch evangelical organizations which were formed, including missionary agencies, Bible societies, prison ministries, and Bible study groups, all of which stood outside the denominational structure.[16]

After the Second World War, evangelicals dominated the field of domestic missions. Youth For Christ and Young Life were formed to minister to the nation's high-school students, Bill Bright founded the Campus Crusade for Christ, which evangelized on college campuses, and Billy Graham began his crusades, which would establish a national reputation not only for him but for evangelicalism more generally. In all of these efforts, evangelicals steered a middle course between what they considered the extremes of liberalism and fundamentalism. They were disassociated from liberalism by their doctrine, while their professionalism and moderation separated them from the still-marginal fundamentalists. The rapid growth of evangelical colleges and seminaries highlighted the new-found professionalism of evangelicalism.

Evangelical organizations, old and new, continued to stress the exclusionary doctrines that Jesus was the sole source of salvation and redemption for individuals and that the Bible was the inspired and infallible Word of God. These organizations grew in the 1960s and 1970s, while liberal churches, which self-consciously accommodated their religious doctrines, lost members. The contrast of evangelical growth with the continued decline in liberal church membership shows, as Adrian Hastings notes, that religion and irreligion can be contemporaneous phenomena within a society. A significant percentage of the population in Britain and America abandoned the church altogether in the 1960s and 1970s, but an equally large number became more active than ever before.[17]

By the end of the 1960s, British and American evangelical organizations were well placed from a resource perspective for political mobilization. Evangelicals had formed religious institutions which were as large as or larger than their liberal counterparts, an evangelical leadership had arisen with the capacity to raise material and human resources for a political cause, and evangelical group members were drawn into organizations through a powerful and coherent religious ideology. The only missing ingredient in their political activism was the presence of social issues which threatened to undermine deeply-held values of an evangelical ideology.

The impetus for evangelical political action came with changing social mores during the 1960s and 1970s. Evangelicals became acutely aware of the distance between their beliefs and social practice during the 1960s and 1970s as divorce rates climbed, homosexuality was more openly expressed, prayer and bible-reading were removed from the public schools, birth control and abortion became more widely available, and sexual practices changed dramatically. Divorce rates in America increased from 9.2 per cent per 100 married women in 1960 to 14.9 per cent in 1970 and 22.6 per cent in 1980.[18] In Britain, the number of divorces doubled from 1970 to 1975 and increased by another 20 per cent in the next five years.[19] Premarital intercourse among women aged 15 to 19 jumped from 30 per cent in 1971 to 46 per cent in 1982 in America, while teenage pregnancy among unmarried girls increased by 64 per cent from 1960 to 1977.[20] Abortion rates climbed rapidly in both nations throughout the 1970s.

Evangelicals became aware not simply of the distance between their values and social practice, but also between evangelical and non-evangelical moral views.[21] Liberals and evangelicals had been theologically divided for nearly fifty years, but it was not until the 1960s and 1970s that it became apparent that they were also ideologically divided in terms of moral and cultural values. James Davison Hunter, using data drawn from a Gallup poll on evangelical attitudes conducted in 1979, concluded that, among religious groups, evangelicals ranked highest in their opposition to homosexuality, abortion and divorce. Over 95 per cent of the evangelicals polled viewed abortion as immoral, while 88 and 66 per cent respectively believed that homosexuality and divorce were immoral.[22] A 1984 survey on American evangelicals conducted by Stuart Rothenberg and Frank Newport and a 1984 poll on British religious opinions done by Roger Jowell and

Colin Airey showed that evangelicals were far more conservative than non-evangelicals on abortion, pornography, divorce and pre-marital sex.[23]

Evangelicals formed political organizations to oppose social practices which were inimical to religious values, and because mainline churches and political elites supported the new moral ideology. As the British and American governments expanded their influence into wider areas of daily life, the moral and political tension between evangelicals and secularists increased. In order to see more clearly how an evangelical ideology helped legitimate the formation of political organizations, I will review evangelical activism on three issues: abortion, pornography, and the place of religion in state-supported schools. A similar pattern of evangelical activism emerges for each issue in each nation. A liberalization or legalization of a social practice led to evangelical ideological discontent. Evangelicals formed groups on the basis of what they believed to be biblically immoral and socially dangerous behaviour and because liberal denominations and political elites supported the new laws and social practices.

EVANGELICAL IDEOLOGY AND ABORTION

The United States Supreme Court granted women the right to abort a foetus in its 1973 decisions *Doe v. Bolton* and *Roe v. Wade*. Prior to those rulings, the majority of states (44) allowed abortions only if the pregnant woman's life would be endangered if the pregnancy were carried to term. In four states (Washington, New York, Alaska and Hawaii), there was a more liberal policy of allowing abortions for reasons of maternal health or mental well-being of the mother. The court overturned the laws of all of the states by ruling that a woman had an absolute right to an abortion in the first trimester of her pregnancy. After the second trimester the state could regulate and even forbid abortions. In fact, states have not been willing or able to regulate late-term abortions. I will return to a more detailed description of the politics which led to the legalization of abortion in the next chapter.[24]

Evangelical organizations blamed the liberal government and churches for allowing such a court doctrine to exist. The Christian Action Council, an evangelical pro-life group, claimed about abortion that 'the government has turned its back on their silent screams. But God has not.'[25] Evangelicals concluded that liberal church leaders and structures were deeply implicated as pro-choice advocates. In fact, none of the major Protestant churches opposed the court's decision. In some cases, Protestant clergy helped legitimate abortion reform through their work in the Clergy Consultation Service (CCS). Ministers formed the Service to refer women seeking abortion to the clinics and hospitals of New York City after New York liberalized its abortion law. At its height, the CCS operated in twenty states.[26] Randall Terry, founder of the pro-life group Operation Rescue, claimed that liberal church support for abortion rights showed that those denominations had 'bowed to the knee of the god of self. Humanism is the worship of man. It makes life man-centered instead of God-centered.'[27]

The Catholic Church immediately mobilized opposition to the court's decision in *Roe v. Wade*. Evangelicals did not organize as quickly, but by the end of the 1970s they were as public as Roman Catholics in their opposition to abortion. The major pro-life organizations which formed were: Christian Americans for Life (1972), National Committee for a Human Life Amendment (1974), March For Life (1974), Christian Action Council (1975), National Pro-Life Political Action Committee (1977), Life Amendment Political Action Committee (1977), Methodists for Life (1978), American Life Lobby (1979), and Operation Rescue (1986). Evangelical pro-life activism also occurred in the 1980s through all-purpose organizations such as Christian Voice (1978), Religious Roundtable (1978), Moral Majority (1979), and Christian Coalition (1989), an organization founded and led by one-time presidential candidate Pat Robertson. The Catholic Church has provided the greatest resources for the Pro-Life Movement, but evangelical Christians have also generously contributed to the movement. The Christian Coalition, with a membership of over 400 000, the Christian Action Council, with 300 000 members, Methodists For Life, with 20 000 members, Christian Americans for Life, 15 000 members, and Operation Rescue are predominantly made up of evangelicals. The non-sectarian American Life Lobby, with 300 000 members, also has a large evangelical constituency. Membership figures are probably inflated, but they provide a rough estimate of the pro-life organizational strength.[28]

The evangelical pro-life movement in Britain has followed the pattern described in America. Abortion became legal in Britain in 1967 through a private member's bill sponsored by David Steel. Although the law has not given women the right to choose an abortion, the grounds for abortion are wide and the practice is relatively liberal. With the approval of two registered doctors, a woman can have an abortion up to 28 weeks in term. The number of abortions performed has risen from 49 000 in 1969, to 101 000 in 1976, and 127 000 in 1983. The law has been upheld despite parliamentary challenges.[29]

It was clear to evangelicals that political and religious elites would not provide opposition to the Steel Bill. As a private member's bill, the Steel bill needed the tacit support of the government in order to pass. The Labour government provided extra time so that the bill would not be talked out by opponents.[30] No major Protestant church was totally opposed to abortion reform. In 1965, two years before Steel introduced his abortion bill, the Church of England Board of Social Responsibility issued a pamphlet entitled 'Abortion: An Ethical Discussion'. The pamphlet recognized that there were certain circumstances under which abortions could be justified. Other major Protestant churches – the Methodists, United Reform/Presbyterian, and even the Baptists – were supportive of a liberalization in the abortion law. To date, the churches are deeply divided on the issue, although the Church of England has moved in a decidedly more conservative direction in the past fifteen years.[31]

The two largest pro-life organizations in Britain are the Society for the Protection of Unborn Children (SPUC) and LIFE. Both are officially nonsectarian groups, but their support comes largely from Catholics and evangelical Christians. SPUC claims a membership of 30 000, and there are probably as many official members of LIFE, but in both cases the figures underestimate actual support. LIFE has two special-interest groups within it – Evangelicals for Life and Life Anglicans – which draw support entirely from the evangelical community. SPUC also attracts evangelical support, especially in many of its 250 local branches where evangelicals are most strongly represented. Evangelicals are also active in the Pro-Life Movement in such all-purpose organizations as the Evangelical Alliance (1845), Christian Action Research and Education (CARE, 1971), Christian Affirmation Campaign (1974), the Conservative Family Campaign (1978); and the London Institute for Contemporary Christianity (1981).[32]

Evangelical moral values about parenthood, family life, human sexuality and the place of God in human affairs provide the basis for their opposition to abortion.[33] The evangelical stress on what they call 'traditional' family values sheds light on believers' opposition to abortion. Evangelicals believe that the family is the most important institution in society. Ordained by God, the family is comprised of a husband and wife, each with clearly-defined obligations. Husbands provide the monetary support for the family while wives are primarily responsible for the nurture and care of children. Children are celebrated in this view as 'miraculous gifts of God'[34] who enable mothers and fathers to assume their proper parental roles. This particular conception of family life is described by a British evangelical to be a reflection of 'the moral order'.[35] Men and women, in short, are not the ultimate arbiters of what constitutes parenthood and a family. That role is reserved for God.

Legalized abortion threatens this morality because it provides women with the power to control when they will have children and allows for a redefinition of the family and parenthood. The language of choice contravenes the notion that the 'traditional' family is ordained by God as part of the moral order and thereby undermines the evangelical claim that the proper role for women is raising children. Although there is no evidence to suggest that most abortions are performed because women want to pursue a career, the importance given to this justification in evangelical pro-life literature suggests that groups view the issue in terms of the proper role of women and men. A pamphlet of the Christian Action Council asks, 'how can we justify unbridled abortion policies because of a desire to pursue one's career?'[36]

In the evangelical view, it is not simply immoral for a woman to have an abortion, it is unnatural. Women are meant to raise children, which is why evangelicals simply cannot understand the idea that women should have a choice to abort a foetus. 'Abortion', according to one publication, 'robs us of the blessings which children can bring.'[37] By contrast to women who choose to follow a career, evangelical pro-life organizations highlight 'the unsung and unrecognized mothers of America who have devoted their lives to their families'.[38] Public opinion polls show that American evangelicals are significantly more conservative than non-evangelicals on questions related to the role of women in society.[39]

Legalized abortion is similarly a threat to an evangelical sexual ethic. Sexual intercourse, in an evangelical ideology, is exclusively reserved for heterosexual marriages. Abortion violates this value because it enables people to have sex outside marriage, without bearing the responsibility of children. Evangelical pro-life literature frequently claims that legalized abortion is responsible for what believers perceive to be a decline in sexual morality in Britain and America. According to the Christian Action Council, 'God's design is for sex and children within the marriage bond. The problem begins with irresponsible intercourse.'[40] What constitutes 'responsible intercourse', for evangelicals, is sex within marriage. In so far as legalized abortion violates those norms it is to be opposed.

The value placed upon 'traditional' moral values is often an unstated but implied assumption in the arguments made by evangelical groups. A report of the Religious Roundtable in 1981 connected the abortion issue to family morality: 'The Roundtable is a pro-family organization in the biblical sense. As such, we oppose abortion as an act of murder.'[41] The two sentences do not necessarily have anything to do with each other, nor does the literature provide an extended discussion to explain how being pro-family in the biblical sense necessarily entails an opposition to abortion. Readers of the report who accept evangelical values relating to family life and gender roles provide the logic necessary to connect the two claims. If one accepts that children are a miraculous gift of God and that women and men are meant to have children, it follows that abortion is an act of murder and unnatural.

Group leaders explicitly related political activism to the preservation of Christian values. The Christian Affirmation Campaign in Britain claimed that it was founded 'to offer resistance to the attacks on Christian morality and the undermining of the family as the basic unit of society'.[42] The Religious Roundtable in America argued that 'we are seeking the survival of Christian families and institutions'.[43] Evangelicals perceived that the formation of political organizations would help them protect their value system and religious convictions in a rapidly changing social world. The Traditional Values Coalition stated its purpose precisely in those terms: 'The coalition was established to help reinstate traditional values in all levels of our government. . . . We seek to educate individuals, churches, and other community groups on the moral and Biblical issues upon which government impacts.'[44] These organizations believed that the solution to social problems lay in a reinvestment in traditional family and sexual morality. Christian Voice put the matter succinctly in a publication mailed to group members in 1988: 'In a society rooted in strong families, schools and religious institutions – a society which holds individuals responsible for their actions and has a well defined understanding of the difference between right and wrong – such a problem (abortion) could hardly have reached its current proportion.'[45]

The most distinctive feature of evangelical pro-life literature is the biblical mandate used by group leaders to justify their position. The Christian Action Council is explicit about the place of scripture in its organization: 'the Christian Action Council raises a clear, biblical standard defending the sanctity of human life'.[46] Abortion is never mentioned directly in the Bible. There is no clear injunction against abortion, as there is in the case of murder or theft. This is not to suggest that evangelical leaders create a biblical argument against abortion where one does not exist. Instead, group leaders link evangelical cultural values about human sexuality to a plausible biblical interpretation on abortion.

Evangelical groups justify their pro-life position in two phases: first they establish that the Bible teaches that life begins at conception and then claim that the biblical principle of the sanctity of life applies to the unborn child. The most frequently-cited biblical passage quoted by evangelical pro-life groups is Psalm 139: 'For you created my inmost being; you knit me together in my mother's womb. I praise you for I am fearfully and wonderfully made.' (Psalm 139:13–14). A second passage often referred to is Jeremiah 1:5: 'Before I formed you in the womb, I knew you; and before you were born I consecrated you; I appointed you a prophet to the nations.'

Pro-life groups use these passages to show that in the Bible, the foetus is considered a human and that God has a purpose for each person before birth. The Christian Action Council quotes Psalm 139 as evidence that 'in the bible humanness is present from conception'.[47] Billy James Hargis and Dan Lyons, founders of Christian Crusade, claim about the relationship between abortion and the Bible: 'the scripture is not silent on the question of the origin of human life. . . . It begins at conception. The Word of God is clearly opposed to the taking of human life, including the lives of unborn babies.'[48] Independent evidence shows that supporters of pro-life organizations accept the claim that abortion violates God's law. A poll conducted in 1990 reported that according to members of pro-life groups, the most convincing argument against abortion was that 'abortion is against God's law'.[49]

In an important way, the evangelical biblical hermeneutic helps in the process of group formation. When evangelicals cite Psalm 139 as an argument that life begins at conception they imply that the Bible is the appropriate place to discover moral principles and that the scriptures can and should be read at face value. Biblical passages are read as straightforward injunctions; there is no elaborate interpretive process necessary to discover the meaning of scriptures. Psalm 139 is not read, as it is in most liberal Protestant circles, as a metaphorical description of God's participation in the creation process, but as an actual account of how God forms human life. The passage is not critiqued using the literary, historical or interpretive tools of modern biblical exegesis. The moral authority of the Bible is so significant among evangelicals, that group leaders can win evangelical sympathy and support by demonstrating a biblical opposition to elective abortions.

Evangelical pro-life groups do not weigh the biblical evidence against what they consider the non-scriptural considerations of the rights of women or the problems of legislating abortion. Non-biblical arguments might be used to strengthen a case for or against abortion, but in the final analysis what the bible declares is of pre-eminent importance for evangelicals. The language of rights upon which the *Roe* decision was adjudicated is therefore rejected because 'a woman has no God-given right to decide on her own to have an abortion. Such thinking is alien to Christianity. According to biblical dictate, a woman's body is not her own to do with as she pleases.'[50] The bible has primacy in social and political matters when there is a conflict between what the scriptures say and other moral considerations, such as a woman's right to control her own reproductivity. It is therefore 'irrelevant' that the Supreme Court established the legality of abortion because, as Randall Terry argues, 'God's laws can never be made null and void by men. Never!'[51]

The literature of most evangelical pro-life groups only talks about rights in terms of the foetus's right not to be aborted, which is in fact less a claim about rights and more an assertion that the foetus is human and that abortion violates the biblical proscription against taking innocent life. As one group claims, 'it is the status of the unborn that must be defined before personal rights become meaningful'.[52] Once evangelicals assume that abortions 'cause the death of a living human',[53] it is possible for group leaders to make the connection between abortion and murder. Hargis simply asserts, 'nowhere in the Bible can there be found any reference that even hints that murder, or abortion, is favourable in God's eyes'.[54] To contravene that belief by supporting abortion is to violate what is a clear biblical mandate. Pro-life organizations consciously legitimate their views in terms of the religious ideology of their members. American Life League President Judie Brown asserts, 'the American Life League was founded because I know that human life is a gift from God, and that only He can make the decision to end that life'.[55] The 300 000 people who have joined her organization share that conviction.

Evangelical pro-life literature asserts that the Bible teaches that abortion is not only a personal sin but also a corporate evil. There is a difference. It is one thing to claim that abortion is morally wrong and that no believer ought to have one, and quite another to assert that Christians have a positive responsibility to legislate that view nationally. Groups appeal to the responsibility members are supposed to feel toward the unborn foetus and to God's unchanging morality. Group members are reminded that evangelical Christians are obliged to bring 'every area of our life under the Lordship of Jesus Christ', including the area of political involvement against legalized abortion.[56] The 'true' believer is the one who recognizes that abortion is so great an immorality that 'the Christian has a biblical duty to oppose it'.[57] The participation of evangelicals in pro-life groups follows, consequently, not because group members believe that they will gain some benefit from membership, but because believers accept the proposition that they have an obligation to join. This sense of obligation follows from an evangelical ideology which teaches believers that they have a responsibility to show their commitment to Christian ethics and their love for God in tangible acts of service. Social groups form among the committed who believe that they have a duty to the divine law, as determined through the scriptures, to help the unborn.

The explicit appeal in group literature to biblical norms is especially important since some of the more radical pro-life organizations ask their members to break the law, a political action which is costly, time-consuming, and potentially dangerous. Operation Rescue and the Non-violent Action Project support civil disobedience at clinics and hospitals as a way of disrupting abortion services. People need a powerful motive to consider such an extreme form of activism. These groups make strong appeals to the religious ideology of members, asking believers to consider the idea that they have a duty to oppose sins against God. Group members are urged to believe that their action, while illegal in the eyes of the state, is legal and honorific by the standard of God's ethical imperative. Randall Terry justifies his group's civil disobedience in precisely those religious terms: 'rescues are not merely civil disobedience, they are biblical obedience'.[58] This is not to suggest that all, or even most, evangelicals show the depth of their commitment to God's mandate by breaking the law. Most evangelicals have not in fact been arrested at abortion clinics. The appeal to civil disobedience can, nevertheless, be a powerfully motivating and educative tool for evangelicals, who are forced to think through the implications of a faith which tells them that biblical values must take precedence over cultural norms in a person's life.

A case is made in group literature that the sin of omission (the lack of opposition to legal abortions) is as great as the sin of commission (actually having an abortion). The Nonviolent Action Project claims, 'the mandate in scripture is clear. . . . Enough looking. Enough talking. Enough ignorant evasion of responsibility. When you know that an innocent and helpless child is about to be killed, you must intervene.'[59] Evangelical pro-life groups assert that taking a public stand against abortion is a way of witnessing to God's higher laws. Keith Tucci of Operation Rescue wrote about an upcoming rescue mission in Wichita, Kansas: 'Friends, let's declare the Lordship of Jesus over our lives. I want you prayerfully to consider giving the week of July 15–20 for missionary service. When we take a public stand against abortion, we are not only standing for the children and mothers but also as witnesses of God's righteous laws.'[60] The thousands of people who were arrested in Wichita in the summer of 1991 are evidence that the appeal to a religious ideology is not inconsequential.

The importance of a religious ideology and commitment for a pro-life position is underscored in the public-opinion data on attitudes towards abortion. Data compiled by Baker, Epstein and Forth on American views shows that religiosity – as measured by church-attendance – is the best predictor of abortion preferences. The study finds that the degree of personal religious involvement and commitment is the best predictor of a pro-life position. Demographic, political, and social-class variables are much less valuable as indicators of preferences on legalized abortion. This data underscores my claim that an evangelical religious ideology, with its emphasis on a high degree of personal commitment and involvement, helps legitimate pro-life activism.[61]

The Bible is the unifying thread of the British evangelical opposition to abortion, as it is for American groups. Pro-life British evangelicals, like their American peers, frequently quote scripture to legitimate their pro-life position. The scriptures provides what Life Anglicans calls 'awesome truths' that life begins at conception.[62] Evangelicals for Life claims that 'the Bible forbids the taking of innocent life. The sanctity of human life and the gravity of any assault on the image of God is upheld throughout scripture.'[63] SPUC is well aware of this biblical argument when it describes itself as a 'political pressure group whose activities are directed towards upholding the most fundamental of all rights – the right to life itself'.[64] What matters most for these groups is the 'biblical bedrock'[65] which teaches an opposition to abortion.

British groups also show a commitment to establishing a scriptural basis for a political opposition to abortion. Group literature emphasizes the moral obligation to oppose abortion which evangelical members are supposed to feel. The Public Morals Committee of the Evangelical Presbyterian Church claims that 'every Christian must recognize that abortion is a sin which they must not commit, advise, or participate in. Positively we have a responsibility to do something about the evil of abortion in our society.'[66] Not every moral value of evangelical Christians elicits efforts to legislate that view nationally. The biblical proscription against extra-marital affairs has not led to the formation of evangelical groups to punish offenders of that sin. Why is abortion such a special case? In the words of John Ling, founder of Evangelicals for Life, 'abortion is in a different league – it strikes at the very root of the value of human life, of who we are'.[67] Evangelical group literature assumes that the reader shares an ideology and a language which answers the question of 'who we are' with, 'We are God's', and that as God's people we have a responsibility to serve Him by opposing abortion. 'In truth there is only one evangelical motive', claims Ling, 'and that is to honour God.' And evangelicals honour God by fighting the 'horror of abortion'.[68]

EVANGELICAL IDEOLOGY AND PORNOGRAPHY

American and British evangelicals also opposed the proliferation of pornographic materials in the 1960s and 1970s. Although there is no generally accepted definition of what constitutes pornography, an increase in pornography, however defined, occurred during the past several decades. American evangelicals saw the complicity of political elites in the new liberal attitude toward pornography. In 1970, an American Presidential Committee published a report on obscenity and pornography laws. The commission concluded that pornography was not harmful and should be freed from restraint and censorship. John Court, an evangelical active in the anti-pornography movement, claimed that the report was 'the most influential defense of pornography ever published'.[69]

In Britain, television programmes showed more sex and violence as the BBC relaxed its monitoring standards in the 1960s. Evangelicals argued that the government chose not to strengthen pornography laws or prosecute offenders with existing laws. Few British religious leaders have openly supported a liberalization in pornography laws, but there have also been few actively trying to restrict those laws. The liberal leadership of the major churches left unquestioned the conclusion of the Williams Committee of 1979 which stated that there was no evidence to link pornography with violent or asocial behaviour. Whether or not the Committee's conclusions were correct, the evangelical anti-pornography activist Mary Whitehouse was upset by the 'considerable reluctance within the church to get involved'.[70]

In the absence of religious or political opposition to the liberalization of pornography standards, American and British evangelicals formed their own anti-pornography groups. In America, the largest organizations formed were: Morality in Media (MIM, 1962), Citizens Against Pornography (1982), and the National Coalition against Pornography (1983). MIM is a nation-wide inter-faith organization with 55 000 members: CAP and NCAP, each with 5000 members and NFD, are regional evangelical groups. Evangelicals were also active in the anti-pornography campaign in larger all-purpose organizations such as Phyllis Schlafly's Eagle Forum (1972), Beverly Lahaye's Concerned Women of America (1979), the Traditional Values Coalition (1982), and Dr James Dobson's hugely successful Focus on the Family (FOF). Concerned Women of America and Focus on the Family have been the largest pro-family groups in America, with 500 000 members each, and, in the case of Focus on the Family, an annual budget of nearly 60 million dollars.[71]

In Britain, the largest and most significant anti-pornography organization has been The National Viewers and Listeners Association (NVALA) with a membership of 31 000 in 1976. It grew out of the Clean-Up TV Campaign (CUTV), founded in 1965 by two housewives, Mrs Mary Whitehouse and Mrs Norah Buckland, who deplored the 'dirt that the BBC projects into millions of homes through the television screen'.[72] The CUTV was specifically interested in the policies at the BBC, but the NVALA broadened the scope to include an opposition to any liberalization in pornography, obscenity, film censorship, blasphemy, homosexuality and divorce laws. Mrs Whitehouse has a notoriety in England not shared by any other religious activist. NVALA has been joined in its effort by other all-purpose evangelical groups, most notably CARE, the Conservative Family Campaign, The Christian Affirmation Campaign, and the Christian Broadcasting Campaign (1983).[73]

The evangelical opposition to pornography in Britain and America follows from a set of religiously-grounded values. The American group Citizens Against Pornography notes, 'pornography attacks the dignity of men and women created in the image of God (Genesis 1:27). It distorts God's gift of sex which should be shared only in the bonds of marriage (1 Corinthians 7:2–3). And it frequently promotes sexual perversion which is condemned by God.'[74] This group, along with most evangelical organizations, includes the scripture in the text of the literature to underscore the importance of a biblical legitimation. For evangelicals, the Bible provides a well-ordered set of values on marriage, the family, and the proper expression of sex.

The debate around pornography is implicitly a conflict around moral claims about the family and human sexuality. Evangelicals place a great value on the 'traditional' family, where the parental roles are clearly circumscribed. The father provides monetary support for the family, while the mother is primarily responsible for the nurture and care of children. British evangelical Graham Webster of the Conservative Family Campaign argues, 'if we turn to the Good Book which guides the Christian faith we find that we were not meant to live alone. The moral order is for one husband and one wife in a secure, lifelong, stable relationship.'[75] In terms of those values, pornography is, as John Court argues, 'anti-relationship and thus anti-family. Pornography carefully avoids any recognition of the value of family relationships.'[76] Pornography, with its emphasis on sexuality outside marriage, distorts evangelical claims about the sacredness of the marital bond and the sinfulness of sex outside marriage. In contrast, evangelical groups argue that the Bible upholds the marital bond and the sinfulness of lustful desires.

Pornography is an obvious challenge to this ideal because it shows and celebrates sex outside marriage. A publication of an American anti-pornography organization wonders aloud how an ethic of sex reserved for marriage can be propounded when 'pornography is polluting the environment in which we are trying to raise our children'.[77] The problem with pornography, according to a British organization, is that it 'affirms an immoral ethos of promiscuity, fornication, homosexuality, is anti-marriage, and encourages children to experiment with sex rather than buttressing children against those pressures'.[78] For evangelicals, pornography is not simply an issue about the publication of 'dirty' pictures. Instead, the pornography debate implies a set of values relating to human sexuality and family life.

Similarly, a publication of Citizens Against Pornography claimed that what was at stake in the pornography debate 'is the future of the family itself'.[79] The readers of the pamphlet who share an evangelical ideology have particular values relating to marriage and family life which enable them to perceive pornographic literature as necessarily an attack on the family. In equally clear language, the National Association of Evangelicals asserted, 'much of our society seems to accept sexual freedoms and perverted lifestyles as normal and healthy; depict the traditional family as obsolete; and view respect for authority as old-fashioned'.[80]

Evangelicals do not view sex as inherently evil. In fact, they go to great lengths to accord sexual relations a biblical status. CARE, a British all-purpose evangelical group, notes, 'The Bible is clear that God invented sex! . . . Abundant life in Christ includes abundant sexual life *in the godly context*'[81] (my emphasis). In America, Beverley and Tim Lahaye use statistical data which purports to show that Christians are more sexually satisfied than non-Christians. Marabel Morgan's book, *The Total Woman*, extols the virtues of a healthy Christian sex-life. For evangelicals, the issue is the proper expression of sex, which is, for them, within 'the context of heterosexual lifelong commitment'.[82] Citizens Against Pornography succinctly states, 'from a biblical perspective, sexual intercourse is exclusively reserved for marriage',[83] an opinion which was shared by 82.6 per cent of the American evangelicals polled in a 1979 survey.[84]

Evangelicals argue that sexuality is healthy within marriage while misdirected expressions of sex (pornography) are opposed because they violate the biblical values of family and marriage. Pornography is misdirected because it portrays sex outside marriage, which undermines the marital union by creating 'lustful desires and the adultery of the heart that Jesus speaks about'.[85] Christians are urged to 'keep themselves pure by fleeing the immorality (1 Corinthians 6:18) of pornography'.[86] Pornography is also deemed sinful because it highlights what are considered illicit sexual orientations: 'pornographic themes emphasize sex in multiple arrangements of people. Bisexuality is praised as more liberated than exclusive heterosexuality,'[87] In all cases, pornography devalues the biblical teaching on the sacredness of the marital bond, the sinfulness of homosexuality and bisexuality, and the proper place of sex within marriage.

The impetus for the formation of the anti-pornography groups NVALA, CARE, Citizens Against Pornography and Focus on the Family came from the concern among evangelicals that widespread pornography threatened their biblically-derived religious values. These groups and their members placed a high value on the biblical celebration of marriage and family and believed that pornography threatened to undermine the realization of those values within their own communities. Evangelicals viewed pornography not simply as a threat to American society, but also to evangelical families and institutions. Falwell claims that 'many men and women are being brainwashed and demoralized by pornography',[88] which implied that he believed that even evangelicals were not immune to the dangers of pornography.

Evangelical anti-pornography groups do not see themselves as 'imposing' their morality on everyone else, as much as they believe that a liberal tolerance of pornography will distort the realization of Christian values within their communities. Richard Enrico, founder of Citizens Against Pornography, stated in a 1989 sermon, 'our whole society is designed to stir up passions that cannot be fulfilled by God's standards. . . . We have allowed that to happen and the body of Christ has gotten caught up in that.'[89] In a rapidly changing world, evangelicals, who recognize that they are not exempt from the debilitating effects of pornography, want to limit pornography in order to protect their values and style of life. As with abortion, evangelical anti-pornography groups appeal to believers' obligation to live in conformity with the divine law. Evangelical groups form among believers who want to protect and defend their religious values in a world in which they are increasingly not represented.

RELIGION IN STATE-SUPPORTED SCHOOLS

Public schools have been the focus of tremendous evangelical pressure in the United States in the past three decades. Despite the official separation of church and state in America, public schools have not historically been secular in character. Whenever a religious group established a majority within a community, the public schools reflected the values of that religion. A change occurred in the 1960s as public schools were 'secularized' with the removal of overt religious teaching from the classroom. In *Engel v. Vitale* (1962) the court ruled that reciting a prayer in public schools violated the Establishment clause of the First Amendment. A year later, in *Abingdon Township School District v. Schempp* (1963), the court ruled that bible-reading was also a violation of the Establishment Clause. In 1968, in

Epperson v. Arkansas, the Court overruled an Arkansas law which prohibited the teaching of evolution in the public schools. Evangelicals also opposed what they believed to be the moral relativism of public school curricula.[90]

Public schools became unsafe to evangelicals in academic and moral terms with the removal of religious symbols and ideology in the 1960s, yet political and religious elites provided little opposition to the court's decisions. Randall Terry sarcastically wrote about school prayer, 'two and a half decades ago when the Supreme Court banished school prayer and Bible reading from public schools, did the church offer much resistance?'[91] They did not. The National Council of Churches and most mainline denominations supported the Supreme Court decisions, arguing that the constitutional separation of church and state required removing religion from the public schools.[92]

As with abortion and pornography, the lack of church opposition to changes in public education led to the organization of evangelical protest groups, the most prominent of which were Mel and Norma Gabler's Educational Research Analysts Program (1961), the Creation Research Society (1963), the Bible Science Association (1963) and Phyllis Schlafly's Eagle Forum (1972). The antagonism against public schools is not surprising. Schools are perhaps the most influential public institution with which Americans have contact. Schools do not simply educate children; they also, by necessity, pass on a set of social values. Evangelicals interpreted the removal of prayer and bible-reading and the addition of courses on values-clarification in the 1960s and 1970s as a threat to their religious ideology. Evangelicals claimed that the removal of religious symbols and teaching from the curricula made public schools a captive to an ideology of 'secular humanism'. This philosophy which, in the words of the Religious Roundtable, 'denies the Word of God as the reliable guide for the life of man on earth',[93] was 'imposed' on evangelicals through the tax-supported public schools. Evangelicals argued that it became more difficult for parents to pass religion on to their children since schools used a curriculum which was 'anti-religious'. Phyllis Schlafly, a conservative Catholic, wrote in words evangelicals accepted that 'the textbook says that what is right or wrong depends more on your judgement than on what someone tells you to do. That's a direct attack on religion.'[94] Instead, evangelicals wanted a public school curriculum which would more accurately reflect their religious and cultural values.

The biblical argument that evangelicals use to justify their position on abortion and pornography is also important in the case of public schools, although it is made more by implication than in the previous cases. A constant concern cited in evangelical literature is that the Bible declares that believers are obliged to pass on the faith to their children. Falwell writes, 'The Bible declares that parents are to instruct their children and bring them up in the discipline and instruction of the Lord.'[95] More important than a single biblical quotation, however, is the strength of the evangelical commitment to a religious ideology. Truth is not relative for these believers and they want the public institutions they engage to avoid moral and religious ambiguity. Falwell claims that 'our children need to acknowledge that there is a Supreme Being, that man did not get here by chance, and that we are here to glorify God'.[96] Evangelicals are not unique in wanting to inculcate their children with a religious or cultural world-view. Catholic secession from public schools occurred in the nineteenth century because the public schools taught an alien religious ideology. In contemporary America, however, evangelicals are one of the few religious groups whose shared doctrine has led them to engage in ideological struggle over the public schools.

Evangelicals believe that a 'secularized' public school system has the potential to undermine the religious values of their children. A significant motive for evangelical activism in the public-school debate is their conviction that schools have an anti-religious bias which threatens an evangelical religion. The Religious Roundtable claims that 'the prevailing religion of secular humanism which guides the thinking of many public policy makers promotes deviant lifestyles and undermines the moral teachings of parents'.[97] Randall Terry makes the argument most apparent when he writes: 'more and more, Christians and Christian principles are being mocked, scorned, and attacked in magazines, newspapers, television shows, classrooms . . . and sooner or later this barrage of anti-Christian bigotry will take its toll on us.'[98]

The number of 'Christian day schools' rose dramatically in the 1960s and 1970s as evangelical parents became dissatisfied with public schools. The best estimate is that there are, at present, between 9000 and 11 000 such schools with a student population of nearly 1 000 000. These schools are not shy about the religious instruction they intend to accomplish. They consciously avoid heterogeneity by having a shared religious doctrine as the criterion for admission and as the goal of the educational endeavour. The curricula of these schools are designed in such a way that the centrality of Christ and the Bible in the life of the believer is manifest in all the courses taught.[99]

These schools have been a constant point of friction between the government and evangelical educators on issues such as teacher qualifications, facilities and textbooks. The most dramatic threat from the government came in 1978 when the IRS and the Carter Administration considered a proposal to establish stiffer non-discrimination policies for private schools wishing to retain tax-exempt status. This tangible threat from the government proved to be a powerful mobilizing stimulus for evangelicals who worried about the preservation of Christian schools. Carter's initial support for the IRS proposal served to alienate the Democratic president from an evangelical constituency that had voted for him in 1976.[100]

The battle over public schools has not abated despite the rapid growth of Christian day-schools. Some states have passed so-called 'balance treatment' laws which allow for the teaching of the biblical account of creation in science classes. Most notably, the states of Arkansas and Louisiana passed laws which, in effect, mandated that Creationism be given near-equal time to Darwinism. Both laws were struck down by the courts.[101] Evangelicals have also pressured state Boards of Education. In many local areas, most notably Texas and California, evangelicals have pressured the state Boards to recommend that schools give some treatment to the biblical account of Creation. The guidelines set by Boards of Education have a tremendous impact on the writing of science textbooks in their state. In Texas and California the recommendations can have a national impact since they dominate the schoolbook market.[102]

Evangelicals in Britain have also tried to influence the character of state-supported schools. Their mobilization has, however, been less organized and coherent than among American evangelicals. Since Christianity has been a compulsory element of the curriculum in all British schools under the Education Act of 1944, there has been less reason for evangelical opposition to schools. Under the provisions of that Act, each school day was to begin with a collective act of worship and religious instruction. There has been no serious challenge to the 'legality' of the Act, as was the case in America with Supreme Court rulings which removed bible-reading and school prayer from the public schools. British schools have, however, chosen curricula in the past two decades which reflected the dominant values of British society and which many evangelicals considered dangerously secular.[103]

British activist Mary Whitehouse described the contemporary school curricula as 'a maelstrom of atheist humanist claptrap'.[104] As state-supported schools adapted their teaching to reflect modern values, evangelicals began to consider the idea that schools were no longer a safe preserve to send their children. The Conservative Family Campaign lamented that 'our schools have traditionally been based on the observance of the Christian ethic . . . (now) our teaching has departed from this Christian ideal'.[105] British evangelicals have been motivated by the same concern as their American counterparts: they want public institutions which do not threaten their religious values.

The place of religious education in British schools has mobilized evangelicals recently because of the Education Reform Bill of 1988. The debate surrounding the bill brought into focus just how far the state schools had fallen from the mandate on religious instruction in the 1944 Act. Some schools ignored the requirement that each day begin with an act of worship, while many others removed any specific Christian content to the daily worship service. John Burns and Colin Hart noted, 'there is no doubt that at present the 1944 requirements with regard to religious education are being flagrantly flouted'.[106] Evangelicals hoped that the new bill would continue to define religious education as predominantly Christian despite the increasing number of alternative faiths in Britain. In giving greater autonomy to local areas to determine the curricula of the schools, the 1988 Act increased the visible activism of evangelicals. CARE urged believers to become 'informed about the curriculum and challenge teaching which denies the existence of God'.[107] The new opportunities for local activism on education have made state schools a focus for evangelical activism in Britain.

THE RELIGIOUS EFFECT OF PROMOTING CHRISTIAN VALUES

For evangelicals, the 'erosion' of moral values symbolized a deeper problem with American and British society: people had ceased to be religious. In the minds of many believers, the moral chaos they saw around them proved that their cultures had become wholly secular. The Religious Roundtable claimed that 'during the past few decades America has forsaken God. As a nation we have turned away from Him, and have given our souls to secular humanism'.[108]

The question is, why did evangelicals come to believe that the solution to their problems lay in political action rather than a religious reformation? Historically, evangelicals had consistently claimed that sin could only be overcome by a religious conversion. Did evangelical organizations inadvertently contribute to the secularization of religion through their political action which implicitly supplanted a political for a spiritual goal? A related question is, why did evangelical pro-life and anti-pornography organizations use arguments about the social problems associated with particular practices rather than relying solely on the religious claim that abortion and pornography were to be opposed because they were sinful?

A comparison between the most current evangelical activism and the temperance movement a century earlier is informative. In the late nineteenth century, evangelicals opposed drinking on two accounts: evangelicals believed that drinking alcohol was a personal sin and they believed that alcohol posed a considerable danger to their norms of religiosity, sobriety and hard work. As the Prohibition Movement gained momentum in Britain and America, evangelical activists came to rely more and more upon arguments about the social dangers of alcohol. Believers never ignored the spiritual claim that drinkers needed to be saved from their sin, but their emphasis on the legislative solutions to the alcohol problem implied that evangelicals accepted that drinking was more a technical than a moral problem. The unique evangelical idea that the drinker needed radically to be converted from his sin receded into the background.

In the contemporary case, evangelicals have argued that abortion, pornography and the removal of religion from public schools are biblically-defined sins. Evangelical groups have retained this religious justification over time, but they have come to rely more heavily on arguments about the social dangers associated with legalized abortion, the proliferation of pornography and a secularized school system, such as sexual promiscuity, domestic violence and increasing divorce rates. Evangelicals have modified their arguments in part to reinforce their own convictions and to persuade non-believers of the dangers of particular social practices.

Some organizations try to retain this distinctive religious argument. James Dobson's Focus on the Family sent a pamphlet to group members which argued that the abortion issue must begin with a discussion of sin and forgiveness: 'In the simplest terms, God's forgiveness, from the biblical perspective, requires that an individual (1) agree with God that what was done was utterly wrong, (2) be genuinely sorrowful over the deed, and then (3) accept God's immediate, total and final provision for all sin through Christ's death on the cross.'[109] Many other groups confuse religious and social claims about abortion, pornography and public schools, and may in fact contribute to the secularization of their religion.

In part, such a discourse is required by the demands of a pluralistic political universe. In America and Britain, evangelicals cannot assume that the audience shares their moral values. In order to increase the scope of their support, evangelicals have come to rely on arguments about the social costs associated with 'sinful' behaviour. This shift of emphasis from a religious to a social claim has led evangelicals to conclude that abortion and pornography can be resolved legislatively, which implicitly undermines believers' religious conviction that sinners can only be saved from their sin by a radical conversion of the heart. From an evangelical religious perspective, the stress ought to be on reformation of the sinner rather than the reform of his or her social world. The use of social arguments by evangelicals, however, is indicative of the extent to which groups have been affected by the political demands of democratic, pluralistic political environments.[110] Equally important is the fact that an evangelical ideology does not clearly demarcate the proper relationship between political and religious activism. Group leaders were needed to make clear to believers how and why religious and cultural values ought to be brought to bear on political questions.

ALTERNATIVE THEORIES

Psychological, status, and resource mobilization theories of collective action have also been used to describe the recent activism of evangelical Christians. Theorists adopting a psychological model have argued that activism occurred because evangelicals were fearful of the social change of the 1960s. These theories do not, however, describe in great detail the frustration which led evangelicals to mobilize. David Edgar and Peter Jenkins describe British evangelical activism of the 1980s as 'a backlash against the social radicalism of the 1960s'.[111] Furio Colombo argues that the Moral Majority and related groups were 'fueled by the frenzy of moral righteousness'.[112] Ronald Inglehart claims that anxiety and strain were the causes for the rise of religious-group activism in the United States.[113] The terms used in a psychological theory to describe evangelical activism imply that the mobilization of protest groups was an irrational response on the part of affected believers.

Psychological models fail to appreciate that evangelical activism can be interpreted as a rational response to social change based on a common ideology and shared values rather than an irrational identity crisis. It was not 'moral frenzy', cognitive 'anxiety', or irrational 'backlash' against liberal morality which led evangelicals to mobilize protest groups, but a common interest in promoting a well-defined set of values which were being undermined by social and political change.

Traditional status interpretations of evangelical activism have focused on the threat believers experienced with the moral pluralism of the 1960s. Status theory claims that evangelical mobilization occurred because of a specific threat believers felt to their social status in light of the new liberal legislation. Andrew Merton argues that the pro-life movement in America was animated by concerns about 'the status of women themselves'.[114] The impetus for the pro-life movement, according to this account, was status discontent among evangelicals.

Sociological accounts have recently broadened the concept of status politics to include a focus on a group's cultural values, lifestyle and worldview.[115] These theorists have correctly noted that evangelicals mobilized to 'protect' themselves from political and religious institutions which 'imposed' a foreign set of values on them. Mores have changed and laws have increasingly reflected a value system which is antithetical to evangelical social views. Evangelicals formed groups to promote social values which were threatened by legalized abortion, the proliferation of pornography, and the removal of religion from public schools. Collective action against abortion and pornography and in favour of religion in public schools represented a concern for shared religious and cultural values.

This chapter has built upon these earlier works with a focus on how the Bible provided evangelicals with a source to shape their social response to changing moral norms. Evangelicals used the Bible to legitimate their opposition to abortion and pornography and to support their view that religion belonged in state-supported schools. The social and moral dislocation of British and American society was an important factor for evangelical activism, but only because specific changes deeply affected evangelical values.

Resource mobilization theory offers another explanation for evangelical activism. The emergence of a social movement for resource theorists is linked to the 'availability of religious infrastructures'.[116] This religious infrastructure reduced the cost of access to potential group members and enabled a new organization to raise the resources necessary for group mobilization. Robert Liebman has described the mobilization of Moral Majority in these terms. Its success was its ability 'to forge strong links with a national network of fundamentalist clergy'.[117] In fact, evangelical political organizations did benefit from the fact that evangelicals were already mobilized at local levels through religious organizations. The fundamentalist institutions of churches, schools, journals, and radio and television media allowed for Jerry Falwell, Pat Robertson, and others to contact potential group members. Religious institutions did use their moral authority and their organizational strength to influence opinion and raise resources. Resource theories are correct to highlight the important role which existing religious networks of interaction played in allowing the formation of new political organizations.

Institutional networks did not, however, create an evangelical social movement. While they may have created the potential for group mobilization, institutions did not create the ferment neccssary for evangelical activism. To understand why evangelicals in Britain and America turned to the well-established structures of interaction, we must first appreciate why they felt it necessary to engage in social activism. In order to do that, it is necessary to return to the ideological justification evangelicals gave for group formation. Evangelicals mobilized in Britain and America because they shared an ideology which opposed abortion on demand, pornography and the removal of religious symbols from public schools. They believed it was their religious responsibility to oppose those practices in the strongest terms.

CONCLUSION

Abortion, pornography, and religion in state-supported schools were particularly salient issues to evangelicals because they represented an important struggle for the definition of proper parental roles and human sexuality, and the place of religion in public institutions. British and American evangelicals perceived a disruption in their moral order and a threat to their religious values when their society condoned the proliferation of pornographic literature, abortion, and the removal of religious symbols from the classroom. The Bible provided the means through which evangelicals interpreted a liberal morality as sinful as well as giving to believers a mandate to form political protest groups against the new social practices. Evangelicals formed protest groups in the hope that they could sustain their values, ideology and style of life in a rapidly changing environment. Without the shared norms of their religious ideology, evangelicals would not have had a basis upon which to judge the changing morality as religiously sinful and socially dangerous.

British and American believers shared an ideology which justified their political involvement, but they did not share identical opportunities for activism. Different sets of political institutions created different conditions for evangelical mobilization. In the next chapter, I show how differing political structures influenced the political success of British and American evangelicals. While it was important that these transatlantic believers shared a religious ideology which led them to form protest groups, this shared ideology did not determine the political expression of those values nor the political success of evangelical groups.

6 Political Structures and Evangelical Activism

Chapter 5 demonstrated that group ideology was the catalyst which structured believers' moral and political views around the issues of abortion, pornography, and religion in state-supported schools and legitimated the formation of social movement organizations to represent those values. The arguments used by American and British evangelicals against abortion and pornography and in support of religion in public schools were nearly identical regardless of the setting. In each nation, the issues became crystallized as a moral and religious debate about human life, the proper expression of sexuality and the place of God in human affairs. Political pressure groups became the vehicle for evangelicals who wanted to change public laws to conform with group values.

This chapter applies the second aspect of my theory of social movements, the influence of state structures on the political behaviour of movement organizations, to the British and American pro-life movements. In each nation, the politics around abortion were symptomatic of evangelical activism on related moral issues. The evidence presented supports the conclusion that the characteristics of the British and American political regimes affected how evangelicals mobilized around abortion and helps explain the political success and failure of pro-life groups. The comparison demonstrates how political institutions influenced the ability of social movement organizations to influence public policy. Group ideology provided the necessary motivation for the formation of pro-life political pressure groups, but state structures shaped the objective possibility that groups would achieve their political goals.

American pro-life groups have successfully placed procedural obstacles on abortions since abortion was decriminalized in 1973. Federal funding for abortions has been eliminated and restrictions on access to abortions at the state level have been imposed. The law passed in Pennsylvania in 1989, for example, requires spousal notification, a 24-hour waiting period, and counselling about foetal development. The law passed in Louisiana prohibits virtually all abortions except to save the life of the mother or in certain cases of rape or incest. British pro-life organizations have been less able to shape the policy process dealing with abortion. The only restriction on universal access to abortions which has been imposed since abortion was decriminalized in 1967 is the 1991 Human Fertilization and Embryology Act which reduced the latest time that a woman could have an abortion from the 28th to the 24th week of pregnancy. All other efforts of pro-life groups to restrict the grounds or funding for abortion have failed.

The divergent patterns of government regulation dealing with abortion in Great Britain and the United States are best explained by looking at the differences in the formal institutions of government and political party structures. Simply put, America's federal political system and weak political parties provided more opportunities for effective participation by evangelical pro-life interest groups than Britain's unitary polity and strong political parties. American evangelical organizations took advantage of a political system which had multiple points of access for interest groups. American groups pressured Congress to pass restrictive abortion laws, attempted to influence the regulatory process at the White House, and challenged particular legislation in the courts. Since abortion also affected state and local government units, the opportunities for evangelical mobilization were multiplied further. In Britain the number of places at which pro-life groups could intervene to influence public law were more limited. Evangelical groups discovered that it was difficult to penetrate the Executive Branch and the Whitehall bureaucracy which dominated public policymaking and which was insulated from pressure from all but a few well-established organizations. The experience of British and American pro-life groups demonstrates the importance of state structures for social movements as they seek to bring about political change.

THE MARKET FOR CONSERVATIVE MORALITY IN BRITAIN AND AMERICA

The fact that evangelicals successfully pursued a political agenda in America but not in Britain should not obscure the similarities between the two countries. Evangelicals in each nation mobilized dynamic grass-roots organizations against legalized abortion, liberal pornography laws and the removal of religion from public schools. A study of British pressure groups conducted in 1976 by Chris Bazlington and Anne Cowens showed that the Society for the Protection of Unborn Children (SPUC), LIFE, and the National Viewers and Listeners Association were in the top 10 per cent in membership among British promotional groups. Only business groups and trade unions consistently had higher membership totals.[1] The American Life Lobby and the Christian Action Council, each with over 300 000 members, were among the largest promotional groups in America.

The market for conservative morality was also nearly identical in the late 1970s and 1980s; equivalent majorities in each nation opposed abortion on demand. In 1980, 75 per cent of the total British population supported the Corrie bill, a private members' bill to reduce the upper time-limit for abortion from 28 to 20 weeks. In a 1987 poll, 62 per cent of the women and 71 per cent of the men favoured David Alton's bill which proposed an 18 week limit. Data from NORCs General Social Survey indicated that Americans also supported a restriction of abortion rights. When asked whether or not it should be possible for a pregnant woman to obtain a legal abortion if the woman wanted it for any reason, a majority of Americans polled, 62 per cent in 1977, 59 per cent in 1982, and 63 per cent in 1985, believed that women should not have such a right. A majority in each nation supported abortions for 'hard' reasons – maternal health, rape and foetal deformity, but sizeable majorities favoured reforming abortion laws to make abortions more difficult to obtain.[2]

There was almost no difference between the two nations in the level of commitment which believers exhibited to working for the pro-life cause. In each nation, pressure groups staged elaborate public demonstrations. In 1970 and in 1987 evangelical Christians challenged the values of the 'permissive British society' with large public protests against abortion, pornography, and liberal sexual ethics. Called 'Festivals of Light' by the recently-converted broadcaster, Malcolm Muggeridge, evangelicals held rallies throughout the country to illuminate the dangers of permissive legislation and morality.[3] Annual demonstrations led by the American pro-life group March for Life in Washington, DC, on the anniversary of the *Roe* decision and the civil disobedience of Operation Rescue similarly brought tens of thousands of American evangelical activists together in protests against liberal abortion laws.

An important difference between the United States and Great Britain which might be expected to explain the different political fortunes of pro-life groups was the number of evangelical Protestants and Roman Catholics, religious groups most likely to oppose abortion, in Britain and America. Only 10 to 15 per cent of Britain's population were even church members by 1980. At most, half of that membership was in Roman Catholic and evangelical Protestant churches. In America, evangelicals represented between 10 and 15 per cent of the total population, and Roman Catholics another 25 per cent. American pro-life group leaders had a much larger constituency to mobilize when they formed political pressure groups than their British counterparts. Certainly it is logical to expect that the different political fortunes of pro-life groups in the two nations had something to do with this radically different membership base. What incentive would British politicians and policymakers have for responding to the pressure of a religious constituency which represented less than 10 per cent of Britain's total population?

American political elites did respond to pro-life groups in order to attract evangelical votes, which undoubtedly speeded up the process of abortion reform at state and national levels. In Britain political leaders did not have the same electoral incentive, which certainly did not help pro-life organizations. The different size of the evangelical constituency was politically significant, but it was not the only nor even the primary cause for the political success and failure of American and British pro-life organizations. British promotional interest groups had succeeded in the past without a mass membership. At its height, the Abortion Law Reform Association (the largest pro-choice group in Britain), had less than three thousand members, yet the group successfully pressured for a reform of the abortion law. In Britain, there is no necessary connection between the size of a political pressure group and its ability to win policy concessions from the state.

Even if British evangelicals had been as numerous as their American counterparts, the political success of the British pro-life movement would not have been any different. British organizations were frustrated in their efforts less by their lack of size than by the absence of support from key political elites and the paucity of opportunities for meaningful activism which their political system afforded them. The British state dominated the policymaking process on abortion, which meant that pro-life groups could not succeed against state resistance and without state support. With its concentration of power in the hands of the Prime Minister and the Cabinet, Britain's parliamentary regime placed few obstacles to abortion reform if the Conservative Party leadership had political or ideological reasons to support them. Mrs Thatcher's Conservative Party did not actively oppose pro-life efforts, but the party did nothing to help those groups.

American groups, by contrast, succeeded not simply because of their electoral size but because America's weak state allowed them direct access to the policymaking process at local, state and national levels. It became apparent in the aftermath of the *Roe* decision that the national state did not have the capacity to impose policy coherence on abortion, a sign of state weakness which provided pro-life groups the opportunity to organize their efforts against a number of state officials and institutions.

The fact that there have been such divergent political fates for pro-life groups in America and Britain calls into question traditional sociological and political theories which explain the development and success of social movement organizations in terms of their capacity to mobilize political resources, gain popular support, recruit committed activists, and develop skilled organizations. A closer review of the politics of the pro-life movement in each nation will sustain my argument that state structural differences explain the political success and failure of political pressure groups.

THE BRITISH PRO-LIFE MOVEMENT

Abortion was decriminalized in Britain in 1967 through a private member's bill sponsored by David Steel, who was at that time a member of the Labour Party. Steel's reform law liberalized the grounds for abortion, enabling women, with the approval of two registered doctors, to have an abortion up to 28 weeks in term. Although Steel's bill did not strictly give women the right to choose an abortion, the practice has been relatively liberal. The Steel bill passed despite the determined opposition of several prominent MPs who unsuccessfully used parliamentary delaying tactics to kill it. Harold Wilson's Labour Government did not officially support the bill, but the government did provide additional time to allow the necessary stages of legislation to be completed. The parliamentary time allocated for private members' bills was so limited and the delaying tactics of opponents so prolific, that ordinarily only non-controversial reforms could be carried through by private members. The Government rarely gave any of its parliamentary time for the consideration of private members' legislation. Wilson's Government, which also provided extra time for bills dealing with the decriminalization of homosexuality, the abolition of the death penalty and the liberalization of the divorce law, was unique in that it encouraged the reform laws proposed by private members.[4]

The mobilization of the pro-choice organization Abortion Law Reform Association (ALRA) helped speed up the process of abortion reform. The ALRA was not, however, a mass membership organization. In 1966, the group only had 1000 members. What the ALRA did have was a skilled leadership which influenced elite and public opinion, developed contacts with MPs and Government ministers, and eventually persuaded Steel to introduce abortion reform legislation when he drew a favourable position in the private members' ballot. Wilson's Government did not want to propose a liberalized abortion law, but it was apparent that the Prime Minister and most Cabinet members supported a reform in existing law. The ALRA did not, however, propose that Steel introduce a bill to repeal the existing abortion law. The ALRA leadership reasoned, quite correctly, that a repeal bill would not help them gain public or elite support, because the majority of the British population in the late 1960s opposed the absolute right of women to choose an abortion. The ALRA opted rather for a reform bill to liberalize the grounds for abortions, a compromise which public opinion polls demonstrated was popular.[5]

The Steel bill was not viewed by most people as a radical departure from existing policies. The grounds for abortion were extended, but the bill continued to recognize the need for medical approval for abortions. In this regard, the debate surrounding the bill was very different from that in America where the decision in *Roe v. Wade* was recognized by all concerned as a marked departure from existing law. *Roe* abolished the idea that there could be grounds for the state to limit abortions in the first trimester. As I will show later in this chapter, American pro-life groups mobilized more quickly than British organizations in part because abortion reform came so quickly and decisively in America.[6]

The success of the ALRA showed what a political pressure group could accomplish in the absence of a mass mobilization. The ALRA was an elite organization which relied for its success upon the skill of its leaders and the contacts they developed in the House of Commons and Whitehall.[7] The Steel bill did not succeed in the Commons because the public demanded abortion reform. Instead, the bill passed because the ALRA persuaded Wilson and the Labour Party leadership to give extra time during the debate on the bill. As a political pressure group, the ALRA did not have the capacity to impose its policy preference upon a recalcitrant state. The British state dominated the policymaking process on abortion; if state elites had wanted to oppose abortion reform they could easily have succeeded in doing so. At a minimum, the ALRA needed the state not to oppose its political efforts. As the debate on the Steel bill ensued, however, it became apparent that the ALRA was going to need more than state neutrality to pass an abortion reform law. Without the extra time provided by Wilson's Government the bill would not have passed because private members' bills could not succeed in the face of determined opposition.

Pro-life organizations did not organize a mass opposition to the Steel bill while it was being debated. As noted above, the majority of the British population supported a liberalization in the grounds for abortion. Most people accepted the idea that a reform of the existing abortion law was necessary to eliminate discrepancies and inefficiencies in abortion services. Liberal religious elites did not provide any opposition to the liberalization of abortion law. In fact, no major Protestant denomination was totally opposed to reform. In 1965, two years before Steel introduced his bill, the Church of England Board of Social Responsibility issued a pamphlet entitled 'Abortion: An Ethical Discussion'. The pamphlet recognized that there were certain circumstances under which abortions could be justified. Other major Protestant churches – the Methodists, United Reform/Presbyterian, the Baptists – and the ecumenical British Council of Churches supported Steel's reform bill.

Two large pro-life groups formed in the wake of the passage of the Steel bill, the Society for the Protection of Unborn Children (SPUC) in 1967 and LIFE in 1970. The membership of these groups was initially small, but escalated as group leaders publicized the growing number of legal abortions performed under the Steel bill, from 49 000 in 1969, to 110 00 in 1973, 119 000 in 1979, and 186 000 in 1990.[8] LIFE and SPUC have effectively argued that abortion on request has become the *de facto* policy of the National Health Service, a claim which is not necessarily true but which serves to mobilize the population which continues to oppose a woman's absolute right to choose an abortion. Each group has a membership of 30 000, primarily made up of Catholics and evangelical Protestants.

The primary political goal of SPUC and LIFE has been to overturn the abortion reform law. Following the example of the ALRA, pro-life groups have publicized their cause, lobbied MPs, exploited inefficiencies in the existing law, and highlighted the growing number of abortions performed, in the hope that they would create a groundswell of support for reform. Pro-life groups have had some success in initiating legislative debates on abortion through private members' bills, the only meaningful avenue of legislative activism for interest groups. SPUC and LIFE were instrumental in the introduction of bills by Norman St John-Stevas in 1969, James White in 1975, John Corrie in 1980 and David Alton in 1988 to restrict abortion services. During the debate on each of the bills, the pro-life lobby coordinated letter-writing campaigns to MPs and organized a mass lobby of Parliament. During the debate on the Corrie bill, 15 000 to 18 000 converged on Parliament in what David Marsh and Joanna Chambers described as 'one of the largest mass lobbies in the history of the House of Commons'.[9] In each case, the bill failed because of the skilful work of the pro-choice lobby and because the Government refused to give extra time for the bill's consideration. The Alton bill was typical of efforts by pro-life groups to restrict abortion rights.

The first reading of the Alton bill before the House of Commons took place in November 1987. It was written to establish a limit of 18 weeks of pregnancy beyond which abortions would not be allowed except in an emergency to save the life of the mother, in cases of rape or incest resulting in the pregnancy of a girl under 18, and in cases where the child would be born severely handicapped. Pro-choice and pro-life groups mobilized support for the the Second Reading of the bill which was scheduled for 22 January 1988. Pro-choice organizations focused their strategy on securing the support of MPs, the medical establishment, the media and the

Labour Party leadership. The Labour Party had adopted defence of the 1967 Abortion Act as party policy at its 1977 Party Conference. The Labour Party's position has been an important bonus to the pro-choice lobby which has been able to use party resources and political pressure to lobby Labour MPs. Pro-choice groups also secured the support of the three major British professional medical organizations, the British Medical Association, the Royal College of Obstetrics and Gynaecologists, and the Royal College of Nurses, which further helped legitimate their cause.[10]

The political strategy of SPUC and LIFE has been to mobilize opposition to abortion within constituencies and to pressure MPs to vote for the amending legislation. In part this 'outsider' strategy was forced upon SPUC and LIFE because they could not secure the support of 'established' medical or political institutions. The Conservative Party, for example, has been resolute in its position that it will not make abortion a party or government matter. In the absence of party support, SPUC and LIFE organized public demonstrations of Parliament and a massive mailing campaign throughout the nation. SPUC distributed 5000 copies of a particularly graphic pro-life pamphlet per constituency toward the end of the Alton debate. SPUC and LIFE also used the resources of Roman Catholic and evangelical Protestant churches to publicize their pro-life message.

The Alton bill passed the Second Reading in the Commons by a vote of 296 to 251, a vote which was remarkable not only because it showed that a majority in Parliament supported a restriction of abortion rights, but also because the number of MPs voting was so high. This large number was a testimony to the lobbying efforts of pro-choice and pro-life groups, who convinced MPs to vote on an issue which was not officially a party matter. The bill was then referred to the Committee stage where several prominent pro-life MPs worked to complete that stage with the least possible amendments added to the bill. The bill returned to the full House on 6 May for its final approval before being sent to the House of Lords. The Alton bill did not complete this final stage in the House of Commons. Opponents introduced amendments which failed to change the features of Alton's legislation but which succeeded in delaying and eventually blocking the bill's progress. The Alton bill ran out of time at the Report stage in the Commons and the Conservative Government decided not to provide pro-life MPs with extra time to work the bill through the House.

Pro-life groups have grown increasingly frustrated with the political system as they have been unable to pass amending legislation to abortion. SPUC credited the defeat of the Alton bill to pro-choice tactics: 'Once again we see an important pro-life bill which has majority support in the House being blocked by opponents manipulating Parliamentary procedures.'[11] LIFE referred to the outcome as an indictment on the anti-democratic nature of private members' legislation: 'We have only been defeated by delaying tactics. The greatest testimony to our parliamentary majority is the fact that we have never been allowed to come to a vote.'[12] There is some evidence to support the argument of pro-life activists. As has been noted, public opinion polls and parliamentary sentiment seem to be in favour of a restriction on abortion services. Had the Thatcher Government provided extra time for the Alton bill, it would likely have passed. What is more difficult to determine is the sincerity of the parliamentary support for abortion reform. Members of Parliament were in the unique position of being able to vote for the Alton bill, knowing that it would never pass without the help of the Conservative Government. MPs essentially were free to placate their vociferous pro-life constituents without fearing that the Alton bill would ever become law.

The Conservative Party has consistently refused to give extra time for private members' bills. David Mellor, then Minister of State for the Department of Health, put the views of the party succinctly during the Alton debate: 'We (the Conservative Party) continue to regard abortion as a matter for private members' business, and to believe that it would not be appropriate for the Government in any way to seek to take over responsibility. We also stand by the decision that no private members' legislation would be given government time.'[13] Sir Bernard Braine, Conservative MP from Castle Point, correctly pointed out that such a view ensured that there would be no amendment to the Steel bill. Braine argued: 'it (a principled opposition to giving extra time) means that the substantive act of 1967, which got onto the statue books only with government help, is written in letters of stone. It will never be amended because time will never be found to do so.'[14] SPUC complained after the Alton bill was defeated that, 'the government was quite prepared to see the bill founder due to lack of time even though the Abortion Act had only been passed in 1967 because of the extra time that was then given'.[15] Until pro-life groups persuade the Conservative Government to change its policy on granting extra time for private members' bills, there will be no change in abortion law in Britain.

Initially, pro-life groups believed that Prime Minister Thatcher was open to their cause. In a 1988 speech she seemed to sympathize with a pro-life position: 'Christians accept the sanctity of life, the responsibility that comes with freedom and the supreme sacrifice of Christ.'[16] Her rhetorical support for the pro-life lobby, however, did not match her political behaviour. While she wanted to resurrect the link between religious values and economic policy in justifying her turn to privatization, Mrs Thatcher never supported a reform of the abortion law and did nothing to facilitate the pro-life movement. When asked about her position on a bill to restrict abortion rights during a question time, Mrs Thatcher admitted that she would not herself vote for the bill: 'Speaking for myself, as the bill is drafted at present, I could not support it.'[17] In the absence of support from the Conservative Party or the British state, pro-life groups had to search for alternative ways to affect abortion policy.

The Conservative Government of John Major did propose national legislation in 1991 to reduce the grounds under which abortion would be allowed. The Human Fertilization and Embryology Act reduced the latest time that a woman could have an abortion from the 28th to the 24th week of pregnancy and was supported by pro-life groups. In truth, however, the law will only pertain to a handful of cases each year and is not nearly as restrictive as pro-life groups would like.

THE BRITISH POLITY AND PRO-LIFE ACTIVISM

The very fact that pro-life groups mobilized significant membership support and successfully introduced private members' bills dealing with abortion, shows how recent changes in British politics, especially the decline of partisan alignments based upon class, have created new opportunities for interest group activism. British promotional pressure groups have been more politically active than at any other time in the postwar era. The defeat of the Alton bill, however, also underscored the degree to which interest groups continue to be dependent upon government support for their political success and the extent to which the British polity limits the opportunities for pressure group activism.

Because of Britain's unitary polity, local political authorities lack real independence and have little role in the policymaking process. Pro-life organizations have had no incentive to lobby locally-elected officials, who have no significant power on any aspect of abortion. The existence of local authorities with some autonomy from the central government has been regarded as a necessary check against abusive state power and has been protected. The local bodies which do exist, metropolitan, district, county, and parish councils, however, are constitutionally subject to the will and dictates of a sovereign Parliament which can, and has, created and abolished local governments through legislation. Local government units do not have any power on the abortion issue; they cannot vote to restrict access or funding for abortions within their region.[18] In over thirty interviews I conducted with interest group leaders in Britain, not one leader mentioned electoral pressure they exerted at local levels.[19]

Models of pressure group politics in Britain have traditionally stressed the point that, because of the strength of the British state, effective interest group activism is primarily directed to national political institutions, especially the executive branch, which dominates the policymaking process.[20] The Prime Minister and the Cabinet make public policy; power is not shared equally among branches of government. While there is a nominal separation of powers among the executive, legislative and judicial branches, the executive, in fact, dominates. A government with a healthy majority in the House of Commons can do just about anything it wants because MPs are expected to vote as instructed by their party whip on any government bill. According to this theory, business groups and labour unions in the 1960s and 1970s, which controlled resources, personnel and information which the government relied upon, established close contacts with governments of both political parties and shared the responsibility for making and implementing public policy. This consensus politics was marked by a high degree of compromise and bargaining between the political parties and the major interest groups. For the most part, promotional or cause groups were locked out of this compromise and consensus and did not receive the attention of scholars. These groups did not have access to the same level of resources as business groups and labour unions and were therefore unable to establish close contacts within Whitehall.

The proliferation of protest groups in the past several decades and the rapid decline of the influence of business groups and labour unions has called into question this corporatist model of interest group behaviour.[21] Pressure group activity no longer conforms to the single pattern described in traditional models. Extra-parliamentary groups have emerged and challenged the close ties that existed between British industry, labour unions, and government with respect to the making of public policy. Environmental groups, the peace movement, animal welfare organizations, and abortion protest groups have learned how to use mass demonstrations, the media, educational campaigns and professional lobbyists to produce a shift in public opinion and to pressure Members of Parliament. It is difficult to disagree with Michael Moran's conclusion that it is 'increasingly easy to enter the political arena using a pressure group as a vehicle'.[22]

The mobilizing effort of the British Peace Movement during the 1970s and 1980s is often cited as evidence for a new-found vitality of promotional pressure groups.[23] The Campaign for Nuclear Disarmament (CND) is the leading organization in the peace movement, which had over a quarter of a million members by 1982. Membership in the CND grew rapidly in the late 1970s and early 1980s as East–West tensions increased sharply after the Russian invasion of Afghanistan in 1979 and NATO decided to modernize its nuclear weaponry in Europe. The CND opposed the British government's decision to accept 160 new cruise missiles to be based at Greenham Common in Berkshire and at Molesworth in Cambridgeshire. Instead, the CND supported the idea of a neutral Britain which would unilaterally disarm itself of all nuclear weaponry. In 1983, the Labour Party endorsed the ideas of the CND and included in its party platform a plank supporting unilateral British disarmament. The CND was able to accomplish what few cause groups had done for several decades in Britain: win the active support of a major political party. The CND's success would seem to offer other promotional groups, such as LIFE and SPUC, a model for infiltrating the policy process.

The question remains, however, as to the political effectiveness of the CND and the potential for other groups to follow its model. By American standards, the development and political power of British pressure groups remain modest. The political success of the CND, for example, was determined by its relationship with the Labour Party; even a social movement as large as the British Peace Movement relied upon support from key state elites for political power. Without this support, there were few formal ways in which the CND could intervene to influence public policy. Because local authorities lacked autonomy and because MPs had no real independence from their party it made sense for the CND to pressure the Labour Party; the group had few other political options at its disposal.

The same is true of related pressure groups. While there has been an explosion in the number of promotional groups in the past few decades which has called into question a corporatist model of interest group activism, there have been no institutional changes to alter the ability of these groups directly to influence public policy. Groups continue to be constrained by Britain's unitary polity and tradition of strong political parties. Britain's political structures restrict the places at which organized groups can intervene in the policy process. Because it has been difficult for promotional groups to translate their newly-discovered popular support to political institutions, there is still much to recommend traditional models of British politics which emphasize the centralization of political authority and lack of opportunities for pressure group involvement. What a corporatist model failed to predict were the capacity of interest groups to mobilize support and their willingness to use non-traditional forms of political protest to win public support. Britain's polity is no more receptive and open now to pressure group involvement than it was two decades ago, however, so groups have had to adopt the tactics of mass pressure, civil disobedience and even violence to gain political attention.

In America, pro-life groups have had success in limiting abortion services by pressing for change through the judicial system. British organizations have been unable to follow this model because the judiciary is not a national institution of policymaking in Britain. Judges have neither the political power nor the autonomy to overturn legislative decisions or establish a distinct public policy on abortion. SPUC and LIFE have focused their attention on lobbying Parliament and organizing massive public demonstrations against legalized abortion. Pro-life groups have been able to initiate legislative debates on abortion through private members' bills but, as the Alton debate demonstrated, the government controls the success of such bills.

In theory, moving the debate to Parliament could have helped the pro-life lobby, but only if it had received the active support of the government in power. The irony for interest groups is that while they can accomplish almost nothing by themselves, the backing of a government with a healthy majority in the House of Commons virtually assures them of success. The pro-choice group ALRA won its legislative victory because it secured the support of the party leadership; it was never a mass membership organization which relied upon the force of public opinion to bring about reform. Official aid from the Labour Party and Cabinet ministers insured ALRA of resources, publicity and access to the institutions which could affect political change. More recently, British environmental interest groups received an unexpected benefit when Mrs Thatcher became acutely concerned about environmental pollution late in her tenure as Prime Minister. She hosted an international conference on the ozone layer in London in 1989 and used the occasion to call for stricter standards for reducing the use of damaging chemicals. With Mrs Thatcher's leadership, Britain adopted the target of a complete ban on these chemicals by the end of the century, a victory environmental groups could never have won without her pledge of support.[24]

Without the tacit support of the government, however, an issue as controversial as restricting abortion services will fail because opponents can defeat it by delaying it. Marsh and Read conclude that the limitations of the private members' bills procedure 'is merely a reflection of executive dominance in the British system'.[25] The lack of responsiveness of Britain's polity to political pressure has left pro-life groups searching for alternative ways to publicize the abortion issue.

THE BRITISH PARTY SYSTEM AND PRO-LIFE ACTIVISM

The traditional picture of British promotional interest groups as powerless adjuncts to the political system was due in large part to the characteristics of the party system. The Labour and Conservative parties dominated politics in Britain between the 1920s and the 1960s. Political loyalties were based upon class, and the dominant instrument of representation was the political party, not the pressure group. The attributes of this two-party system included the following: the parties were programmatic – they put forward a detailed manifesto to the public at each election; MPS from both parties voted as disciplined blocs in the House of Commons; the parties were national in scope; and in both parties, the parliamentary party had considerable autonomy from extra-parliamentary mass organizations. The interest groups which received attention in this model were labour unions and business groups, which reinforced the partisan division of the major parties. Cause groups were treated as marginal to the political process.[26]

The decline of class politics in the 1970s and 1980s has called into question the utility of this model.[27] The Labour and Conservative parties have experienced a decline in their popular base as voter turnout has fallen, and as they have lost support to competing political parties. Moreover, there has been a partisan dealignment in the past several decades as fewer people vote on the basis of membership of a social class. The weakening of partisan alignments has created the conditions necessary for a renewal of interest group mobilization. Michael Moran correctly argues that 'once established class and party identification weakens, citizens are free to enter politics in an almost infinite variety of roles'.[28] In fact, there has been an extraordinary expansion in the number and the influence of pressure groups which have formed to fill the void created by gradually weakening political parties. A class model of interest group activism which implied that promotional groups were nothing more than marginal adjuncts to the political process cannot explain this development.

Political parties have gradually begun to open themselves up to pressure from extra-parliamentary organizations. The Labour Party has been particularly willing to respond to organized groups and has recently taken official stands on peace and environmental issues. Both the Trades Union Congress (TUC) and the Labour Party are on record defending the 1967 Abortion Act and calling for abortion on request.[29] Pro-life groups have tried to take advantage of the relative openness of TUC and Labour Party structures to exert their own pressure. LIFE urges its members to 'change TUC policy. . . . Trade unions are democratic organizations. It is up to you to take positive action to win your colleagues over to your pro-life view.'[30] The Conservative Party, on the other hand, has been less willing to involve pressure groups in the formation of party policy. Despite the efforts of pro-life activists, the Conservative Party has never taken a position on abortion.

Mrs Thatcher simply ignored the pressure of evangelical interest groups while she was in power. While her rhetoric seemed ideal for an evangelical constituency, her actions alienated her from evangelicals who hoped for explicit government support on abortion, pornography and related social issues.[31] Mrs Thatcher clearly demonstrated her political opposition to evangelical causes when she supported the elimination of Sunday trading restrictions in 1985.[32] The Sunday closing laws in Britain were haphazard by 1983. The Shop Acts of 1950 stated that 'every shop shall, save as otherwise provided by the part of this act, be closed for the serving of customers on Sunday', but the law was unevenly enforced, opposed by business groups, and full of strange anomalies. In 1983, the Government commissioned an inquiry to investigate what to do about Sunday trading. The committee concluded that the removal of all restrictions was the best way to proceed and in the 1985/86 parliamentary session the Conservative Government introduced legislation to deregulate Sunday trading. Mrs Thatcher and the Conservative Party leadership pressured party MPs to vote for the legislation, and with a 144-seat majority in the House of Commons, it seemed impossible that the Government would be defeated. The bill's eventual defeat was, as Marsh and Read conclude, 'an almost unprecedented set-back for the Government'.[33]

Evangelicals saw deregulation as an attack on the family and the Christian day of rest and they formed the 'Keep Sunday Special Campaign' to fight the bill. Evangelicals interpreted Mrs Thatcher's position as a capitulation of religious ideals to free-market principles. The Shops Bill had been conceived as a part of Mrs Thatcher's privatizing programme. John Roberts, executive director of the Lord's Day Observance Society, the oldest and most active Sabbatarian group in Britain, said in an interview, 'twenty-five years ago the Conservative Party supported our position, but now we look to the Labour Party. The commercial world is the biggest contributor to Thatcher. Business is our greatest enemy, as is an unchecked free-market ideology.'[34]

There was little or no electoral incentive for Mrs Thatcher to respond to evangelical voters, who were neither numerous nor willing, it appeared, to abandon the Conservative Party on moral issues such as abortion and Sunday Trading alone. The Labour Party was even less sympathetic to evangelical moral concerns, which allowed Mrs Thatcher to retain the support of religious voters with minimal effort. Some evangelical group leaders believed that a third party, particularly the Liberal/Social Democratic Alliance Party, would be the best place for evangelical voters, but rank-and-file evangelicals remained conservative.[35] American evangelicals were better placed, electorally, to gain political attention from Republican Party leaders. President Reagan appealed to evangelicals on moral issues in order to win them away from the Democratic Party, which they had historically supported.

The decline of class in British politics has pointed in the direction of a more fragmented system of representation. Pressure groups such as LIFE, SPUC, and CARE have arisen to challenge the supremacy of political parties in the policy process, and the centralization of Parliamentary authority. By American standards, however, British parties remain strong and the British polity is not as open to interest group penetration in the formation of policy. British institutions have not responded to the mobilization of new protest groups by making policy decisions highly responsive to organized interests. The institutional obstacles to interest group intervention in the policy process remain formidable.

British parties control virtually all of the resources a candidate desires and most of the sanctions she fears. Parties select candidates for a general election and finance and organize the campaign. Voters do not choose party candidates for the general election in political primaries; instead, candidates are selected by a small group of party members in each parliamentary constituency. David Denver claims that in the Conservative Party the final choice for a candidate in a local constituency is made by as few as 60 people.[36] There are no residency requirements for parliamentary candidates (which is not the case in the United States), so parties have a wide range of choice in selecting candidates. Political parties try to select candidates who reflect the interests of the local electorate, and in some cases this requires that the candidate establish some autonomy from the party if a specific policy conflicts with the wishes of local voters. British interest groups are effectively deprived of two of such groups' most important functions in the United States: financing campaigns and exerting pressure in primary elections.

Candidates who win a general election remain dependent upon the party while in office. Party cohesion is assured through an incentive system which punishes members who vote against the wishes of party leaders. The party, specifically the Prime Minister, controls nearly all of the rewards an MP seeks while in office, including the selection of coveted cabinet, ministry, and party-leadership positions, which in turn encourages the acquiescence of parliamentary members to their party. MPs have recently shown greater willingness to vote against the wishes of the party leadership. Backbench MPs have exhibited a greater voting independence in the past two decades, revolting against party policy on such issues as the setting of rates, student financing, the poll tax, and Sunday trading. In theory, such independence provides an opening for interest group activism. Should MPs no longer feel compelled to vote as dictated by the party leadership, pressure groups would have greater recourse directly to pressure individual MPs. In practice, however, MP revolts have been few and have not, in the words of Peter Riddell, 'represented a fundamental challenge to the government'.[37]

Pro-life groups have also tried to bypass the parties and exert their own pressure on individual MPs. A non-party issue such as abortion does provide latitude for Conservative MPs to establish their own position, which in turn makes the pressure of promotional groups potentially important. But SPUC and LIFE discovered that the tactic of pressure politics was of limited utility because they do not have an electoral sanction with which to threaten a recalcitrant MP. Some MPs publicly complained during the Alton debate that the lobbying of pro-life groups was itself contemptible. According to Andrew MacKay, Conservative MP from Berskshire, East, pro-life groups, 'had the impertinence and cheek to persuade their zealot supporters – the ayatollahs who parade under the banner of the Society for the Protection of Unborn Children – to write to churches and newspapers in our constituencies suggesting that we were filibustering'.[38] MacKay, it seems, did not feel it necessary to heed the pressure of pro-life interest groups. Protest groups continue to rely upon the good graces of parliamentary members. Bridget Pym correctly notes that 'no group has any MP in its pocket. The extra-parliamentary group is entirely dependent on MPs and peers for its success, but the reverse is not true.'[39]

It could be argued that the Conservative Party did not respond to the pressure of pro-life groups because those voters were not of sufficient size to command the attention of party leaders. There is some truth to this claim, but only if one accepts that MPs and party leaders always make their political decisions based upon constituent pressure. State-centred theories have demonstrated, however, that the state should be viewed as far more autonomous from societal pressure than pluralist theories have imagined. The strength of the British state and political party structures has effectively shielded elected officials from the pressure of promotional interest groups. Public policy on non-economic issues such as abortion has not been made in reaction to the pressure of interested social groups, and the Conservative Party to date has been able to resist the pressure of pro-life groups.[40]

If class issues continue to decline in importance in British politics, pressure groups might find themselves well-situated to mobilize citizens based upon any number of social roles. Dennis Kavanagh suggests that one legacy of Thatcherism in Britain is that non-economic issues will become more important in future British elections. Kavanagh argues that the Labour Party, because of the popularity of Thatcher's economic programme, will be unable to abandon Conservative economic principles. The party will, instead, fight on a new ground of 'post-materialist issues like the environment, public services, citizens' rights and duties, and women's rights'.[41] If the post-materialist trend continues and economic issues no longer divide the British electorate, the Conservative and Labour Parties will have an incentive to divide on moral issues such as abortion and the environment because of the capacity of those promotional groups to mobilize voters. What is less apparent is whether or not the British polity will become more receptive and open to intervention by interest groups in the process of policy formation.

The failure of British pro-life groups to pass restrictions on abortion services relates directly to the strength of British political parties and the centralization of political authority in the hands of a few state institutions. The British state and the major political parties have not wanted to restrict abortion rights, and pro-life groups have not had the ability to impose their preferences against an unwilling state. The British state is, as the comparison with the American pro-life movement demonstrates, relatively autonomous from the political pressure of promotional groups, which continue to rely upon the support of key state elites and institutions to bring about social change.

THE AMERICAN PRO-LIFE MOVEMENT

American pro-life groups have used the openness of America's federal political system, weak political party structures, and division of sovereignty among branches of the national government to become a much more vital force than British organizations. Abortion was decriminalized in America in the 1973 Supreme Court decision *Roe v. Wade*. Prior to that ruling, a large majority of states (44) allowed abortions only if the pregnant woman's life would be endangered if the pregnancy were carried to term. The court overturned the laws of all the states by ruling that a woman had an absolute right to an abortion in the first trimester of her pregnancy. After the second trimester, the state could regulate and even forbid abortions.[42]

There are a number of differences between the pro-choice movements in America and Britain. First, the fundamental objective of the leading organizations in the American movement, The National Association for the Repeal of Abortion Laws (NARAL) and the National Association for Women (NOW), was the repeal instead of the reform of existing abortion laws. American pro-choice groups, unlike the ALRA in Britain, reasoned that the complete legalization of abortion was the only way to ensure a woman's right to choose an abortion, a position which put these groups at odds with public opinion. The American Law Institute (ALI) had written a model abortion bill in 1962 which recommended that a doctor be permitted to terminate a pregnancy for therapeutic reasons. As Judith Blake has noted, throughout the 1960s and early 1970s public opinion polls showed that the majority of Americans supported abortions along the lines advocated by the ALI but opposed abortion on demand.[43]

A second obvious difference between Britain and America was the way in which abortion reform came to the two nations. Mary Ann Glendon has correctly pointed out that, from a comparative point of view, abortion policy in the United States is distinctive because abortion rights were not worked out through the legislative process.[44] Pro-choice groups effectively used America's court system to push the reform process through the judicial branch. Borrowing the tactics of civil rights groups of the 1950s and 1960s, pro-choice groups initiated law-suits to bring their case to state and federal courts before they had the support of any other branch of government. As Kristin Luker notes, 'the court ruled on abortion because abortion reform advocates cared enough about the issue to press it to the top of the judicial system'.[45]

The strategy succeeded for two important reasons. First, America's courts were open to the well-organized pressure of pro-choice groups. The judiciary has often been the first institution to feel pressure to make changes in existing laws, because individuals and small organizations can litigate a matter before a court. Reformers challenged state abortion laws in 30 lower federal and state courts, a process which was less expensive and more effective than lobbying state legislatures. Second, the judicial branch had the power to impose a coherent policy on abortion in a manner not shared by any other branch of government. In a series of decisions which culminated in *Roe v. Wade*, the Supreme Court ruled that women had a constitutional right to privacy and that state laws restricting abortions were therefore unconstitutional. In overturning existing abortion laws of all the fifty states, the Court seemed to be creating a national public policy on abortion.[46]

Without judicial review, the assured legal status of abortion in America would not have occurred for many years. The grounds for abortion had slowly been liberalized, and in the cases of Washington State, Hawaii, and New York City abortion had been fully legalized. The majority of states, however, continued to impose some restrictions on access to abortion. In no other Western nation were the grounds for abortion completely eliminated as they were in America, nor did any other country rely upon the language of rights to justify abortion policy. The Court's decision in *Roe* was well ahead of public opinion at the time, a fact which pro-life groups widely publicized.[47]

Given the public opposition to abortion on demand, it was not difficult for pro-life groups to mobilize an intense opposition to the Court's decision. Catholics and evangelical Protestants were at the forefront of the opposition to the Court's doctrine. Mainline Protestant churches did not publicly oppose the legalization of abortion. In 1962, eleven years before *Roe*, the United Presbyterian Church had urged liberalization in abortion laws; in 1963 the American Lutheran and Unitarian Universalists followed suit. The American and Southern Baptists, Methodists, and the United Church of Christ initially supported the *Roe* decision.[48] The major American pro-life organizations which formed after the *Roe* decision have been: Christian American for Life, National Committee for a Human Life Amendment, Christian Action Council, National Pro-Life Political Action Committee, American Life Lobby, Christian Voice, and Operation Rescue. The American Life Lobby and the Christian Action Council, with 300 000 members per organization, are the largest pro-life groups.[49] Pro-life activism also occurred in the 1980s through all-purpose political organizations such as Christian Voice, Religious Roundtable, Christian Coalition and Moral Majority.

The Supreme Court did not resolve the abortion dilemma in America nor did it depoliticize the issue. As Tatlovich and Daynes note, the court's decision actually spurred other public institutions to become involved in the issue. Prior to the *Roe* ruling, abortion was a matter left to the discretion of the states; after the decision Congress and the President became intimately involved in the issue, especially in the matter of federal financing for abortions.[50] Since 1978, Congress has voted to restrict federal funds for abortions for women whose life is at risk and, with the help of President Reagan, Congress voted to bar employees of federally-financed family planning clinics from all discussions of abortion with their patients, an administrative order which the Supreme Court upheld in 1991 in *Rust v. Sullivan*.[51] President Clinton has recently eliminated the so-called gag rule and promised to support public funding for abortions and a Freedom of Choice Act, but he faces stiff congressional opposition on both proposals.[52]

President Reagan, by contrast to Mrs Thatcher, gave credibility to the pro-life cause with his public opposition to legalized abortion: 'We cannot proclaim the noble ideal that human life is sacred, then turn our backs on the taking of some 4,000 unborn children's lives every day. Abortion as a means of birth control must stop.'[53] Reagan welcomed the involvement and support of pro-life leaders and organizations, and he promised to make himself available to them: 'As long as I'm president, your groups and others who stand up for Judeo-Christian values will be welcomed here (at the White House) because you belong here.'[54]

State officials have remained key players for pro-life groups, who have been able to use their power in certain states to pass restrictive legislation. Eva Rubin notes that 80 bills dealing with abortion were introduced into state legislatures in the first five months after the court's decision in *Roe*.[55] Pro-life group influence has been so strong in some regions that abortions are virtually unavailable. North Dakota, for example, has imposed severe restrictions on women seeking abortions. A minor wanting an abortion in North Dakota must first get the consent of both parents or go to court to get a judge's approval. The state allows no public financing for abortions and prohibits abortions at public hospitals. Public sentiment against abortion in North Dakota has been so strong that only one doctor in the entire state agreed to perform abortions, and he recently retired. Louisiana passed a law in 1991 which would prohibit virtually all abortions except those to save the life of the mother or in certain cases of rape or incest. States as diverse as Minnesota, Pennsylvania and Idaho have seen the abortion issue upset the political alignments of the state.[56]

American pro-life groups have also used political pressure to restrict abortion services at the city and county level. One popular tactic has been to use legal and illegal political, economic and psychological pressure to create 'abortion-free zones'. Abortion-free zones are defined as 'any geo-graphical–political unit in which abortions do not take place. This is meant to include any state, county, congressional district, legislative district, city, town, suburb or neighborhood in our country.'[57] Groups picket hospitals and abortion clinics which, because they are private facilities, are faced with the sometimes difficult dilemma of whether or not to provide abortion services in the face of community hostility. Pro-life protesters also picket the homes of abortion-providers and, in one case, a doctor was murdered by a pro-life advocate. Clinics are now having difficulty finding doctors willing to provide abortion services.[58] Pro-life group influence has been so successful in some regions that abortions, while legal at the state level, are effectively not available in many places throughout the state. The centralization of medical care in Britain means that National Health Service hospitals and clinics do not have the right to refuse to perform an abortion.

THE AMERICAN POLITY AND PRO-LIFE ACTIVISM

The dispersion of authority in America's federal polity has created the conditions necessary to make pro-life interest groups politically powerful. As has often been noted, America's political structures fragment and weaken the power of the state, and thereby encourage the involvement of interest groups in the policy process at local and national political levels.[59] Interest groups have greater autonomy to advance claims directly against the government when political institutions are weak and political authority is dispersed among various branches of government. As James Q. Wilson notes, 'the greater the decentralization of power, the greater the incentive for the formation of many voluntary associations'.[60] Organizations have the opportunity to act on group interests in city, county, state and national politics.

The importance of state and local government in America stands in stark contrast to the highly-centralized power of the British national government. As a federal nation, the United States has a dispersion of power between national and state governments. All power which is not actually vested in the national government in the federal constitution is delegated to the states. In theory, this division of power means that states have the freedom to go their own way on a wide variety of social policies. In fact, the scope and significance of the American federal state has increased dramatically in the twentieth century. Local governmental units in America, however, continue to have a political significance and autonomy which is not shared by local government authorities in Britain. American states dominate issues such as law-enforcement, health care, education, and taxation, which in turn gives interest groups an opportunity and an incentive to pressure state and local political officials.

Pro-life interest groups have been able to make abortion a salient political issue because the Supreme Court did not impose a universal standard in the same way that the British Parliament did. State legislatures have the power to determine if public funds will be used to perform abortions for poor women, whether or not minors need to notify parents to receive an abortion, or if public hospitals will be used for performing abortions, while the courts have assumed the power to determine the constitutionality of those laws. The Supreme Court's 1989 decision in *Webster v. Reproductive Health Services*, which upheld the legality of state restrictions on abortion, has given states even more latitude in determining how and when abortions are performed within their borders.[61]

Policymaking on abortion is not restricted to national political bodies in America, as it is in Britain, which has encouraged pro-life groups to mobilize dynamic organizations at local levels. Tens of thousands of people gathered in Wichita, Kansas in the summer of 1991 for the purpose of pressuring the state to pass a restrictive abortion law and to close a clinic which performed late-term abortions. Pro-life groups have also used state initiatives and referenda in order to introduce restrictive abortion laws at the state level, an opportunity which British organizations simply do not have. Because American groups had the capacity to influence abortion policy in the city of Wichita and the state of Kansas, pro-life activists had an incentive to organize a mass protest at the local level.

The effect of a federal system on interest group mobilization can be significant. Michael McCann has noted that reform groups can work more effectively and attract a more committed membership if they can bring together the communal and political life of their members.[62] American pro-life organizations have the capacity directly to affect political outcomes in local political regions and are therefore better able to mobilize support than British groups. British pro-life groups cannot attract group members by connecting their community life to their local political activity on abortion, which remains a national political issue.

The fact that political power is shared among the three branches of the federal government in the United States also increases the opportunities and power of organized interest groups. The judicial branch competes with the executive and legislative branches to make public policy.[63] The court has been central to the raising of cultural issues and the creation of cultural conflicts which have been so important to evangelical Christians. Pro-life groups knew that the legality of their restrictive state abortion laws would be challenged, but they counted on using the litigation which would arise from those laws to overturn *Roe v. Wade*. In the case of an Idaho law in 1990 which passed both houses of Congress but was eventually vetoed by the Governor, the legislation was specifically written to persuade Justice O'Connor to overturn the landmark ruling that legalized abortion nationwide. Initiating lawsuits and implicit appeals to Supreme Court justices have become part of the pro-life political strategy in the abortion dispute.[64] Ironically, pro-life groups have succeeded most through the same institution which initially guaranteed abortion rights: the Supreme Court. British pro-life organizations are not able to litigate the abortion question because British courts do not stand in a position analogous to American courts; they do not have the power to overturn parliamentary laws and thereby shape public policy.

The division of authority between the President and Congress also acts to weaken the power of the American state and increase the power of interest groups.[65] The President and the legislature are elected separately, and the President's party may or may not control either house of Congress. In fact, divided government has been the norm since the end of the Second World War.[66] Both the Senate and the House can initiate or block legislation, propose amendments to existing bills, or bargain with other institutions. This political freedom makes both houses of Congress a target for extensive lobbying by interest groups. American interest groups know that pressuring Congress can be an effective way to influence policy choices in the absence of support from the President or the courts.

There is almost no limit to the points of access for social organizations in America. Groups can lobby the President, senators, congressmen and judges. If they are not successful with national politicians, organizations can turn to state governments and pressure the Governor, state senators and representatives, county commissioners, state judges, city councils and school boards. The Anglo-American contrast is important not simply because there are many more public offices in America than Britain, but because those offices in America provide elected officials with greater political autonomy and authority than their British peers.

American interest groups can succeed in the absence of presidential support in a way that British groups cannot if they fail to win over the Prime Minister. American environmental groups, for example, continued to have an impact in the 1980s despite the fact that Presidents Reagan and Bush supported easing environmental protection laws. Environmental interest groups turned their attention to Congress, which used its powers to block many of Reagan's and Bush's policy initiatives and formulated its own environmental policy in the absence of executive action, and the courts, where groups used litigation to ensure compliance with state and federal environmental regulations.[67]

American pro-life groups have been able to impose limits on abortion services in state and local areas and have won the sympathy and support of individual politicians. They have been unsuccessful, however, in their primary political objective: passing a constitutional amendment banning abortion. A 1983 proposed constitutional amendment, which would have overturned the *Roe* decision, failed to get the necessary two-thirds majority needed to pass the measures.[68] The failure of pro-life groups to pass national restrictions on abortion underscores an important point about the American polity. America's dispersed polity makes it relatively easy for groups to win local victories, but much harder to create a uniform national policy. A constitutional amendment requires a coordinated effort of disparate elements in the polity and substantial electoral majorities; pro-life groups did not have either of them. Efforts to pass a constitutional amendment exposed the national weakness of pro-life groups. This is one way in which British groups, theoretically, have a political advantage over American groups. Had Mrs Thatcher been strongly committed to the pro-life cause, the political obstacles to implementation would have more easily disappeared.

THE AMERICAN PARTY SYSTEM AND PRO-LIFE ACTIVISM

Generally speaking, the stronger the party system, the less opportunity interest groups have to influence politicians. American political parties are weak by British standards and have grown weaker in the past few decades.[69] British political parties shield politicians from interest group influence in two ways: by selecting candidates for nomination to public office and by financing political campaigns. British politicians have less need for the resources which interest groups offer them than American politicians, and they have less reason to fear the sanctions a group threatens. American political parties are weak, by contrast, which creates more opportunities for social organizations to influence politicians.

American parties do not select the candidate who will run for public office and they do not finance political campaigns. Nominees for a general election in each political party are selected through primary elections. Parties cannot determine who runs for nomination and they are powerless to control voting in primary elections. Any US citizen can run for public office, with or without the blessing of the party.[70] The rise of primaries as the means of selecting party candidates has deprived parties of an important source of influence over elected officials. As Gary Jacobson notes, in being unable to determine who runs under the party label, political parties 'cannot control what the label represents'.[71] To say that American political parties are weak is, as Nelson Polsby argues, 'to say little more than that state and local party elites have lost influence over some of the processes most important to their collective life, such as making political nominations'.[72]

Interest groups have helped to fill the vacuum created by weakened political parties. Candidates no longer depend upon the party for nomination and so they build their own personal organizations with the help of volunteer workers and interest groups. Successful candidates create a winning coalition by forging a plurality through the addition of disparate interest groups. Candidates will, if necessary, run against the party to win an election. In 1990, Ed Rollins, the chairman of the Congressional Republican Party, actually encouraged GOP candidates to distance themselves from President Bush for reneging on his 'no new taxes' pledge. British MPs would never be given the licence to forge policy positions so independent of the Prime Minister and the party leadership.

Candidates for public office also rely upon interest groups to finance and staff political campaigns. National political parties contribute less than ten per cent of the total cost of an election; individual donors and political action committees (PACs) finance the remainder of what are increasingly expensive campaigns.[73] By necessity, candidates become individual entrepreneurs searching for resources and votes without the benefit of a dynamic party organization behind them. American pro-life groups have contributed liberally to literally thousands of campaigns throughout the nation. The frequency of elections and the desperate need which candidates have of the resources controlled by interest groups has made it possible for American pro-life groups to pressure individual politicians in a way not possible in Britain.

It is the accepted norm that interest organizations will try to hold their representatives accountable for their voting behaviour. Richard Viguerie, a fund-raiser for the New Right, advises his followers: 'Let your representatives know you're watching them like a hawk, waiting to see how hard they fight to pass those amendments. Don't let up on them until you win their active support.'[74] American pro-life groups have learned to target politicians for their votes on abortion in a way that is perfectly consistent with virtually all pressure groups. Christian Voice annually compiles a 'Congressional Report Card' which rates members on their votes on abortion. The group is not shy about its justification: 'Our report card is the only mass distributed tool in America to enable millions of Christians to hold their representatives accountable for their actions in Congress.'[75] Given the weakness of American political parties, a candidate has every incentive to placate the wishes of a well-organized interest group within his or her constituency. From the candidate's perspective, interest groups can help finance and staff a campaign, or they can threaten his or her position by supporting the opposition. American political parties have neither the incentives which public officials desire nor the sanctions they fear.

The plethora of elected offices in America has provided ample opportunities for pro-life electoral activism. Operation Rescue, an evangelical pro-life group which tries to stop women from having an abortion by blocking clinic doors, even pressures locally-elected judges. Members of Operation Rescue pledge to get themselves arrested in order to shut down an abortion facility for that day. In some areas, the police and judges have been more aggressive in prosecuting group members for criminal trespass than in others. Since judges are locally elected in many American states, pro-life groups have the political opportunity to pressure those officials. Movement founder Randall Terry remarked on this in a 1990 mailing: 'Would you rather have judges who fear God, and permit the defense necessary at a trial, as in Missouri, or judges who throw lawyers in jail for mentioning 'God' or 'babies' during rescue trials, as in San Diego?'[76] The implication of Terry's letter is clear: pro-life advocates vote for judges who do not aggressively prosecute Operation Rescue activists.

American pro-life organizations have also taken advantage of the openness and responsiveness of political parties to organized pressure. A large measure of group success has been due to the relationship forged with the Republican Party during the 1980s. Conservative Christians opposed the liberal social changes of the 1970s, but neither the Democratic nor the Republican party was particularly sympathetic to their goals in the 1970s. The cultural issues of abortion, school prayer, women's rights and pornography cut across the social base of both parties, and they were content to let the Supreme Court resolve issues which had the potential to disrupt existing partisan formations.

In 1976, evangelicals enthusiastically voted for Jimmy Carter, the first born-again candidate, in the hope that he might reverse key court decisions on school prayer and abortion. Carter proved to be more liberal than evangelicals expected on moral issues such as abortion, however, and they turned to Ronald Reagan in 1980 who promised greater fealty to conservative moral principles and policies. Carter had little room to manoeuvre on cultural issues as the active wing of the Democratic Party became overwhelmingly pro-choice. Republicans capitalized on the discontent of pro-life Democrats by courting leaders of conservative moral organizations.[77]

The Republican Party platform throughout the 1980s reflected Reagan's commitment to evangelicals. Jerry Falwell said of the 1980 plank that it 'is just like I wanted it'.[78] Much the same could be said for the Republican Party platform of 1992 which included conservative moral statements on abortion, family values and homosexuality. There is no simple translation between a party's platform and the policies it will propose once in office. At a symbolic level, however, a party platform can legitimate the issues of a constituent group. This is what the Republican Party platform did for evangelical Christians throughout the 1980s. Even more important than platform statements, however, was the public sympathy and even admiration which Reagan and fellow Republicans displayed toward evangelicals. Republican support for evangelicals shaped the national debate on abortion, homosexuality and women's rights, and gave much-needed credibility to evangelical positions on those issues. The contrast with the British Conservative Party is marked. Mrs Thatcher and the Conservatives avoided taking a position on abortion and related social issues, claiming that they were non-party matters.[79]

President Reagan and the Republican Party had compelling political reasons to support the pro-life cause. In public opinion surveys, evangelical Protestants and conservative Catholics (target groups for Reagan throughout his presidency) were consistently more conservative on the abortion issue than was the general public.[80] The heavy concentration of evangelicals in the historically Democratic southern states made them an attractive target for Republican party activists who concluded that they had to win the south in the 1980 election. Reagan appealed to evangelicals and the leadership of the Roman Catholic Church on issues such as abortion, pornography and school prayer to win their votes away from the Democratic Party whose liberal positions on those issues alienated many believers.[81]

Reagan kept his promise to conservative groups with frequent speeches about school prayer, pornography, abortion and the place of religion in public life. President Reagan supported an amendment to the constitution allowing prayer in public schools: 'I want to see the Congress act on our constitutional amendment permitting voluntary prayer in America's classrooms'.[82] He seemed sympathetic to the view that America faced not only economic problems, but a moral crisis as well: 'In recent years, we must admit, America did seem to lose her religious and moral bearings, to forget that faith and values are what made us good and great.'[83] Finally, Reagan publicly defended evangelicals from their critics who were worried about the political involvement of religionists. At a prayer breakfast at the Republican National Convention in 1984, Reagan asserted that religion and politics 'are necessarily related'.[84] The evidence suggests that Reagan's electoral strategy succeeded; evangelical voter turnout increased dramatically and evangelicals became closely identified with the Republican Party by the mid-1980s. Robert Wuthnow notes that in the 1980 and 1984 elections a significant positive correlation existed between evangelical religiosity and political participation.[85] Northern and southern evangelicals voted overwhelmingly for Reagan in both elections, 67 per cent in 1980 and 76 per cent in 1984, and evangelicals increasingly came to identify themselves as Republicans. Corwin Smidt concludes that, while a plurality of evangelicals classified themselves as Democrats prior to Reagan's election in 1980, 'a plurality of evangelicals classified themselves as Republican when Reagan began his second term of office'.[86]

In responding to the organized pressure of pro-life groups, President Reagan and the Republican party were not behaving in an abnormal or irrational manner. As pluralist theories of American politics have long argued, the weakness of the American state encourages political parties and elected officials to react to interest group pressure. It was not simply the size of pro-life groups that was important, but also the fact that in America these groups inherited a weak polity which fostered a close alliance between organized pressure and politicians. As with most public policy in America, abortion policy was made in response to the pressure of interested social groups. The comparison with Britain is marked. The relative strength of Britain's state and political party structures effectively shielded politicians and policymakers from constituent pressure. State officials had less reason to heed to constituent demands.

Reagan, in fact, had much to gain and very little to lose in courting evangelical voters on moral issues such as abortion. He could give pro-life groups the rhetorical support which they wanted but, in practical terms, Reagan had no effective power on the abortion issue beyond the question of federal financing of abortions for poor women. The Supreme Court, in claiming that women had a constitutional right to first-trimester abortions, had stripped the President and the Congress of the power to adjudicate abortion's legality. Reagan's 'powerlessness' on abortion served his political purposes well. He could claim sympathy for the pro-life cause, but since he could not propose legislation to outlaw abortions, he also did not need to alienate any pro-choice sentiment within his party.

Pro-choice Republicans had little to fear from Reagan's social conservatism, because the courts had seemingly upheld the idea of abortion as a fundamental constitutional right in the *Roe* decision. This was a luxury which George Bush did not enjoy in the aftermath of the Supreme Court decision in *Webster v. Reproductive Services* (1989). The Court ruled that states would be given wide latitude in determining the grounds under which abortion would be allowed. Pro-choice groups, recognizing that they could not count on the courts to ensure a woman's fundamental right to an abortion, began to pressure for a national Freedom of Choice Act.[87] The renewed activism and politicization of the pro-choice movement disrupted the Republican Party in 1992 in much the same way that pro-life activism polarized the Democrats a decade earlier. Pro-lifers had become a powerful force in the Republican Party by 1992, but their uncompromising moral views alienated the moderate wing of the party. It remains to be seen what the Republican Party will do with pro-choice groups in the aftermath of Bush's 1992 presidential defeat.[88]

The contrast with Prime Minister Thatcher and the Conservative Party is stark and reveals a great deal about Mrs Thatcher's institutional incapacity to remain neutral on moral issues. British pro-life groups contended, quite correctly, that Mrs Thatcher had it within her power to support the Alton bill and impose a restriction on abortion services. Because she controlled the amount of time allocated for a private members' bill, Mrs Thatcher bore some responsibility for the success of the Alton bill. Abortion was a concern of the national government in Britain, which made it impossible for her to claim, as did President Reagan, that she was politically powerless to restrict abortion services. In the end, Mrs Thatcher concluded that pro-life groups were not important enough to warrant her support.

Reagan and Bush used evangelicals for their political purposes, but they also served as conduits for the pro-life movement. The advantages which accrued to American pro-life organizations because of Reagan's initial support were numerous: access to government officials, publicity, legitimacy in the public eye, and a greater potential to recruit group members. Reagan gave public credibility to the pro-life cause and helped interest groups raise awareness and resources for the cause. Pro-life groups exploited their relationship with Presidents Reagan and Bush. The Christian Action Council wrote in a 1989 newsletter, 'The CAC commends President Reagan for declaring National Sanctity of Human Life Day on our behalf since 1984.'[89] At least until 1992, evangelicals and the Republican Party concluded that they benefited from their symbiotic relationship.

British pro-life groups have been deprived of virtually all of these rewards because neither of the major political parties, and no significant political figure, has supported a reform of the abortion law. Even Mrs Thatcher, who seemed rhetorically sympathetic, proved to be politically unhelpful to British pro-life groups. The opinion expressed by Clive Calver, Executive Director of the Evangelical Alliance, reflects this discontent: 'Thatcher appears to be in favour of what she likes to call "moral values". Her support among evangelical leaders is, however, not great. She has alienated us on a wide variety of issues.'[90]

The important contrast between Britain and America was not only that Reagan and Bush supported the pro-life cause while Mrs Thatcher opposed it, but that support from key political elites was essential for British organizations, but not for American groups. Because Britain has a unitary polity, and since neither Mrs Thatcher nor one of the major political parties supported restricting abortion rights, pro-life groups were doomed to be politically ineffective. American pro-life groups certainly benefited from the support of Reagan and Bush, but they, unlike British groups, had recourse to other means of political action in the absence of state support. If Reagan and Bush had not wanted to restrict abortion rights, pro-life groups, because of America's polity, could still have focused political pressure on the courts, Congress, state and local governments and public officials. This will be the likely political strategy for pro-life groups if the Republicans become a party of 'inclusion' on the abortion issue in 1996.

EVANGELICAL ACTIVISM: EDUCATION AND PORNOGRAPHY

The different trajectories of British and American pro-life groups are symptomatic of the variant fortunes of evangelical political organizations in the two countries for the past two decades. Protest groups which mobilized around religion in state-supported schools and pornography have been more successful at influencing public policy in America than in Britain. American groups have used the openness of America's federal polity and the responsiveness of politicians and institutions to organize pressure to win numerous political victories. British groups, by contrast, inherited a unitary polity and a relatively strong state which has not been as responsive to promotional group pressure. These groups have been less successful in affecting policy choices on pornography and education.

Surveys on people's attitudes toward pornography reveal a similar level of potential support for anti-pornography groups in the two nations. In 1981, 45 per cent believed that pornography was a 'very serious social problem' in Britain. In the same survey, 51 per cent concluded that the right to show nudity and sex in films and magazines had 'gone too far'.[91] In a 1986 survey, 76 per cent of those asked believed that the use of pornography 'can trigger off sexual assault'.[92] Fifty-four per cent of those polled in a 1980 American survey said that 'sexual materials lead people to commit rape'. Forty per cent believed that 'there should be laws against the distribution of pornography whatever the age'. In all of the surveys, members of Christian groups were consistently more conservative than the general public.[93] If interest groups relied only upon public sentiment for their political success, anti-pornography groups in Britain and America ought to have experienced similar fortunes because they had nearly identical popular support. The fact that American groups were more successful than British groups cannot be explained only in terms of public opinion.

Dynamic anti-pornography organizations such as Morality in Media, Citizens Against Pornography, the National Coalition Against Pornography, Concerned Women for America, and the Traditional Values Coalition formed to limit the publication and distribution of pornographic materials. The Supreme Court, in broadening the concept of free speech, has given greater protection to pornography in the past several decades. The Court has continued to recognize, however, that the state has an interest to control obscene material and that local political communities are best equipped to determine what is obscene. In *Miller v. California* (1973), the court came up with an obscenity test which elevated the idea of applying 'contemporary community standards' to decide what constitutes patently offensive pornographic material. Anti-pornography groups have taken advantage of the court's reliance on this notion of community standards to press restrictive laws in Florida, Minnesota, Ohio and Indiana. Since pornography remains primarily a local police matter, anti-pornography groups have been able to use their resources to keep the issue salient in state and local politics.[94] National politics and politicians have also not been immune to the pressure of anti-pornography groups, as has been demonstrated in the recurring debate around qualifications for federal funding by the National Endowment for the Arts.

In Britain, anti-pornography groups have had some success in limiting the publication of pornographic materials, but those restrictions are nowhere near as severe as in selected American states and cities. Mrs Mary Whitehouse and her organization, the National Viewers and Listeners Association, effectively campaigned for the passage of the Child Protection Act of 1978, a private members' bill sponsored by the Conservative MP Cyril Townsend, which added new regulations to the production and distribution of child pornography. NVALA campaigned for the measure and presented a petition to Parliament signed by 1.6 million voters who supported the legislation. Initially, the Labour Party showed little enthusiasm for Townsend's Child Protection Act. Moodie and McCarthy have correctly noted that the bill eventually succeeded because the Labour Party and individual MPs, while not necessarily supportive of the restrictions in the law, found it difficult publicly to support the pornography industry.[95] Despite the efforts of Mrs Whitehouse and other British anti-pornography groups, pornography remains a marginal political issue in British politics. One of the greatest obstacles to anti-pornography activism follows from Britain's unitary polity, which does not allow organized groups to bring political matters to local voters through referendums or initiatives.

In America, the increased state interest in education in the 1960s bred significant opposition among evangelicals, who resisted Supreme Court decisions removing prayer and Bible-reading from public schools. The imposition of a universal standard on any aspect of education was novel in America where local regions historically had the power to establish their own guidelines. Some evangelicals responded by founding their own schools where religious teaching was central to the curriculum. A new area of contention arose between the state and church schools on the applicability of federal and state regulations to those schools. Evangelicals who chose not to opt out of public schools also had a considerable influence over local schools through the activism of protest groups formed to shape the public-school curriculum in numerous school districts across the country. Evangelical groups have increasingly focused attention on local school-board elections as a way of impacting public schools.[96] Since education is still primarily a local political matter in America, organized groups continue to have a tremendous influence in how education is conducted.

Evangelical groups, with the help of the Reagan and Bush administrations, pressed lawsuits to the Supreme Court challenging the 20-year-old precedents which removed Bible-reading and prayer from the public schools.[97] As with the abortion issue, however, evangelicals had less success in national than in state and local politics. Congress rejected a 1984 proposed constitutional amendment to permit organized, recited prayers in public schools. The 56 to 44 vote in favour of the amendment fell 11 votes short of the necessary two-thirds majority.[98]

The 'return' of British evangelicals to the education field in recent years has come about because of the neglect of religious education in schools. Groups became disenchanted with the unwillingness of many local schools to comply with the 1944 Education Act which stipulated that religious instruction be a compulsory part of the school curriculum. In 1988, the Conservative Party introduced the Education Reform bill to decentralize the educational system by giving parents more choice in choosing their own schools and local areas more power to set their own school curriculum, including the area of religious education.[99]

Many evangelicals responded angrily to a change which would have abandoned the principle of the 1944 Act that religious instruction be included in all schools. The Government eventually changed course, and returned religious education to the national curriculum, but it left vague what the content of that instruction would be. Evangelical groups responded by calling on the Government to define religious education as Christian: 'Parliament should amend the present Education Reform bill in such a way that Religious Instruction is defined as being predominantly the study of Christian religion.'[100] Groups also recognized that the new law would allow organized interests to have a prominent say in the curriculum of local schools. The national state, in limiting its power in education, created increased opportunities for meaningful local activism. As CARE noted, 'It is very important that Christians should understand this new situation and take the opportunity to become fully involved. . . . We are being presented with a new way of making sure the Christian voice is heard clearly within the education system.'[101]

CONCLUSION

The Anglo-American comparison is important not only for what it tells us about the political successes and failures of American and British evangelical organizations, but also for what it teaches about the political opportunities and incentives for interest group mobilization provided by different kinds of political institutions. Abortion, pornography and the place of religion in state-supported schools were issues which mobilized British and American evangelicals into social movement organizations in the 1970s and 1980s. The ability of these groups to affect public policy was greatly influenced, however, by the structure of state institutions and the level of state power which groups inherited. Britain's unitary polity raised the cost of group mobilization, limited how groups could politicize moral issues, and forced interest groups into a national debate where their weaknesses (principally the absence of elite support) were exposed. British evangelical interest groups did not have the opportunity to have a genuine impact on abortion or pornography at local levels which has in turn helped keep these groups organizationally weak.

America's federal polity, weak political parties and divided powers at the national level have helped keep the American state weak and have provided myriad opportunities for interest group influence in the policymaking process. American evangelicals formed more powerful pressure groups than their British counterparts not simply because American believers were more numerous, but because the American political regime gave organized interests the capacity to become more influential than did the British polity. America's weak state created the conditions necessary for powerful and independent interest groups; Britain's relatively strong state restricted interest group authority and forced them to rely upon the support of political elites to bring about social change.

7 The Future of Evangelical Social Movements

Evangelical Christians in Britain and America formed dynamic social movement organizations to combat drinking a century ago and abortion in the past several decades. An evangelical ideology proved to be a powerful mobilizing force for British and American Christians who joined protest groups and fought for their cause with dedicated fervour. Without this religious ideology and the cultural values which followed from it, evangelicals would have had no compelling reason to organize such dynamic political protest groups.

At a minimum, British and American evangelicals agree that Jesus is the sole source of salvation and redemption for individuals, that the Bible is the inspired word of God, and that believers are obliged to integrate religious convictions into activities of their daily lives. Evangelical religion has been affected by social and political change, but shared beliefs and cultural values have been the basis for evangelical activism for the past two hundred years. A shared commitment to these religious principles shaped adherents' political preferences and encouraged believers to form and join political protest groups.

What does the future hold for evangelical social movements? The ideological and political cleavages based upon religion will not disappear. Religious ideologies always have been and always will be socially and politically meaningful. Evangelicals are deeply divided from liberal Christians and secularists on religious, moral and political issues. Evangelicals have distinct beliefs and values which will continue to have the capacity to mobilize believers into movement organizations. As these cleavages become entangled with political questions, group mobilization and political conflict is inevitable. For heuristic and social purposes, it is essential to acknowledge and begin to understand how and why ideological conflicts of interest and social movement mobilization based upon religion arise.

The demise of class-based politics in Britain and America should encourage the rise in the kinds of moral and political disputes which would elicit evangelical activism. Both American and British society are increasingly polarized on moral issues such as Gay Rights, abortion, equal rights for women and the place of religion in public life. The intensification of these so-called 'culture wars' will likely witness persistent evangelical social and political participation. Moreover, the gradual expansion of governmental power and authority into more areas of personal life will create disputes about the meaning and direction of that involvement. Evangelicals will continue to oppose the introduction of values into daily life to which they object.

In terms of resources and manpower, evangelicals are well placed for social and political mobilization. Evangelicalism has largely eclipsed liberal Protestantism as the dominant religious perspective in Britain and America. Evangelical churches, schools, ministries to young people, publishing houses, summer camps and media are growing rapidly, while liberal organizations are still in decline. Evangelicals have shown a willingness and an ability to use those resources for political purposes. Perhaps even more important, evangelicals, after a fifty-year hiatus from social activism, are once again in agreement on the importance of political participation.

Evangelical unity has thus far been maintained by a shared dissatisfaction with liberal Christianity, secularism and certain aspects of modernity. Evangelicals do share basic theological premises, but historical, religious and, increasingly, educational differences exist among believers. Evangelicals have put aside divisive debates about biblical inerrancy, pre- and postmillenialism, and ecclesiology in the past thirty years in the interest of a shared religious and social agenda. There is no guarantee that these issues, which have balkanized evangelicals in the past, will not fragment them in the future, particularly if divisive class and religious differences emerge among wings of evangelicalism. Evangelicals, who are increasingly represented in the middle and upper middle classes, will be pressured and possibly fragmented by the forces of secularism and modernity. The evangelical ability to act in concert politically, socially and religiously will be determined, to a great extent, by the capacity of evangelical leaders in Britain and America to make a persuasive case that particular social issues are unambiguously related to biblical teaching.

Political realities and structures will also continue to influence how evangelicals engage in politics. The pattern established in the past decade by evangelical groups in Britain and America will continue into the next decade. American evangelical organizations will continue to be a more imposing political force than their British counterparts, in part because they represent a larger constituency, but also because American groups will be able to take advantage of a political system which encourages their activism. America's federal polity and weak political parties will continue to give evangelicals opportunities for effective political involvement in the policymaking process. Britain's unitary polity and strong political parties will continue to frustrate evangelical political efforts.

The election of a Democratic President in 1992 means that evangelicals will not have a sympathetic ear in the White House for the first time since 1980. President Clinton capitalized on internal divisions within the Republican Party on moral issues in 1992 to make a persuasive case that he was the moderate candidate. Clinton called himself a 'New Democrat' and implied that he would be more conservative than previous Democratic presidential candidates on cultural and family-values issues. Once in office, however, Clinton forged ahead with liberal, and controversial, proposals on Gay Rights and abortion, specifically The Freedom of Choice Act. Evangelicals have tried to focus on these moral issues to take advantage of persistent tensions in the Democratic Party and pressure the Republicans to continue support for evangelical moral views.

Given the debate within the Republican Party on moral issues, however, evangelicals cannot rely upon the level of elite support they received from Presidents Reagan and Bush and the Republicans in the 1980s and early 1990s.[1] The Supreme Court's decision in *Webster v. Reproductive Services*, which upheld the legality of state restrictions on abortion, galvanized the pro-choice movement. Pro-choice organizations renewed their lobbying of Republican Party candidates and voters. The 1992 presidential elections demonstrated that the party is currently deeply divided on moral issues such as abortion and school prayer. Forces within the Republican Party have urged a moderate position on abortion, and since evangelicals now vote overwhelmingly Republican, future party candidates may have greater freedom to adopt moderate positions on controversial matters.

American parties are, however, still vulnerable to organized, disciplined, and active social movements. Evangelicals have established themselves as an important wing of the Republican Party. They have a base of support, dedication, and resources which will continue to influence Republican platform positions. There is no guarantee, in fact, that evangelicals, because they have become so active in party politics, will not take over some state organizations. The Republican Party in California, Colorado and Oregon has recently faced a division over an evangelical moral agenda.[2]

The prospects are dim that an evangelical candidate will win the Republican Party nomination. Pat Robertson's unsuccessful candidacy in 1988 underscored the limitations of an evangelical candidate in national politics. Robertson's following was large enough to pack party caucuses, but not large enough to win party primaries.[3] More likely is the rise of a candidate who will try to combine a culturally conservative programme with an economic vision of limited government and private enterprise.

American evangelical groups will try to shift the debate on moral issues to state and local politics where groups have been more successful in the past. Ralph Reed, Executive Director for the Christian Coalition, has made a concerted effort to turn his group's attention to local activism. Evangelical groups, working with motivated activists and with impressive resources, have a good chance to mobilize voters and have an impact on local races. In local elections, where voting turnout is historically low, evangelicals have the capacity to become a powerful force in many parts of the country. In California, Virginia, Washington and many other states, evangelicals have successfully elected sympathetic people to school boards, city councils and state legislatures.[4]

British evangelical organizations will continue to have only a marginal impact in national politics. There is no indication that either the Conservative Party or John Major is at all interested in supporting evangelical moral concerns on issues such as abortion and pornography. Nor are British parties as open to outside agitation and influence as their American counterparts. In the absence of elite or party support, evangelical groups cannot accomplish much. British evangelicals will have no reason to turn to local activism, because local governmental bodies do not have any meaningful political power or autonomy. The best hope for British groups is that elections and partisan affiliations would, in the future, be based less on issues of class and more on questions of culture. If this post-materialist trend becomes evident in electoral politics, evangelical groups will be well-situated to represent conservative moral and cultural viewpoints.

This is not to suggest that the only way to view the success of British or American groups is to measure their political impact. The limit of an institutional interpretation of social movement mobilization is that such a theory often fails to recognize that individuals and groups have political and symbolic goals in mind when they engage in collective action. The meaning of evangelical political activism is to be found in the action itself as much as in the movement's political result. Evangelical groups want to bring political change to their society, but membership itself provides participants with a sense of meaning and worth which is not eliminated if the group fails to achieve a set of political objectives. Evangelicals participated in the temperance and pro-life movements because they believed that activism was consistent with their religious values, regardless of their political success. Participation brought its own reward for believers whose activism served to re-establish the veracity of their religious, moral and cultural order. The issues which mobilize believers can and will change over time, but it is unlikely that evangelical political groups will disappear in America or Britain.

Notes

1 INTRODUCTION

1. William E. Schmidt, 'U.S. Abortion Protesters Shunned by British', *New York Times*, 15 April 1993: p. A2.
2. Some of the best treatments include, Robert C. Liebman and Robert Wuthnow (eds), *The New Christian Right* (New York: Aldine Publishing Company, 1983); Kenneth D. Wald, *Religion and Politics in the United States* (New York: St. Martin's Press, 1987), Chapter 7; Steve Bruce, *The Rise and Fall of the New Christian Right* (Oxford: Clarendon Press, 1988); Wilcox, *God's Warriors: The Christian Right in Twentieth Century America* (Baltimore, MD: The Johns Hopkins University Press, 1992); and Allen D. Hertzke, *Echoes of Discontent: Jesse Jackson, Pat Robertson and the Resurgence of Populism* (Washington, DC: Congressional Quarterly Press, 1993).
3. Bruce, ibid., imagines what such a comparison might look like, but does not systematically compare evangelical politics in Britain and America. The importance of state structures has been recognized in a comparative analysis of abortion politics in Canada and the United States. See Mildred Schwartz, 'Politics and Moral Causes in Canada and the United States', in Richard F. Tomasson, *Comparative Social Research* (Greenwich, CT: JAI, 1981): pp. 65–90.

2 THEORIES OF SOCIAL MOVEMENT MOBILIZATION

1. Richard Hofstadter, *The Age of Reform* (New York: Alfred A. Knopf, 1955); Neil J. Smelser, *Theory of Collective Behavior* (New York: The Free Press, 1962); and Joseph Gusfield, *Symbolic Crusade* (Urbana: University of Illinois Press, 1963).
2. Mancur Olson, *The Logic of Collective Action* (Cambridge: Cambridge University Press, 1965); Terry Moe, *The Organization of Interests* (Chicago: Chicago University Press, 1980); Kenneth A. Shepsle and Barry R. Weingast, 'Structure-Induced Equilibrium and Legislative Choice', *Public Choice* 37 (1981): 503–19; Michael Hechter, *Principles of Group Solidarity* (Berkeley: University of California Press, 1987).
3. Mayer N. Zald and John D. McCarthy (eds), *Social Movements in an Organizational Society* (New Brunswick: Transaction Books, 1987); William Gamson, *The Strategy of Social Protest*, 2nd edn (Belmont, California: Wadsworth, 1990).
4. Stephen Krasner, *Defending the National Interest: Raw Materials Investment in United States Foreign Policy* (Princeton, NJ: Princeton University Press, 1978); Charles Tilly, *From Mobilization to Revolution* (Reading, Mass., 1979); Theda Skocpol, *States and Social Revolutions* (Cambridge: Cambridge University Press, 1979); and Peter B. Evans, Dietrich Rueschemeyer

and Theda Skocpol (eds), *Bringing the State Back In* (Cambridge: Cambridge University Press, 1985).

5. See Donald C. Clelland and Alan Page, 'The Kanawha Textbook Controversy: A Study of the Politics of Life Style Concern', *Social Forces* 57 (1978): 265–81; Roy Wallis, *Salvation and Protest: Studies of Social and Religious Movements* (London: Frances Puritan, 1979); Louise Lorentzen, 'Evangelical Life Style Concerns Expressed in Political Action', *Sociological Analysis* 41 (1980): 144–54; and Clyde Wilcox, *God's Warriors: The Christian Right in Twentieth Century America* (Baltimore: Johns Hopkins University Press, 1992).

6. James Q. Wilson has noted that the decisive problem faced by all social groups is organizational maintenance. As I show in this chapter, the ideology of a purposive organization shapes when groups form and influences the strategy used by group leaders to maintain the group over time.

7. Richard Hofstadter, *The Age of Reform*.

8. Joseph Gusfield, *Symbolic Crusade*. It should be noted that Gusfield tries to distinguish himself from Hofstadter and Lipset by separating status and symbol as analytical devices. For my purposes he can be combined with status analysts because of his commitment to measuring a group's status-ascent or decline and explaining political behaviour in those terms.

9. Seymour Martin Lipset and Earl Raab, 'The Election and the Evangelicals', *Commentary* (March 1981): 25–31; Donna Day-Lower, 'Who is the Moral Majority?', *Union Seminary Quarterly Review* 37 (1983): 335–47; James David Fairbanks, 'The Evangelical Right: Beginnings of Another Symbolic Crusade?', paper delivered at the 1981 Annual Meeting of the American Political Science Association; Ronald Inglehart, *Culture Shift in Advanced Industrial Society* (Princeton: Princeton University Press, 1990), Chapter 6.

10. Alan Clarke, 'Moral Reform and the Anti-Abortion Movement', *Sociological Review* 35 (February 1987): 123–49.

11. Gusfield, *Symbolic Crusade*, p. 20.

12. Ibid., p. 17.

13. Ibid., p. 6.

14. Ibid., p. 167.

15. Ibid., p. 174.

16. Neil J. Smelser, *Theory of Collective Action*.

17. Ibid., p. 71.

18. Ibid., p. 65.

19. Status theory is critiqued by resource mobilization theory for its inadequate treatment of organizations in collective-action movements. See, for example, Charles Tilly, *From Mobilization to Revolution*; Mayer N. Zald and John D. McCarthy (eds), *Social Movements in an Organizational Society*; and Doug McAdam, *Political Process and the Development of Black Insurgency* (Chicago: University of Chicago Press, 1982), Chapter 1. For a good analysis of the weakness of status theory on the issue of group ideology, see Roy Wallis, *Salvation and Protest*; and Steve Bruce, *The Rise and Fall of the New Christian Right*, Chapter 1.

20. Smelser, *Theory of Collective Behavior*, p. 48.

21. Seymour Martin Lipset and Earl Raab, *The Politics of Unreason* (Chicago: University of Chicago Press, 1970), p. 29.

22. Smelser, *Theory of Collective Action*, p. 11.
23. Wallis, *Salvation and Protest*, p. 97.
24. Ibid., p. 96.
25. Clifford Geertz, *The Interpretation of Cultures* (New York: Basic Books, 1973), p. 219.
26. See Page and Clelland, 'The Kanawha County Textbook Controversy'; Lorentzen, 'Evangelical Life Style Concerns Expressed in Political Action'; and John Simpson, 'Moral Issues and Status Politics', in Robert C. Liebman and Robert Wuthnow (eds), *The New Christian Right* (New York: Aldine, 1982), pp. 188–205. For a good review of these theories, see Kenneth D. Wald, Dennis E. Owen, and Samuel S. Hill, 'Evangelical Politics and Status Issues', *Journal for the Social Scientific Study of Religion* 28 (1989): 1–16.
27. Page and Clelland, 'The Kanawha County Textbook Controversy', p. 266.
28. Lorentzen, 'Evangelical Life Style Concerns Expressed in Political Action', p. 147.
29. Mancur Olson, *The Logic of Collective Action*.
30. See David Gartell and Zane Shannon, 'Contacts, Cognitions, and Conversion: A Rational Choice Approach', *Review of Religious Literature* 27 (September 1985): 32–47, for the application of Olson's analysis to the study of religious conversions.
31. Olson, *The Logic of Collective Action*, p. 2. Olson directs his argument to pluralist theories of group behaviour, but the same logic applies to status theory on the question of group formation.
32. Ibid., p. 51.
33. Ibid., p. 9.
34. Ibid., pp. 161–3.
35. William Gamson, *The Strategy of Social Protest*, pp. 153–5.
36. Terry Moe, *The Organization of Interests*; Terry Moe, 'Toward a Broader View of Interest Groups', *The Journal of Politics* 43 (1981): 531–43; and Shepsle and Weingast, 'The Institutional Foundations of Committee Power'.
37. Moe, *The Organization of Interests*, p. 47.
38. Ibid., p. 117.
39. Michael Hechter, *Principles of Group Solidarity*.
40. Ibid., p. 33.
41. Aaron Wildavsky, 'Choosing Preferences by Constructing Institutions: A Cultural Theory of Preference Formation', *American Political Science Review* 81 (1987): 3.
42. Rogers M. Smith, 'If Politics Matter: Implications for a New Institutionalism', paper prepared for the 1991 Annual Meeting of the American Political Science Association.
43. Randall Terry, *Operation Rescue* (Binghamton, New York: Operation Rescue, 1988), p. 209.
44. For a theoretical review of resource mobilization theory, see Zald and McCarthy, *Social Movements in an Organizational Perspective*; and Gamson, *The Strategy of Social Protest*. For the application of a resource model to specific social movements, see McAdam, *Political Process and the Development of Black Insurgency*; Pamela Johnstone Conover and Virginia Gray, *Feminism and the New Right* (New York: Praeger, 1983); Robert C. Liebman and Robert Wuthnow (eds), *The New Christian Right* (New York: Aldine,

1983); and Norris Johnson, David Choate and William Bunis, 'Attendance at a Billy Graham Crusade: A Resource Mobilization Approach', *Sociological Analysis* 45 (Summer 1984): 383–91.

45. Zald and McCarthy, ibid., p. 11.

46. Gamson, *The Strategy of Social Protest*, p. 172.

47. Jack Walker, 'Origins and Maintenance of Interest Groups in America', *American Political Science Review* 77 (1983): p. 403.

48. McAdam, *Political Process and the Development of Black Insurgency*, p. 44.

49. John D. McCarthy, 'Pro-Life and Pro-Choice Mobilization: Infrastructure Deficits and New Technologies', pp. 49–66, in Zald and McCarthy, *Social Movements in an Organizational Perspective*.

50. Johnson, Choate and Bunis, 'Attendance at a Billy Graham Crusade', p. 385.

51. McCarthy, 'Pro-Life and Pro-Choice Mobilization'; and Liebman and Wuthnow, *The New Christian Right*.

52. Zald and McCarthy, *Social Movements in an Organizational Perspective*, p. 20.

53. Gamson, *The Strategy of Social Protest*, p. 6.

54. Zald and McCarthy, *Social Movements in an Organizational Perspective*, p. 21.

55. For good accounts of state structure theory, see J. P. Nettl, 'The State as a Conceptual Variable', *World Politics* 20 (July 1968): 559–92; Stephen Krasner, *Defending the National Interest;* Peter Evans, Dietrich Rueschemeyer, and Theda Skocpol (eds), *Bringing the State Back In*; and Peter Hall, *Governing the Economy: The Politics of State Invention in Britain and France* (Cambridge: Polity Press, 1986).

56. Stephen Krasner, *Defending the National Interest*, p. 10.

57. Peter Hall, *Governing the Economy*, p. 19.

58. Theda Skocpol, *States and Social Revolutions*; Ann Shola Orloff and Theda Skocpol, 'Why Not Equal Protection? Explaining the Politics of Public Social Spending in Britain, 1900–1911 and the United States, 1880–1920', *American Sociological Review* 49 (December 1984): 726–50; Ira Katznelson, 'Working-Class Formation and the State: Nineteenth-Century England in American Perspective', in Evans, Ruschemeyer and Skocpol (eds), *Bringing the State Back In*, pp. 257–84; and Robert Wuthnow, 'State Structures and Ideological Outcomes', *American Sociological Review* 50 (December 1985): 799–821.

59. Wuthnow is put into the state structural camp by virtue of the article he wrote on the English and French Reformation Movements. In his recent book on cultural analysis (1987), however, Wuthnow tries to construct a theory of social movements which appreciates the ideological and structural component of group activism. I argue that he relies too heavily on a structural analysis to explain the production of group ideas and, in the process, dismisses an autonomous role for ideology in social group behaviour. Wuthnow's own critique of structural theory, however, is persuasive, and I borrow his insights from Chapter 2 in this section of my work.

60. Wuthnow, 'State Structures and Ideological Outcomes', pp. 805–6.

61. Ibid., p. 811.

62. Theodore J. Lowi, *The End of Liberalism: Ideology, Policy and the Crisis of Public Authority* (New York: W. W. Norton, 1969); James Q. Wilson, *Political Organizations* (New York: Basic Books, 1973); Robert Dahl, *Dilemmas*

of Pluralist Democracy (New Haven: Yale University Press, 1982). For a good critique of state structure theory, see Eric A. Nordlinger, Theodore J. Lowi and Sergio Fabbrini, 'The Return to the State: Critiques', *American Political Science Review* 82 (September 1988): 875–901.

63. Evans, Rueschemeyer and Skocpol, *Bringing the State Back In*, p. 253.

64. Skocpol, *States and Social Revolutions*, p. 285. In her recent work, Skocpol has begun to recognize the role of individual activism in social movements. For an example, see Margaret Weir, Ann Shola Orlaff and Theda Skocpol (eds), *The Politics of Social Policy in the United States* (Princeton: Princeton University Press, 1988).

65. Peter Hall, *Governing the Economy*, p. 277.

66. It should be noted here that not all state structure theorists are ignorant of ideological formation. Robert Wuthnow, for example, deals extensively with the origin of ideologies which compete for social power.

67. Gamson, *The Strategy of Social Protest*, Chapter 3.

68. Alberto Melucci, 'The Symbolic Challenge of Contemporary Movements', *Social Research* 52 (Winter, 1985): 789–815.

69. Wildavsky, 'Choosing Preferences by Constructing Institutions', p. 2.

70. For good discussions of ideology, see Clifford Geertz, *The Interpretation of Cultures*, Chapter 8; Robert Wuthnow, *Meaning and Moral Order: Explorations in Cultural Analysis* (Berkeley: University of California Press, 1987), Chapter 5; and Raymond Boudon, *The Analysis of Ideology* (Oxford: Polity Press, 1989).

71. Thomas Kuhn, *The Structure of Scientific Revolutions*, 2nd edn, enlarged (Chicago: University of Chicago Press, 1970).

72. Norman Cohn, *The Pursuit of the Millennium* (Oxford: Oxford University Press, 1961).

73. Robert Wuthnow, *Meaning and Moral Order*, p. 154.

74. For a good description, see Ellis Sandoz, *A Government of Laws: Political Theory, Religion and the American Founding* (Baton Rouge: Louisiana State University Press, 1990), pp. 34–6.

75. For a good analysis, see James C. Scott, *The Moral Economy of the Peasant* (New Haven: Yale University Press, 1976), pp. 5–6.

76. Clifford Geertz, *The Interpretation of Cultures*, p. 231.

77. Scott, *The Moral Economy of the Peasant*, Chapter 1.

78. James Q. Wilson, *Political Organizations*, p. 7.

79. See Geertz, *The Interpretation of Cultures*, Chapter 8; Page and Clelland, 'The Kanawha County Textbook Controversy'; Lorentzen, 'Evangelical Life Style Concerns Expressed in Political Action'; and Wuthnow, *Meaning and Moral Order*, Chapter 5.

80. Geertz, ibid., p. 219.

81. 'No Cheap Solutions', pamphlet of the Prolife Nonviolent Action Project, 1984, p. 14.

82. This does not mean that the symbol of Jesus on the Cross will evoke the same meaning for all Christian believers. Ideologies and symbols have a high capacity for interpretation. Jesus on the cross may elicit a message of non-violent resistance at a pro-life rally, but it may have meant victory in armed combat for those who participated in the Crusades. Ideologies are malleable, which partially explains how so many different groups arise from a particular belief system.

83.   James Q. Wilson, *Political Organizations*, Chapter 14, provides an insightful discussion of how different types of groups adopt different political strategies to reach their goal.

84.   For a good discussion of single-issue politics, see Marjorie Randon Hershey and Darrell M. West, 'Single-Issue Politics: Prolife Groups and the 1980 Senate Campaign', in Allen J. Cigler and Burdett A. Loomis, *Interest Group Politics* (Washington: Congressional Quarterly Press, 1983): 31–59. Pro-choice and pro-life groups have experienced an internal conflict between an accommodating wing which has been willing to make strategic choices in pursuit of a political goal, and a radical side which has refused any compromise on their ideological agenda.

85.   See Matthew C. Moen, 'The Political Transformations of the Christian Right', unpublished paper delivered at the 1990 Annual Meeting of the American Political Science Association.

86.   Patrick Seyd, 'Labour: The Great Transformation', in *Britain at the Polls: 1992* (Chatham, NJ: Chatham House, 1993), pp. 70–100.

87.   Peter Hall, *Governing the Economy*, Chapter 1.

88.   Nelson W. Polsby, *Congress and the Presidency* (Englewood Cliffs, NJ: Prentice-Hall, 1971), p. 140. See also Benjamin Ginsberg and Martin Shefter, *Politics by Other Means* (New York: Basic Books, 1990).

89.   Ann Shola Orloff and Theda Skocpol, 'Why Not Equal Protection? Explaining the Politics of Public Social Spending in Britain, 1900–1911, and the United States, 1880–1920'.

3   EVANGELICAL IDEOLOGY AND GROUP-FORMATION

1.   The most influential works using a modernization theory are Bryan R. Wilson, *Religion in a Secular Society* (London: C. A. Watts, 1966); and David Martin, *A General Theory of Secularization* (New York: Harper and Row, 1978).

2.   There are several problems with the public-opinion data on evangelicals in America. The most serious limitation is a lack of systematic data on evangelicals. Until recently very few national surveys asked religious questions. The recent interest in evangelicals has led to more religious questions in polling, but the additional questions have varied from poll to poll. In short, the conclusions drawn from survey research must be tentative. Nonetheless, there is enough uniformity among the various polls to draw conclusions about evangelicals. For an excellent discussion of the problems related to survey research on evangelicals, see Corwin Smidt and Lyman Kellstedt, 'Evangelicalism and Survey Research: Interpretive Problems and Substantive Findings', in Richard Neuhaus (ed.), *The Bible, Politics and Democracy* (Grand Rapids, Michigan: William B. Eerdmans, 1987): pp. 81–102 and 131–67.

3.   For especially fine treatments of the history of British Evangelicalism, see D. W. Bebbington, *Evangelicalism in Modern Britain* (London: Unwin Hyman, 1989); and Kenneth Hylson-Smith, *Evangelicals in the Church of England: 1734–1984* (Edinburgh: T. & T. Clark, 1989). For sources on American evangelicalism, see Sydney Ahlstrom, *A Religious History of America* (New Haven: Yale University Press, 1972); George Marsden, *Fundamentalism and*

American Culture (Oxford: Oxford University Press, 1980); James Davison Hunter, *American Evangelicalism* (New Brunswick: Rutgers University Press, 1983); and A. James Reichley, *Religion in American Public Life* (Washington, DC: The Brookings Institute, 1985).

4. For a good discussion of the distinction between evangelical and Calvinist theology, see John L. Hammond, *The Politics of Benevolence: Revival Religion and American Voting Behavior* (Norwood, NJ: Ablex, 1979).

5. Positing a definition invites a host of problems, many of which emerge in the data, which show a great diversity among American evangelicals. I have purposely left out a 'born-again' criterion in my measurement of evangelicalism, despite the fact that many surveys identify evangelicals on the basis of this identification. Smidt and Kellstedt, ibid., conclude that the term is unreliable when used as a key measure of evangelicalism. I have also excluded Roman Catholics from my definition, despite the fact that a large body of Catholics fits the theological definition of evangelicals in many surveys. These surveys, however, tend to rely on a born-again measurement for evangelicals rather than theological questions. As noted above, I believe that a born-again measurement is not an accurate reflection of evangelicals.

6. The statements are taken from 'Your Church is Needed to Make a Difference in these Difficult Times', undated publication of the National Association of Evangelicals, and 'A World Falling Apart Needs a People Coming Together', undated publication of the Evangelical Alliance. For some scholarly definitions of Evangelicalism see Bebbington, *Evangelicalism in Modern Britain*; James Barr, *Fundamentalism* (London: SCM Press, 1977); R. Steven Warner, 'Theoretical Barriers to the Understanding of Evangelical Christianity', *Sociological Analysis*, 40 (1979): 1–19; Steve Bruce, 'Identifying Conservative Protestants', *Sociological Analysis*, 1 (1983); Hunter, *American Evangelicalism*, Chapter 1; Kenneth D. Wald, *Religion and Politics in the United States* (New York: St. Martin's Press, 1987); and Michael Saward, *Evangelicals on the Move* (London: Mowbray Press, 1987).

7. 'One in Christ: The Prophetic Justice Unit', undated publication of the National Council of Churches of Christ in the USA.

8. Interview with the Rev. Alan Gibson, 21 April 1989.

9. The Rev. David McKinnis, sermon preached at St Aldates, 5 February 1989.

10. Interview with Malcolm Laver, 1 June 1989.

11. 'The British Evangelical Council: Who are We?', undated publication of the British Evangelical Council.

12. The Rev. David McKinnis, sermon preached at St Aldates, 19 February 1989.

13. Bebbington, *Evangelicalism in Modern Britain*, p. 74.

14. Clive Calver, *He Brings Us Together* (London: Hodder and Stoughton, 1987), p. 10.

15. John Stott, *Issues Facing Christians Today* (London: Marshall, Morgan and Scott, 1984), p. 330.

16. Barr, *Fundamentalism*, p. 18.

17. Bebbington, *Evangelicalism in Modern Britain*, p. 5.

18. Jerry Falwell, *Wisdom for Living: Pursuing Right in a World Gone Wrong* (New York: Doubleday, 1982), p. 61.

19. The Rev. David Johnson, sermon preached at St Ebbe's, 12 February 1989.

20. Saward, *Evangelicals on the Move* , p. 3.

172 *Notes*

21. For good reviews of how evangelicals use the Bible, see Donald McKim, *What Christians Believe about the Bible* (Nashville: Thomas Nelson, 1985); Tony Baker, 'Evangelical Approaches to Theological Dialogue', *Churchman* 102 (1988): 44–53; and Mark Burkill, 'The Principles of Biblical Interpretation', *Churchman* 103 (1989): 40–51. For an excellent discussion of the various ways in which scripture is appropriated by Christians, see David H. Kelsey, *The Use of Scripture in Recent Theology* (Philadelphia: Fortress Press, 1975).

22. George Gallup, *Evangelical Christianity in the United States* (Princeton, NJ: The Gallup Organization, 1981), pp. 46 and 132–3. The Gallup poll defines evangelicals as those who believe in the inerrancy of the Bible; who believe that Jesus Christ is both fully God and fully man or is the Son of God; who believe that the only hope for salvation is through a personal faith in Jesus Christ; who read the Bible at least once a month; and who attend religious services at least once per month.

23. Smidt and Kellstedt, 'Evangelicalism and Social Research', p. 143.

24. Baker, 'Evangelical Approaches to Theological Dialogue', p. 45.

25. J. I. Packer, *Fundamentalism and the Word of God* (London: Inter-Varsity Press, 1958).

26. See Gallup, *Evangelical Christianity in the United States*, pp. 27 and 94–5.

27. Interview with Tim Dean, 11 May 1989.

28. 'Welcome to St Ebbe's!', undated publication of St Ebbe's Anglican Church.

29. Interview with the Rev. Alan Gibson, 21 April 1989.

30. 'Making All Things New', undated publication of the National Council of Churches of Christ in the USA.

31. For reviews of liberal Protestantism see, Wade Clark Roof, *Community and Commitment: Religious Plausibility in a Liberal Protestant Church* (New York: Elsevier, 1978); and Wade Clark Roof and William McKinney, *American Mainline Religion* (New Brunswick, NJ: Rutgers University Press, 1987).

32. Hunter, *American Evangelicalism*, p. 9.

33. Hammond, *The Politics of Benevolence*, p. 53.

34. Ahlstrom, *A Religious History of America*, pp. 325–6.

35. Smidt and Kellstedt, 'Evangelicalism and Survey Research', p. 143.

36. Gallup, *Evangelical Christianity in the United States*, pp. 112–19.

37. Smidt and Kellstedt, 'Evangelicalism and Survey Research', p. 141.

38. Max Weber, *The Sociology of Religion* (Boston: Beacon Press), p. 182.

39. Carl Henry, 'Making Political Decisions: An Evangelical Perspective', in Richard John Neuhaus and Michael Cromartie (eds), *Piety and Politics* (Lanham, MD: University Press, 1987), p. 105.

40. 'Leadership Through Cooperation', undated publication of the National Association of Evangelicals.

41. Corwin Smidt, 'Evangelicals and the 1984 Election: Continuity or Change?', *American Politics Quarterly*, 15 (October 1987): 419–44. Also see Bebbington, *Evangelicalism in Modern Britain*, Chapter 9.

42. See, for example, Kenneth Wald, *Crosses on the Ballot: Patterns of British Voter Alignment Since 1885* (Princeton: Princeton University Press, 1983), Chapter 7; and Kenneth D. Brown, *A Social History of the Nonconformist Ministry in England and Wales* (Oxford: Clarendon Press, 1988), Chapter 1.

43. Brian Harrison, *Drink and the Victorians: The Temperance Question in England,* 1815–1872 (London: Faber and Faber, 1971); Bebbington, *Evangelicalism in Modern Britain,* pp. 110–11.

44. Bebbington, *Evangelicalism in Modern Britain,* p. 111.

45. Ahlstrom, *A Religious History of America,* pp. 842–8.

46. Hunter, *American Evangelicalism,* p. 24.

47. For good historical reviews of evangelicals, see Phillip E. Hammond, 'The Curious Path of Conservative Protestantism', *The Annals of the American Academy,* 480 (July 1985): 53–62; Marsden, *Fundamentalism and American Culture;* Hunter, *American Evangelicalism,* Chapter 3; and Reichley, *Religion in American Public Life,* Chapter 5.

48. Hunter, *American Evangelicalism,* p. 33.

49. Bebbington, *Evangelicalism in Modern Britain,* Chapter 6 and Marsden, *Fundamentalism and American Culture,* Part 2.

50. For an excellent comparison of British and American Evangelicalism, see George Marsden, 'Fundamentalism as an American Phenomenon, A Comparison with English Evangelicalism', *Church History* 46 (June, 1977): 215–32.

51. Hunter, *American Evangelicalism,* p. 39.

52. George Gallup, *Evangelical Christianity in the United States;* Hunter, *American Evangelicalism,* Chapter 4; and Smidt, 'Evangelicals and the 1984 Election'. For poll data which suggests that evangelicals and non-evangelicals do not differ in terms of income and educational achievement, see Stuart Rothenberg and Frank Newport, *The Evangelical Voter: Religion and Politics in America* (Washington, DC: Free Congress Research & Education Foundation).

53. Hunter, *American Evangelicalism,* p. 55.

54. Ibid.; and John C. Green, 'Education and Evangelical Activists', paper presented at the Annual Meeting of the American Political Science Association, 1991.

55. Robert Wuthnow, *The Restructuring of American Religion* (Princeton: Princeton University Press, 1988), p. 194.

56. For membership statistics, see Peter Brierley (ed.), *United Kingdom Christian Handbook;* 1992–1993 (P. W. Brierley: London, 1991).

57. David Winter, *Battered Bride?* (Sussex: Monarch Publications, 1988), Chapter 8 and Bebbington, *Evangelicalism in Modern Britain,* Chapter 8.

58. Roof and McKinney, *American Mainline Religion,* Chapter 1.

59. 'Into the 21st Century with the FIEC', pamphlet of the Fellowship of Independent Evangelical Churches, undated.

60. Hylson-Smith, *Evangelicals in the Church of England,* pp. 178–80.

61. Gallup, *Evangelical Christianity in the United States,* pp. 49 and 139–42.

62. Roof and McKinney, *American Mainline Religion,* Chapter 6.

63. 'One in Christ', undated publication of the National Council of Churches of Christ in the USA.

64. For the classic argument linking evangelical doctrine to church growth, see Dean M. Kelley, *Why Conservative Churches are Growing* (New York: Harper and Row, 1972).

65. Harold Lindsell, *The Bible in Balance* (Grand Rapids, Michigan: Zondervan Press, 1979), p. 313.

66. 'What is the Spirit Saying?', A Report from the National Evangelical An-
     glican Celebration, May 1988, p. 7.
67. *The Works of the Reverend John Wesley* (London: John Mason, 1829), Vol.
     VI, p. 303.
68. *Minutes of the Sixty-Ninth Session of the New England Annual Conference of
     the Methodist Episcopal Church* (Boston: James P. Magee, 1868), p. 45.
69. 'Ye Have Been Called into Liberty', undated publication of the Christian Life
     Commission of the Southern Baptist Convention.
70. Max Weber, *The Protestant Ethic and the Spirit of Capitalism* (New York:
     Charles Scribner's Sons, 1958).
71. Max Weber, *The Sociology of Religion*, p. 171.
72. 'A Statement of the Principles for Christian Social Concern and Christian
     Social Action', undated publication of the Christian Life Commission of the
     Southern Baptist Convention.
73. Nigel Cameron, 'The Logic of Christian Political Responsibility', undated
     pamphlet of CARE, p. 7.
74. Carl Henry, 'Making Political Decisions: An Evangelical Perspective', pp.
     101–2.
75. 'What is the Spirit Saying?' A Report from the National Evangelical An-
     glican Celebration, May 1988, p. 5.
76. Interview with Kathryn Ede, 19 April 1989.
77. Steve Bruce, 'Authority and Fission: the Protestants' Divisions', *The British
     Journal of Sociology* 36 (December 1985): 592–603.
78. Kenneth Tucker, 'Ideology and Social Movements: The Contributions of
     Habermas', *Sociological Inquiry* 59 (Winter 1989): 30–47.
79. 'A World Falling Apart Needs a People Coming Together', undated pam-
     phlet of the Evangelical Alliance.
80. Stuart Rothenberg and Frank Newport, *The Evangelical Voter: Religion and
     Politics in America*; and George Gallup, Jr, *The People's Religion* (New
     York: Macmillan, 1989), Chapter 4. See Smidt, 'Evangelicals and the 1984
     Election', for a discussion of these opinion polls.
81. Smidt and Kellstedt, 'Evangelicalism and Social Research', p. 91.
82. For an interesting discussion of the variety of views within evangelicalism,
     see Robert Booth Fowler, *A New Engagement: Evangelical Political Thought,
     1966–1976* (Grand Rapids, Michigan: William B. Eerdmans, 1982).
83. See Jeffrey Hadden, 'Religion and the Construction of Social Problems',
     Sociological Analysis 2 (Fall, 1980): 99–108, for a discussion of ideological
     resources in religious group formation.
84. 'The Third Annual Report of the Virginia Society for the Promotion of
     Temperance', 1829, p. 10.
85. 'Preserving a Free Society', undated publication of Christian Voice.
86. Ibid.
87. Smidt and Kellstedt, 'Evangelicalism and Survey Research', p. 91.
88. Michael Hechter, *Principles of Group Solidarity* (Berkeley: University of
     California Press, 1987).
89. Stott, *Issues Facing Christians Today* , p. 131.
90. Joseph Gusfield, *Symbolic Crusade* (Urbana, Illinois: University of Illinois
     Press, 1963).

4 TEMPERANCE POLITICS IN BRITAIN AND AMERICA

1. *Proceedings of the Baptist World Congress* (London: Baptist Union, 1905), p. 258.
2. 1 Corinthians 6: 9–11. All biblical quotations are from the Revised Standard Version (New York: Oxford University Press, 1973).
3. Quoted in Lilian Lewis Shiman, *Crusade against Drink in Victorian England* (New York: St. Martin's Press, 1988), p. 44.
4. 'An Address Delivered by William Freeman Before the First Temperance Society of Cherryfield, Maine, 1820' (Cherryfield, 1820), p. 58.
5. 'History of Blackburn's First Temperance Society: 1831–1931' (Blackburn, 1931).
6. Shiman, *Crusade against Drink in Victorian England*, Chapter 3.
7. Norman H. Clark, *Deliver Us from Evil* (New York: Norton, 1976); and Jack Blocker, *American Temperance Movements: Cycles of Reform* (Boston: Twayne, 1989).
8. Brian Harrison, *Drink and the Victorians* (London: Faber and Faber, 1971), Chapter 3.
9. Blocker, *American Temperance Movements: Cycles of Reform*, p. 97.
10. *Proceedings of the Baptist World Congress* (London: Baptist Union, 1905), p. 257.
11. 'The Third Annual Meeting of the Virginia Society for the Promotion of Temperance, 1829'.
12. 'Christian Witness Bearing against the Sin of Intemperance' (Edinburgh, 1854).
13. *Proceedings of the Baptist World Congress* (London: Baptist Union, 1905), p. 261.
14. 'The Prohibition Movement: Proceedings of the National Convention for the Prohibition of the Liquor Traffic' (Newcastle-on-Tyne, 1897).
15. 'Minutes of the Seventy-seventh Session of the New England Annual Conference of the Methodist Episcopal Church' (Boston, 1876), p. 25.
16. Quoted in Harrison, *Drink and the Victorians*, p. 182.
17. 'Christian Witness Bearing against the Sin of Intemperance' (Edinburgh, 1854).
18. 'The Design and Constitution of Temperance Societies' (Edinburgh, 1830).
19. 'Minutes of the One Hundred and Tenth Seventy-Session of the New England Annual Conference of the Methodist Episcopal Church' (Boston, 1906), p. 90.
20. *Proceedings of the Seventh Annual Session of the Baptist Congress, 1888* (New York: Baptist Congress, 1889), p. 45.
21. Emory Aldrich, 'Prohibitory Legislation: A Paper Read Before the American Social Science Association' (Saratoga, New York, 1881), p. 8.
22. 'The New Christianity: An Appeal to the Clergy and to All Men' (New York, 1887), p. 25.
23. 'The Prohibition Movement: Proceedings of the National Convention for the Prohibition of the Liquor Traffic' (Newcastle-on-Tyne, 1897), p. 157.
24. 'The New Christianity: An Appeal to the Clergy and to All Men' (New York, 1887), p. 32.

25. 'The Prohibition Movement: Proceedings of the National Convention for the Prohibition of the Liquor Traffic' (Newcastle-on-Tyne, 1897), p. 236.
26. J. M. Stearns, 'The Constitutional Prohibitionist' (New York: National Temperance Society, 1889).
27. Lyman Beecher, quoted in Edwin S. Gaustad (ed.), *A Documentary History of Religion in America* (Grand Rapids, Michigan: William B. Eerdmans, 1982), p. 327.
28. Beecher, quoted in Gaustad, ibid., p. 130.
29. *Proceedings of the Baptist World Congress* (London: Baptist Union, 1905), p. 262.
30. Harrison, *Drink and the Victorians*, Chapter 8 and Jack Blocker, *American Temperance Movements: Cycles of Reform*, p. 24.
31. Irving Fisher, 'Can Prohibition Drive out Drink?', undated pamphlet.
32. E. J. Wheeler, 'Prohibition: The Principle, the Policy, the Party' (New York, 1889), p. 28.
33. Rev. A. M. Richardson, 'Prohibition in Kansas: Its Results and Present Status' (Ottawa, Kansas, 1882), p. 4.
34. Rev. W. H. Ten Eyck, 'Total Abstinence is Not Scriptural Temperance' (New York, 1885).
35. 'Christian Witness Bearing against the Sin of Intemperance' (Edinburgh, 1854).
36. Rev. W. H. Ten Eyck, 'Total Abstinence is Not Scriptural Temperance' (New York, 1885).
37. Rev. Herrick Johnson, 'The Wine of the Word and the Word Concerning Wine' (Philadelphia, 1872).
38. 'Communion Wine: A Critical Examination of Scripture Words' (New York, 1886).
39. Dr John Ellis, 'The Fruit of the Vine: Unfermented or Fermented – Which?' (New York, 1894).
40. *The Temperance Bible Commentary* (National Temperance Publication Depot, New York, 1894).
41. Shiman, *Crusade against Drink in Victorian England*, p. 19.
42. 'Christian Witness Bearing against the Sin of Intemperance' (Edinburgh, 1854).
43. Harrison, *Drink and the Victorians*, p. 181. For an excellent discussion of the religious activism in British temperance groups see Harrison, Chapter 8.
44. Jack S. Blocker, Jr, *Give to the Winds Thy Fears: The Women's Temperance Crusade, 1873–1874* (Westport, CT: Greenwood Press, 1985), Chapter 3.
45. For the best histories of the British Temperance Movement, see Harrison, *Drink and the Victorians*; D. A. Hamer, *The Politics of Electoral Pressure: A Study in the History of Victorian Reform Agitation* (Sussex: Harvester Press, 1977); A. E. Dingle, *The Campaign for Prohibition in Victorian England* (London: Croom Helm, 1980); and Shiman, *Crusade against Drink in Victorian England*.
46. 'The Prohibition Movement: Proceedings of the National Convention for the Prohibition of the Liquor Traffic' (Newcastle-on-Tyne, 1897), p. 53.
47. For a good treatment of local government in Britain, see Howard Elcock, *Local Government: Politicians, Professionals and the Public in Local Authorities* (London: Methuen Press, 1982).

48. Ira Katznelson, 'Working-Class Formation and the State: Nineteenth-Century England in American Perspective', in Dietrich Rueschemeyer, Peter B. Evans and Theda Skocpol (eds), *Bringing the State Back In* (Cambridge: Cambridge University Press, 1985), pp. 44–74.

49. 'The Prohibition Movement: Proceedings of the National Convention for the Prohibition of the Liquor Traffic' (Newcastle-on-Tyne, 1897), p. 258.

50. Ibid., p. 248.

51. See Robert Currie, Alan Gilbert, and Lee Horsley, *Churches and Church-goers in the British Isles since* 1700 (Oxford: Clarendon Press, 1977), p. 25; and D.W. Bebbington, *Evangelicals in Modern Britain: A History from the 1730s to the 1980s* (London: Unwin Hyman, 1989), Chapter 4.

52. For a discussion of these pan-evangelical organizations, see Roger H. Martin, *Evangelicals United: Ecumenical Stirrings in Pre-Victorian Britain* (Metuchen, NJ: Scarecrow Press, 1983); and Kenneth Hylson-Smith, *Evangelicals in the Church of England: 1734–1984* (Edinburgh: T. and T. Clark, 1988), Chapter 6.

53. For some good historical accounts of nineteenth-century English religious history, see Alan Gilbert, *Religion and Society in Industrial England* (London: Longman, 1976); E. R. Norman, *Church and State in England* (Oxford: Clarendon Press, 1976); Currie, Gilbert and Horsley, *Churches and Church-goers in the British Isles since 1700*; David Edwards, *Christian England, Volume Three* (Grand Rapids: Eerdmans, 1984); Adrian Hastings, *A History of English Christianity* (London: Collins, 1986); and G.I.T. Machin, *Politics and the Churches in Great Britain: 1869–1921* (Oxford: Clarendon Press, 1987).

54. Currie, Gilbert and Horsley, *Churches and Churchgoers in the British Isles since 1700*, p. 25.

55. Norman, *Church and State in England*, p. 95; Hylson-Smith, *Evangelicals in the Church of England*, p. 177; Martin, *Evangelicals United*, p. 200; and Bebbington, *Evangelicals in Modern Britain*, p. 97.

56. See Hylson-Smith, ibid., p. 177.

57. David Martin, *A General Theory of Secularization* (New York: Harper and Row, 1978), p. 16.

58. Currie, Gilbert and Horsley, *Churches and Churchgoers in the British Isles since 1700*, p. 107.

59. Kenneth Wald, *Crosses on the Ballot: Patterns of British Voter Alignments since 1885* (Princeton: Princeton University Press, 1983), Chapter 6.

60. 'The United Kingdom Alliance Monthly Papers' (Manchester, 1859).

61. 'The Liquor Question: What the Rival Parties Say and How the Liquor Laws of the World Work' (London, 1893), p. 18.

62. *The London Alliance Review* 2 (July 1899), p. 5.

63. See Hamer, *The Politics of Electoral Pressure*, pp. 27–30.

64. For statistics on the registered electorate, see Anthony Wood, *Nineteenth Century Britain, 1815–1914*, 2nd edn (London: Longman, 1982), p. 437.

65. Samuel Beer, *Modern British Politics* (London: Faber and Faber, 1965), p. 48.

66. See Harrison, *Drink and the Victorians*, Chapter 8.

67. Beer, *Modern British Politics*, Chapter 2.

68. Party votes are defined as ones in which 90 per cent of one party faced 90 per

cent of the other. For excellent discussions of the political effects of electoral reform, see J. P. D. Dunbabin, 'Electoral Reforms and their Outcome in the United Kingdom, 1865–1900 in T. R. Gourvish and Alan O'Day, *Later Victorian Britain, 1867–1900* (London: Macmillan, 1988), pp. 93–125; and John Garrard, 'Parties, Members and Voters after 1867', in Gourvish and O'Day, ibid., pp. 127–50.

69. Dingle, *The Campaign for Prohibition in Victorian England*, p. 14; Harrison, *Drink and the Victorians*, pp. 240–4; and Hamer, *The Politics of Electoral Pressure,* Chapter 10.
70. Quoted in Hamer, *The Politics of Electoral Pressure*, p. 208.
71. Quoted in Shimon, *Crusade against Drink in Victorian England.* p. 28.
72. See Dingle, *The Campaign for Prohibition in Victorian England*, p. 143, and Shiman, *Crusade against Drink in Victorian England*, p. 101.
73. Quoted in Hamer, *The Politics of Electoral Pressure,* p. 235.
74. Harrison, *Drink and the Victorians*, p. 270.
75. Dingle, *The Campaign for Prohibition in Victorian England, p. 20.
76. 'The Prohibition Movement: Proceedings of the National Convention for the Prohibition of the Liquor Traffic' (Newcastle-on-Tyne, 1897), p. 259.
77. Ibid., p. 259.
78. *The London Alliance Review* 3 (October 1899), p. 8.
79. Hamer, *The Politics of Electoral Pressure*, p. 41.
80. Shiman, *Crusade against Drink in Victorian England*, p. 229.
81. 'The Prohibition Movement: Proceedings of the National Convention for the Prohibition of the Liquor Traffic' (Newcastle-on-Tyne, 1897), p. 61.
82. Ibid., p. 58.
83. *London Alliance Review* 3 (October 1899).
84. 'The Liquor Question: What the Rival Parties Say and How the Liquor Laws of the World Work' (London, 1893), p. 18.
85. See Hamer, *The Politics of Electoral Pressure,* Chapter 1.
86. *London Alliance Review* 3 (October 1899), p. 3.
87. 'The Prohibition Movement: Proceedings of the National Convention for the Prohibition of the Liquor Traffic' (Newcastle-on-Tyne, 1897), p. 258.
88. For historical reviews of prohibition in the United States, see Charles Merz, *The Dry Decade* (New York: Doubleday, 1931); Herbert Asbury, *The Grand Illusion* (New York: The Greenwood Press, 1968); Sydney Ahlstrom, *A Religious History of the American People* (New Haven: Yale University Press, 1972), Chapter 51; Norman H. Clark, *Deliver Us From Evil* (New York: Norton, 1976); Austin Kerr, *Organized for Prohibition: A New History of the Anti-Saloon League* (New Haven: Yale University Press, 1985); A. James Reichley, *Religion In American Public Life* (Washington: The Brookings Institution, 1985), Chapter 5; and Jack S. Blocker Jr, *American Temperance Movements* (Twayne: Boston, 1989).
89. For the best treatment of the Women's Christian Temperance Union, see Jack S. Blocker, *Give to the Winds Thy Fears: The Women's Temperance Crusade, 1873–1874* (Westport, CT: Greenwood Press, 1985).
90. Ibid., p. 62; and Kerr, *Organized for Prohibition,* Chapter 2.
91. 'A Prohibition Party: Will it Advance Prohibition?', undated publication of the National Temperance Society.
92. Ahlstrom, *A Religious History of the American People*, Chapter 40; and Reichley, *Religion in American Public Life*, Chapter 5.

93. E. J. Wheeler, 'Prohibition: The Principle, the Policy, the Party' (New York, 1889), p. 169.
94. For a discussion of Rauschenbusch and the Social Gospel Movement, see Ahlstrom, *A Religious History of the American People*, Chapter 47 and Clark, *Deliver Us from Evil*, p. 121. See Kerr, *Organized for Prohibition*, pp. 75–6 for a discussion of church support for the Anti-Saloon League.
95. *The Christian Advocate*, 15 February 1890 (Nashville: General Organ of the Methodist Church South).
96. John G. Woolley, 'Prohibition: With the People Behind it' (Washington, DC, 1911), p. 4.
97. For the best histories of the Anti-Saloon League, see Blocker, *American Temperance Movements*, Chapter 4 and Kerr, *Organized for Prohibition*.
98. Ahlstrom, *A Religious History of the American People*, p. 843.
99. Rev. A. M. Richardson, 'Prohibition in Kansas: Its Results and Present Status' (Ottawa, Kansas: 1882).
100. Clark, *Deliver Us from Evil*, p. 113; and Blocker, *American Temperance Movements*, p. 102.
101. Ernest Charrington (ed.), *The Anti-Saloon League Yearbook* (Westerville, Ohio: The American Issue Press, 1911), p. 19.
102. See Blocker, *American Temperance Movements*, p. 103, and Jimmie Lewis Franklin, *Born Sober: Prohibition in Oklahoma, 1907–1959* (Norman, Oklahoma: University of Oklahoma Press, 1971).
103. For excellent discussions of late-nineteenth-century American politics, see Leonard D. White, *The Republican Era: 1869–1901* (New York: Macmillan, 1958); and Stephen Skowronek, *Building a New American State: The Expansion of National Administrative Capacities, 1877–1920* (Cambridge: Cambridge University Press, 1982).
104. Stephen Skowronek, *Building a New American State*, Chapter 1.
105. Noah McFarland, 'Prohibition in Kansas: Facts, Not Opinions' (Topeka, 1889), p. 18.
106. John G. Woolley, 'Prohibition: With the People Behind it' (Washington, DC, 1911), p. 5.
107. E. J. Wheeler, 'Prohibition: The Principle, the Policy, the Party' (New York, 1889), p. 176.
108. For a good example of such a document, see J. N. Stearns, 'The Constitutional Prohibitionist' (New York, 1889).
109. Katznelson, 'Working-Class Formation and the State'; and Skowronek, *Building a New American State*, pp. 21–2.
110. Clark, *Deliver Us from Evil*, p. 102.
111. See Kerr, *Organized for Prohibition*, pp. 109–13 and Blocker, *American Temperance Movements*, pp. 104–11 for a discussion of the 1905 Ohio gubernatorial campaign.
112. White, *The Republican Era: 1869–1901*; Richard J. Jenson, *Grass Roots Politics: 1854–1983* (Westport, CT: Greenwood Press, 1983); and Skowronek, *Building a New American State*.
113. 'Debater's Handbook on Prohibition' (Washington, DC, 1921), p. 17.
114. Blocker, *American Temperance Movements*, Chapters 6 and 8.
115. Joseph Gusfield, *Symbolic Crusade* (Urbana, Illinois: University of Illinois Press, 1963).
116. Ahlstrom, *A Religious History of the American People*, p. 749.

117. *Proceedings of the Seventh Annual Session of the Baptist Congress, 1888* (New York: Baptist Congress, 1889), p. 90.
118. Paul Kleppner, *The Cross of Culture* (New York: The Free Press, 1970).
119. For an argument which links evangelical ideas to the needs of an expanding capitalist economy, see Charles Foster, *An Errand of Mercy: The Evangelical Front, 1790–1837* (Chapel Hill: The University of North Carolina Press, 1960), Paul E. Johnson, *A Shopkeeper's Millennium: Society and Revivals in Rochester, New York, 1815–1837* (New York: Hill and Wang, 1978); Shiman, *Crusade against Drink in Victorian England*; and A. E. Dingle, *The Campaign for Prohibition in Victorian England.*
120. Shiman, *Crusade against Drink in Victorian England*, p. 2.
121. Ibid., p. 2.
122. Dingle, *The Campaign for Prohibition in Victorian England*, p. 18.
123. Johnson, *A Shopkeeper's Millennium*, p. 81.
124. Ibid., p. 139.
125. Harrison, *Drink and the Victorians*, p. 378.
126. Austin Kerr, *Organized for Prohibition.*

5 THE POLITICAL MOBILIZATION OF EVANGELICALS, FROM 1960 TO THE PRESENT

1. For the best interpretations of this period of American church history, see Sydney Ahlstrom, *A Religious History of the American People* (New Haven: Yale University Press, 1972); Dean M. Kelley, *Why Conservative Churches are Growing* (New York: Harper and Row, 1972); Martin E. Marty, *Religion and Republic* (Boston: Beacon Press, 1987), Part III; James Davison Hunter, *American Evangelicalism: Conservative Religion and the Quandary of Modernity* (New Brunswick, NJ: Rutgers University Press, 1983); Wade Clark Roof and William McKinney, *American Mainline Religion* (New Brunswick, NJ: Rutgers University Press, 1987); Kenneth D. Wald, *Religion and Politics in the United States* (New York: St. Martin's Press, 1987); and Robert Wuthnow, *The Restructuring of American Religion* (Princeton: Princeton University Press, 1988).
2. The best interpretations of contemporary British evangelicalism are Steve Bruce, 'The Persistence of Religion: Conservative Protestantism in the United Kingdom', *The Sociological Review* 31 (1983): 453–69; Paul A. Welsby, *A History of the Church of England* (Oxford: Oxford University Press, 1984); Randall Manwaring, *From Controversy to Co-Existence: Evangelicals in the Church of England* (Cambridge: Cambridge University Press, 1985); Kenneth Hylson-Smith, *Evangelicals in the Church of England: 1734–1984* (Edinburgh: T. and T. Clark Press, 1988), Chapters 20–6; and D. W. Bebbington, *Evangelicalism in Modern Britain* (London: Unwin Hyman, 1989), Chapters 7–9. For accounts from within evangelical circles, see John Stott, *Issues Facing Christians Today* (London: Marshall Morgan and Scott, 1984); Rene Padilla and Chris Sugden, *How Evangelicals Endorsed Social Responsibility* (Brancote, England: Grove Books); Clive Calver, *He Brings Us Together* (London: Hodder and Stoughton, 1987); Michael Saward, *Evangelicals on*

the Move (London: Mowbray Press, 1987); and David Winter, *Battered Bride?* (Estbourne, England: Monarch Publications, 1988).

3. Robert Currie, Alan Gilbert and Lee Horsley, *Churches and Churchgoers* (Oxford: Clarendon Press, 1977), p. 100.
4. Roof and McKinney, *American Mainline Religion*, Chapter 1.
5. Saward, *Evangelicals on the Move*, p. 80.
6. 'Leadership Through Cooperation', undated publication of NAE.
7. Interview with John Ling, 28 April 1989.
8. For good accounts of evangelical church growth, see Dean M. Kelley, *Why Conservative Churches are Growing*; Dean R. Hoge and David A. Roozen, *Understanding Church Growth and Decline: 1950–1978* (New York: Pilgrim Press, 1978); and Wade Clark Roof and William McKinney, *American Mainline Religion*.
9. See Manwaring, *From Controversy to Co-Existence*; Calver, *He Brings Us Together*, and Saward, *Evangelicals on the Move* for a discussion of the role played by the Billy Graham crusades in British Evangelicalism. Graham has made numerous trips to England since 1954, the last taking place in the Summer of 1989.
10. The best estimates of the strength of British evangelicals can be found in Winter, *Battered Bride?*, Chapter 8; Saward, *Evangelicals on the Move*, Chapter 3; and Welsby, *A History of the Church of England*.
11. See Peter Brierley (ed.), *The United Kingdom Christian Handbook 1987/88 and 1992/93*, pp. 226–8 and pp. 16–20 for a list of the groups affiliated with the Evangelical Alliance.
12. For a good discussion of the growth of evangelical organizations in England, see Steve Bruce, 'The Student Christian Movement: A Nineteenth Century New Religious Movement and its Vicissitudes', *The Journal of Sociology and Social Policy* 2 (1982): 67–82.
13. Roof and McKinney, *American Mainline Religion*, p. 23.
14. 'Leadership Through Cooperation', undated publication of the National Association of Evangelicals.
15. Nathan A. Hatch and Michael S. Hamilton, 'Can Evangelicalism Survive its own Success?' *Christianity Today*, 5 October 1992: 20–31.
16. For a description of the growth of evangelical organizations, see Wuthnow, *The Restructuring of American Religion*, Chapter 8.
17. Adrian Hastings, *A History of English Christianity: 1920–1985* (London: Collins, 1986), p. 33; and Marty, *Religion and Republic*, p. 22.
18. *Vital Statistics of the United States, 1987: Vol. III: Marriages and Divorce* (Hyatsville, Maryland: United States Department of Health and Human Resources, 1991).
19. Peter Brierley (ed.), *The United Kingdom Christian Handbook 1992/93*, p. 530.
20. Renata T. Forste and Tim B. Heaton, 'Initiation of Sexual Activity among Female Adolescents', *Youth and Society* 19 (1988): 250–68; and Maria A. Vinovskis, *An Epidemic of Adolescent Pregnancy?* (Oxford: Oxford University Press, 1988).
21. Roof and McKinney, *American Mainline Religion*, p. 70.
22. Hunter, *American Evangelicalism*, p. 85; and *George Gallup Polls America on Religion* (Princeton, NJ: The Gallup Organization, 1981), pp. 55–7 and 160–9.

23. Roger Jowell and Colin Airey, *British Social Attitudes: The 1984 Report* (Aldershot: Gower, 1984), pp. 136–43; and Stuart Rothenberg and Frank Newport, *The Evangelical Voter* (Washington: The Free Congress Research and Education Foundation, 1984).

24. For good reviews of abortion politics in America, see Raymond Tatlovich and Byron Daynes, *The Politics of Abortion: A Study of Community Conflict in Public Policymaking* (New York: Praeger, 1981); Eva Rubin, *Abortion, Politics and the Courts: Roe v. Wade and its Aftermath* (Greenwood, CT: Greenwood Press, 1982); Kristin Luker, *Abortion and the Politics of Motherhood* (Berkeley: University of California Press, 1984); and Christopher Tietze, Jacqueline Danoch Forrest and Stanley K. Henshaw, 'United States of America', in Paul Sachdev (ed.), *International Handbook on Abortion* (Greenwood, CT: Greenwood Press, 1988).

25. 'A Birth Certificate', undated publication of the Christian Action Council.

26. For a discussion of the Clergy Consultation Service, see Andrew Merton, *Enemies of Choice* (Boston: Beacon Press, 1981), pp. 40–60, and Nanette J. Davis, *From Crime to Choice: The Transformation of Abortion in America* (Westport, CT: Greenwood Press, 1985), pp. 129–42. For a more general discussion of the role of the church in the abortion debate, see J. Robert Nelson, 'The Divided Mind of Protestant Christians', in Thomas Hilbers, Dennis Horan, David Mail (eds), *New Perspectives on Human Abortion* (Frederick, MD: University Publications of America, 1981), pp. 387–404.

27. Randall Terry, *Operation Rescue* (Binghamton, New York: Whitaker House, 1988), p. 159.

28. For a description of these organizations, see *The Encyclopedia of Associations* (Detroit: Gale Research, 1988).

29. For good discussions of abortion politics in Britain, see David Marsh and Joanna Chambers, *Abortion Politics* (London: Junction Books, 1981); Victoria Greenwood and Jock Young, *Abortion on Demand* (London: Plato Press, 1983); David Marsh and Joanna Chambers, 'The Abortion Lobby: Pluralism at Work?,' in David Marsh (ed.), *Pressure Politics: Interest Groups in Britain* (London: Junction Books, 1983), pp. 144–65; Colin Francome *Abortion Freedom: A Worldwide Movement* (London: George Allen and Unwin, 1984); and Paul Sachdev (ed.), *International Handbook on Abortion* (New York: Greenwood Press, 1988).

30. Marsh and Chambers, *Abortion Politics*, p. 167.

31. See Marsh and Chambers, *Abortion Politics*, p. 72; and Bridget Pym, *Pressure Groups and the Permissive Society* (Newton Abbot, 1974), p. 56.

32. Interviews with David Paton, Liason Officer, SPUC, 9 May 1989 and Dr John Ling, organizer of Evangelicals for LIFE, 28 April 1989.

33. For an excellent discussion of the relation between opposition to abortion and related social values, see Kristin Luker, *Abortion and the Politics of Motherhood*, Chapter 7.

34. 'There's More You Need to Know', undated publication of Christian Action Council.

35. 'Family Matters', a publication of the Conservative Family Campaign, February 1989.

36. 'Abortion: Where Have All the Babies Gone?', undated publication of Christian Action Council.

37. 'A Birth Certificate', undated publication of Christian Action Council.

38. Billy James Hargis, *Abortion on Trial* (Tulsa, Oklahoma: Americans Against Abortion, 1982), p. 9.

39. Corwin Smidt and Lyman Kellstedt, 'Evangelicalism and Survey Research: Interpretive Problems and Substantive Findings', in Richard Neuhaus (ed.), *The Bible, Politics and Democracy* (Grand Rapids, Michigan: William B. Eerdmans, 1987), p. 91.

40. 'Abortion: Where Have All the Babies Gone?', undated publication of Christian Action Council.

41. 'The Roundtable Report', undated publication of the Religious Roundtable.

42. 'Introducing the Christian Affirmation Campaign', undated publication of the Christian Affirmation Campaign.

43. William H. Marshner, 'The New Creatures and the New Politics', undated publication of the Religious Roundtable, p. 11.

44. 'Working to Restore Traditional Values in America', undated publication of the Traditional Values Coalition.

45. 'Christian Voice Scorecard', a publication of Christian Voice, July/August, 1988.

46. 'Pro-Life Advocate: Magazine of the Christian Action Council', 1989.

47. 'Abortion: Where Have All the Babies Gone?', undated publication of Christian Action Council.

48. Dan Lyons and Billy James Hargis, *Thou Shalt Not Kill . . . My Babies* (Tulsa, Oklahoma: Christian Crusade Publications, 1977), p. 50.

49. Chris John Miko and Edward Weilant (eds), *Opinions 1990* (Detroit: Gale Research, 1991).

50. Lyons and Hargis, *Thou Shalt Not Kill . . . My Babies* , p. 31.

51. Terry, *Operation Rescue*, p. 215.

52. 'Abortion: Where Have All the Babies Gone?', undated publication of Christian Action Council.

53. Ibid.

54. Billy James Hargis, *Abortion on Trial* , p. 31.

55. 'Join the Winning Team', undated publication of the American Life League.

56. Mailing from Keith Tucci, Director of Operation Rescue National, 11 May 1991.

57. Hargis, *Abortion on Trial*, p. 31.

58. Terry, *Operation Rescue*, p. 127.

59. 'No Cheap Solutions', undated publication of the Nonviolent Action Project.

60. Mailing from Keith Tucci, Director of Operation Rescue National, 11 May 1991.

61. Ross K. Baker, Luarily K. Epstein, and Rodney D. Forth, 'Matters of Life and Death: Social, Political and Religious Correlates of Attitudes on Abortion', *American Politics Quarterly* 9 (January 1981): 89–102.

62. 'Life Anglicans', undated publication of Life Anglicans.

63. 'Evangelicals for Life', undated publication of Evangelicals for Life.

64. 'Educational Services for the Schools', undated publication of SPUC.

65. 'Evangelicals for Life', undated publication of Evangelicals for Life.

66. 'Abortion: A Matter of Life and Death', report of the Public Morals Committee of the Evangelical Presbyterian Church, 1981, p. 11.

67. 'Life Newsletter', November 1988, p. 3.

68. Ibid., p. 4.

69. John H. Court, *Pornography: A Christian Critique* (Downers Grove, Illinois:

Intervarsity Press, 1980), p. 13. For a good review of pornography in America, see Susan Gruber and Joan Hoff (eds), *For Adult Users Only: The Dilemma of Violent Pornography* (Bloomington, Indiana: Indiana University Press, 1989).

70. Mary Whitehouse, *A Most Dangerous Woman?* (Tring: Lion, 1982) p. 162.
71. 'No Church, No Ministry, No Pulpit, He is Called Religious Right's Star', *New York Times*, 5 June 1990, p. 22.
72. Whitehouse, *A Most Dangerous Woman?*, p. 13.
73. For a discussion of the anti-pornography movement in Britain, see Roy Wallis, *Salvation and Protest* (London: Frances Pinter, 1979); Roy Wallis and Steve Bruce, *Sociological Theory, Religion and Collective Action* (Belfast: The Queens University Press, 1986); and M. A. McCarthy and R. A. Moodie, 'Parliament and Pornography: The 1978 Child Protection Act', *Parliamentary Affairs* 34 (Winter 1981): 47–62.
74. 'The Peril of Pornography', undated publication of Citizens Against Pornography'.
75. 'Family Matters', newsletter of the Conservative Family Campaign, February 1989.
76. John Court, *Pornography: A Christian Critique*, p. 53.
77. 'Information and Resources for Concerned Citizens', undated publication of the National Coalition Against Pornography.
78. 'Pornography and Your Child', undated publication of the Conservative Family Campaign.
79. 'The Perils of Pornography', undated publication of Citizens Against Pornography.
80. 'Your Church is Needed to make a Difference in these Difficult Times', undated publication of the National Association of Evangelicals.
81. Anna Grear, 'Towards a Biblical View of Pornography', undated publication of CARE, p. 6.
82. Ibid., p. 7.
83. 'The Perils of Pornography', undated publication of Citizens Against Pornography.
84. Hunter, *American Evangelicalism*, p. 85.
85. Raymond Johnson, 'A Biblical View of Pornography', undated publication of CARE.
86. 'The Perils of Pornography', undated publication of Citizens Against Pornography.
87. Court, *Pornography: A Christian Critique*, p. 55.
88. Jerry Falwell, *Listen America* (New York: Doubleday, 1980), p. 198.
89. Richard Enrico, Founder of Citizens Against Pornography, in a sermon titled 'What Does the Bible Say About Sexual Sin?', 14 January 1989.
90. For a good review of the Supreme Court cases dealing with religion, see Philip B. Kurland, 'The Supreme Court, Compulsory Education, and the First Amendment's Religion Clause', *West Virginia Law Review* 75 (April 1973): 213–45; and Kenneth Wald, *Religion and Politics in the United States*, Chapter 5. For a good review of religion and education in America, see James E. Wood (ed.), *Religion, The State and Education* (Waco, Texas: Baylor University Press, 1984). For an argument which claims that public school texts exhibit a bias against religion and traditional family values, see Paul C.

Vitz, 'Religion and Traditional Values in Public School Textbooks', *Public Interest* 84 (Summer 1986): 79–90.

91. Terry, *Operation Rescue*, p. 171.

92. For good discussions of the evangelical protest against public schools, see James C. Carper, 'The Christian Day School', in James C. Carper and Thomas C. Hunt (eds), *Religious Schooling in America* (Birmingham, Alabama: Religious Education Press, 1984), pp. 110–29; and James C. Carper, 'The State and the Christian Day School', in James E. Wood (ed.), *Religion and the State: Essays in Honor of Leo Pfeffer* (Waco, Texas: Baylor University Press, 1985), pp. 211–34. For a good analysis of a Christian day-school, see Alan Peshkin, *God's Choice: The Total World of a Fundamentalist Christian School* (Chicago: The University of Chicago Press, 1986).

93. 'The Roundtable's Position on Controversial Issues', undated publication of the Religious Roundtable.

94. 'The Phyllis Schlafly Report', October 1989, p. 4.

95. Jerry Falwell, *The Fundamentalist Phenomenon* (New York: Doubleday, 1981), p. 147.

96. Ibid., p. 55.

97. 'The Round Table', undated publication of the Religious Roundtable.

98. Mailing from Randall Terry, 16 July 1990.

99. See Carper, 'The State and the Christian Day School', and Peshkin, *God's Choice*, for a good discussion of Christian day-schools.

100. James L. Guth, 'The Politics of the Evangelical Right', paper prepared for delivery at the 1981 Annual Meeting of the American Political Science Association, New York. For a case study analysis of the conflict between a church school and the state, see 'In Nebraska, the War between Church and State Rages on', *Christianity Today* 17 February 1984: 32–36.

101. For an analysis of the Arkansas case, see Langdon Gilkey, *Creationism on Trial: Evolution and God at Little Rock* (San Francisco: Harper and Row, 1985).

102. 'Battle over Teaching of Creation May Rumble Far from California', *New York Times*, 27 July 1989.

103. For a good discussion of British educational policy, see Robert Waddington, 'The Church and Educational Policy', in George Moyser, *Church and Politics Today: The Role of the Church of England in Contemporary Politics* (Edinburgh: T. and T. Clark, 1985), pp. 221–55. For a discussion of Christian day schools in Britain, see Charles Martin, 'Have the Schools Lost Their Way?', Grove Books Pastoral Series No. 4.

104. Mary Whitehouse, *A Most Dangerous Woman?*, p. 47.

105. 'Bringing the Family Back into Focus', undated publication of the Conservative Family Campaign.

106. John Burns and Colin Hart, *The Crisis in Religious Education* (London: The Educational Trust, 1988), p. 20.

107. 'Being a School Governor', undated publication of CARE.

108. 'Is there not a Cause?', undated publication of the Religious Roundtable.

109. 'Help for the Postabortal Woman', undated publication of Focus on the Family.

110. I am indebted to Ken Wald for helping to make this point clear to me.

111. David Edgar, 'The Free of the Good', in Ruth Levitus (ed.), *The Ideology of*

186 *Notes*

the New Right (Cambridge: Polity Press, 1986), p. 56; and Peter Jenkins, *Mrs Thatcher's Revolution* (Cambridge: Harvard University Press, 1988), p. 74.

112. Furio Colombo, *God in America: Religion and Politics in the United States* (New York: Columbia University Press, 1984), p. 53.
113. Ronald Inglehart, *Culture Shift in Advanced Industrial Society* (Princeton, NJ: Princeton University Press, 1990), Chapter 6.
114. Andrew Merton, *Enemies of Choice*, p. 180.
115. Alan L. Page and Donald C. Clelland, 'The Kanawha Textbook Controversy: A Study of the Politics of Life Style Concern', *Social Forces* 57 (1978): 265–81; Louise Lorentzen, 'Evangelical Life Style Concerns Expressed in Political Action', *Sociological Analysis* 41 (1980): 144–54; and John Simpson, 'Moral Issues and Status Politics', in Robert C. Liebman and Robert Wuthnow (eds), *The New Christian Right* (New York: Aldine, 1982), pp. 188–205.
116. Mayer N. Zald and John D. McCarthy, 'Religious Groups as Crucibles of Social Movements', in Mayer N. Zald and John D. McCarthy, *Social Movements in an Organizational Society* (New Brunswick: Transaction Books, 1987), p. 69.
117. Robert C. Liebman, 'Mobilizing the Moral Majority', in Robert C. Liebman and Robert Wuthnow, *The New Christian Right*, p. 58.

6   POLITICAL STRUCTURES AND EVANGELICAL ACTIVISM

1. Chris Bazlington and Anne Cowens, *The Guardian Directory of Pressure Groups and Representative Associations* (London: Wilton House, 1976).
2. Elizabeth Hann Hastings and Philip K. Hastings (eds), *Index to International Public Opinion, 1979–1980, 1980–1981*, and *1984–1985* (Greenwich, CT: Greenwood Press, 1981), pp. 387, 392, and 397; and Floris W. Wood (ed.), *The American Profile: Opinions and Behavior* (Detroit: Gale Research, 1990), p. 549.
3. D. W. Bebbington, *Evangelicalism in Modern Britain: A History from the 1730s to the 1980s* (London: Unwin Hyman, 1989), Chapter 8.
4. For an excellent discussion of private members' bills, see David Marsh and Melvyn Read, *Private Members' Bills* (Cambridge: Cambridge University Press, 1988). For good reviews of the private members' legislation of the 1960s, see Bridget Pym, *Pressure Groups and the Permissive Society* (London: Newton Abbey, 1974); and Peter Richards, *Parliament and Conscience* (London: Allen and Unwin, 1970).
5. For good reviews of abortion politics in Britain, see Victoria Greenwood and Jack Young, *Abortion on Demand* (London: Plato Press, 1983); David Marsh and Joanna Chambers, *Abortion Politics* (London: Junction Books, 1981); and Colin Francome, *Abortion Freedom: A Worldwide Movement* (London: George Allen and Unwin, 1984).
6. For an excellent comparison of abortion policies in Western Europe and America, see Mary Ann Glendon, *Abortion and Divorce in Western Law* (Cambridge: Harvard University Press, 1987). See also, 'A World of Conflict Over Abortion', *World Press Review* (October 1992): 22–4.
7. Francome, *Abortion Freedom*, Chapter 4.

8. Paul Sachdev (ed.), *International Handbook on Abortion* (Greenwich, CT: Greenwood Press, 1988), p. 470; 'A World of Conflict over Abortion', *World Press Review* (October 1992): 22–4.

9. Marsh and Chambers, *Abortion Politics*, p. 156.

10. David Marsh, 'The Abortion Lobby: Pluralism at Work?', in David Marsh (ed.), *Pressure Politics* (London: Junction Books, 1983), pp. 144–65.

11. *Pro-Life Parliamentary Monitor*, May/June, 1988, a publication of SPUC.

12. *Life News*, undated publication of LIFE.

13. *Pro-Life Parliamentary Monitor*, a publication of SPUC, December 1988.

14. Ibid.

15. *Pro-Life Parliamentary Monitor*, a publication of SPUC, January/February 1989.

16. Prime Minister Margaret Thatcher, speech delivered at the 58th Conservative Women's National Conference, 25 May 1988.

17. *Pro-Life Parliamentary Monitor*, a publication of SPUC, December 1988.

18. See, for example, Howard Elcock, *Local Government: Politicians, Professionals, and the Public in Local Authorities* (London: Methuen Press, 1982); Ken Young, 'Local Government', in Dennis Kavanagh and Anthony Sheldon (eds), *The Thatcher Effect: A Decade of Change* (Oxford: Oxford University Press, 1989), pp. 124–33; and Hugh Butler, Ian G. Law, Robert Leach and Maurice Mullard, *Local Government and Thatcherism* (New York: Routledge, 1990). The strife in Britain over the community charge, or 'poll tax', shows how circumscribed is the power of the local government. Local authorities have historically collected revenues through property taxes. The community charge law passed by Parliament in 1989 abolished the property tax and established that the tax for local government services would be the same for everyone, rich and poor, within a community. Local councils were not asked to approve the new measure, nor did they have the power to overturn it; they were simply told to set the rate and collect it. Mrs Thatcher's government abolished a century-long precedent of local government power. Her assault on local government culminated in the abolition of the Greater London Council, a local body which radically opposed her public policies. For a review of the community charge, see Craig Whitney, 'Where All-Powerful Central Government Lives On', *New York Times Week in Review*, 6 May 1990, p. 3.

19. The interviews were conducted between January and June 1989 and included group leaders from SPUC and LIFE.

20. See, for example, Samuel H. Beer, *Modern British Politics* (London: Faber and Faber, 1965); S. E. Finer, *Comparative Government* (New York: Penguin Books, 1970); Richard Rose, *Politics in England* (Boston: Little, Brown and Company, 1980); Samuel Beer, *Britain Against Itself* (New York: W. W. Norton, 1982); Geoffrey Alderman, *Pressure Groups and Government in Britain* (London: Longman, 1984); Ian Derbyshire, *Politics in Britain: From Callaghan to Thatcher* (London: W. and R. Chambers, 1988); and Graham K. Wilson, 'American Interest Groups in Comparative Perspective', in Mark P. Petracca (ed.), *The Politics of Interests* (Boulder: Westview Press, 1992), pp. 80–95.

21. See, for example, David Marsh (ed.), *Pressure Groups: Interest Groups in Britain* (London: Junction Books, 1983); W. N. Coxall, *Political Realities:*

Parties and Pressure Groups (London: Longman, 1986); Michael Moran, 'The Changing World of British Pressure Groups', in Lynton Robins (ed.), *Political Institutions in Britain* (London: Longman, 1987); and Philip Norton, *The British Polity* (New York: Longman, 1991), Chapter 7.

22.   Michael Moran, 'The Changing World of British Pressure Groups', p. 181.

23.   W. N. Coxall, *Political Realities: Parties and Pressure Groups,* Chapter 5; and Lawrence Freedman, 'Thatcherism and Defence', in Dennis Kavanagh and Anthony Sheldon (eds), *The Thatcher Effect: A Decade of Change* (Oxford: Clarendon Press, 1989), pp. 143–53.

24.   Charles Clover, 'Green Thoughts for the Blues', *The Spectator*, February 1989, pp. 8–9; Ronald Bull, 'Tory Green Fingers', *The Times*, 9 February 1989, p. 6; John Hunt, 'Thatcher Calls for Stricter Targets', *The Financial Times*, 6 March 1989, p. 12; and Richard North and Nicholas Schoon, 'Thatcher to Urge Curbs on CFCs', *The Independent*, 2 March 1989, p. 8.

25.   Marsh and Read, *Private Members' Bills*, p. 184.

26.   For characteristic portraits of British political parties, see Robert McKenzie, *British Political Parties*, 2nd edn (London: Heinemann, 1964); S. E. Finer, *Comparative Government;* David Butler and David Stokes, *Political Change in Britain*, 2nd edn (Oxford: Basic Blackwell, 1989); and Philip Norton, *The British Polity*, Chapter 6.

27.   See, for example, Ivor Crewe, 'The Electorate: Partisan Dealignment Ten Years On', in Hugh Berrington (ed.), *Changes in British Government* (London: Case, 1984); Hugh Berrington, 'The Changing Party System', in Lynton Robins (ed.), *Political Institutions in Britain* (London: Longman, 1987); Dennis Kavanagh, *Thatcherism and British Politics: The End of Consensus?* (Oxford: Oxford University Press, 1987); and Michael Moran, 'The Changing World of British Pressure Groups'.

28.   Moran, 'The Changing World of British Pressure Groups', p. 185.

29.   See Marsh and Chambers, *Abortion Politics.*

30.   'Trade Unions and Abortion', undated publication of LIFE.

31.   For good reviews of the Thatcher years, see Philip Norton and Arthur Aughley, *Conservatives and Conservatism* (London: Temple Smith, 1981); Dennis Kavanagh, *Thatcherism and British Politics: The End of Consensus?* (Oxford: Oxford University Press, 1987); Brian Girvin (ed.), *The Transformation of Contemporary Conservatism* (London: Sage Publications, 1988); Anthony Hartley, 'After the Thatcher Decade', *Foreign Affairs* 68 (Winter 1989/90): 102–18; and Dennis Kavanagh and Anthony Sheldon (eds), *The Thatcher Effect: A Decade of Change* (Oxford: Oxford University Press, 1989). For excellent biographies of Thatcher, see Peter Jenkins, *Mrs Thatcher's Revolution* (Cambridge, Mass.: Harvard University Press, 1988); and Hugo Young, *One of Us* (London: Macmillan, 1989).

32.   For good general discussions of Sunday trading restrictions in Britain, see Peter Richards, *Parliament and Conscience*; and John Parker, *Father of the House* (London: Routledge and Kegan Paul, 1982). For discussions of the 1985/86 legislation, see Michael Schluter, *Keeping Sunday Special* (Basingstoke: Zondervan Press, 1988).

33.   Marsh and Read, *Private Members' Bills*, pp. 77–8. For a description of the Act, see, 'Action on Sunday Trading', undated publication of CARE.

34.   Interview with John Roberts, 5 September 1989.

35. There is no polling data on evangelical voting in Britain. The conclusions reached in this paragraph are drawn from interviews with evangelical group leaders, particularly with Tim Dean, editor of the evangelical journal *Third Way*.

36. David Denver, 'Britain: Centralized Parties with Decentralized Selection', in Michael Gallagher and Michael Marsh (eds), *Candidate Selection in Comparative Perspective* (London: Sage Publications, 1988), p. 59.

37. Peter Riddell, 'Cabinet and Parliament', in Dennis Kavanagh and Anthony Seldon (eds), *The Thatcher Effect: A Decade of Change* (Oxford: Oxford University Press, 1989), p. 110.

38. 'Pro-Life Parliamentary Monitor', a publication of SPUC, November 1988.

39. Pym, *Pressure Groups and the Permissive Society*, p. 92.

40. See Peter Hall, *Governing the Economy: The Politics of State Intervention in Britain and France* (Cambridge: Polity Press, 1986), Chapter 1, for a state-centric theory of public policymaking.

41. Dennis Kavanagh, 'The Changing Political Opposition', in Kavanagh and Sheldon, *The Thatcher Effect: A Decade of Change*, p. 98.

42. Raymond Tatlovich and Bryon Daynes, *The Politics of Abortion: A Study of Community Conflict and Public Policymaking* (New York: Praeger, 1981); Eva Rubin, *Abortion, Politics and the Courts: Roe v. Wade and its Aftermath* (Greenwich, CT: Greenwood Press, 1982); and Kristin Luker, *Abortion and the Politics of Motherhood* (Berkeley: University of California Press, 1984).

43. Judith Blake, 'The Abortion Decisions: Judicial Review and Public Opinion', in Edward Manier, William Liu and David Solomon, *Abortion: New Directions in Policy Studies* (Notre Dame, Indiana: University of Notre Dame Press, 1977), pp. 51–82.

44. Mary Ann Glendon, *Abortion and Divorce Law in Western Law* (Cambridge, Mass.: Harvard University Press, 1987), Chapter 1.

45. Luker, *Abortion and the Politics of Motherhood*, p. 142.

46. Tatlovich and Daynes, *The Politics of Abortion*, Chapter 5.

47. Blake, 'The Abortion Decisions: Judicial Review and Public Opinion', p. 52.

48. Robert Nelson, 'The Divided Mind of Protestant Christians', in Hilgers, Horan and Mall, *New Perspectives on Human Abortion* (Frederick, MD: University Publications, 1981), pp. 387–404.

49. For a description of these and other pro-life organizations, see *The Encyclopedia of Associations* (Detroit: Gale Research, 1988).

50. Tatlovich and Daynes, *The Politics of Abortion*, Chapter 5.

51. R. W. Apple, 'An Altered Political Climate Suddenly Surrounds Abortion', *The New York Times*, 13 October 1989, p. 1; and Linda Greenhouse, 'Five Justices Uphold U.S. Rules Curbing Abortion Services', *New York Times*, 24 May 1991, p. 1.

52. Julie Romer, 'Mixed Results on Both Sides Keep Spotlight on Abortion', *Congressional Quarterly*, 7 November 1992: 3591–2.

53. Ronald Reagan, *Abortion and the Conscience of the Nation* (Nashville, Tenn.: Thomas Nelson, 1984), p. 53.

54. Ronald Reagan, *In God We Trust* (Wheaton, Ill.: Tyndale, 1984), p. 12.

55. Eva Rubin, *Abortion, Politics and the Courts*, p. 56.

56. Felicity Barringer, 'Minnesota, Scene of Abortion Battles, Watches High Court for Key Moves', *New York Times*, 25 June 1989, p. 20; Michael

deCourchy Hinds, 'Pennsylvania Passes Anti-Abortion Measure', *New York Times*, 15 November 1989, p. 19; and Isabel Wilkerson, 'North Dakota a Hostile Landscape for Abortion', *New York Times*, 6 May 1990, p. 12.

57. Dick Andrews, 'Abortion-Free Zones: A Battle Plan for Pro-Life America', undated publication of American Life League.

58. Sara Rimer, 'Abortion Clinics Search for Doctors in Scarcity', *Los Angeles Times*, 3 March 1993, p. 7.

59. James Q. Wilson, *Political Organizations* (New York: Basic Books, 1973); Janet K. Boles, *The Politics of the Equal Rights Amendment* (New York: Longman, 1979); Michael McCann, *Taking Reform Seriously* (Ithaca: Cornell University Press, 1986); Byron Shafer, ' "Exceptionalism" in American Politics?' *Political Science* 22 (September 1989): 588–94; and Robert H. Salisbury, 'The Paradox of Interest Groups in Washington – More Groups, Less Clout', in Anthony King (ed.), *The New American Political System* (Washington: American Enterprise Institute, 1990), pp. 203–29.

60. Wilson, *Political Organizations*, p. 89.

61. Linda Greenhouse, 'Supreme Court, 5–4, Narrowing Roe v. Wade, Upholds Sharp State Limits on Abortions', *New York Times*, 4 July 1989, p. 1.

62. Michael McCann, *Taking Reform Seriously*.

63. Richard Neely, *How Courts Govern America* (New Haven: Yale University Press, 1981); and Richard Hodder-Williams, 'Litigation and Political Action: Making the Supreme Court Activist', in Robert Williams (ed.), *Explaining American Politics* (London: Routledge, 1990), pp. 116-43.

64. Timothy Egan, 'Anti-Abortion Bill In Idaho Takes Aim at Landmark Case', *The New York Times*, 22 March 1990, p. A1.

65. For good discussions on the relationship between interest groups and political institutions, see David R. Mayhew, *Congress: The Electoral Connection* (New Haven: Yale University Press, 1974); Nelson W. Polsby, *Consequences of Party Reform* (Oxford: Oxford University Press, 1983); and Gary C. Jacobson, *The Politics of Congressional Elections*, 2nd edn (Glenview, Ill.: Scott, Foresman and Co., 1987).

66. James L. Sundquist, *The Decline and Resurgence of Congress* (Washington: The Brookings Institution, 1981); and David R. Mayhew, *Divided We Govern* (New Haven: Yale University Press, 1991).

67. Henry C. Kenski and Margaret Corgan Kenski, 'Congress Against the President: The Struggle over the Environment', in Norman Vig and Michael Kraft, *Environmental Policy in the 1980s* (Washington: Congressional Quarterly, 1984); James P. Lester, 'A New Federalism? Environmental Policy in the States', in Norman Vig and Michael Kraft, *Environmental Policy in the 1990s* (Washington: Congressional Quarterly, 1990); and Lettie M. Wenner, 'Environmental Policy in the Courts', in Vig and Kraft, ibid.

68. *Congressional Quarterly Annual Almanac: 1983* (Washington, DC: Congressional Quarterly, 1983), pp. 308–10.

69. David R. Mayhew, *Placing Parties in American Politics* (Princeton: Princeton University Press, 1986).

70. There are numerous instances of candidates running for public office without the support of his professed party. The most recent celebrated case comes from Louisiana, where the former Ku Klux Klansman, David Duke, ran in the non-partisan Senate primary race as a self-anointed Republican. Duke was

not supported by the Republican Party. In Britain, by contrast, local party elites select candidates for nomination to the general election, even if some local party members oppose the choice. In a recent case, the Conservative Party selected John Taylor, a 38-year-old black man, to represent the party in the Cheltenham constituency. Party dissidents who opposed Taylor's candidacy tried to change the selection, but to no avail. The party leadership rallied around the candidate and expelled one person from the party for calling Taylor a 'bloody nigger'.

71. Jacobson, *The Politics of Congressional Elections*, p. 20.
72. Polsby, *Consequences of Party Reform*, p. 139.
73. Jacobson, *The Politics of Congressional Elections*, p. 63.
74. Richard Viguerie, *The New Right: We're Ready to Lead* (Falls Church, Virginia: The Viguerie Company, 1981), p. 142.
75. 'Congressional Report Card', undated publication of Christian Voice.
76. Mailing from Randall Terry, 2 April 1990.
77. Byron Shafer, 'Post-War Politics in the G-7: The United States'. Paper Prepared for the Annual Meeting of the American Political Science Association, Chicago, 1992.
78. Quoted in Richard V. Pierard, 'Reagan and the Evangelicals: The Making of a Love Affair', *The Christian Century*, 21 December 1983: 221–5.
79. For good accounts of the Republican Party and evangelical Christians, see Richard V. Pierard, 'Religion and the 1984 Election Campaign', *Review of Religious Literature* 27 (December 1984): 98–114; and Kenneth Wald, *Religion and Politics in the United States* (New York: St. Martins Press, 1987), Chapter 7.
80. George Gallup, *George Gallup Polls America on Religion* (Princeton, NJ: The Gallup Organization, 1981).
81. Samuel S. Hill and Dennis E. Owen, *The New Religious and Political Right in America* (Nashville: Abingdon Press, 1982); Robert C. Liebman and Robert Wuthnow (eds), *The New Christian Right* (New York: Aldine, 1983); and Robert Wuthnow, *The Restructuring of American Religion* (Princeton: Princeton University Press, 1988), Chapter 8.
82. Reagan, *In God We Trust*, p. 42.
83. Ibid., p. 49.
84. Ronald Reagan, 'Religion and Politics are Necessarily Related', *Church and State* 37 (October 1984): 9–11.
85. Wuthnow, *The Restructuring of American Religion*, pp. 237–8.
86. Corwin Smidt, 'Evangelicals in Presidential Elections: A Look at the 1980s', *Election Politics* 5 (Spring, 1988): 2–10.
87. Linda Greenhouse, 'Both Sides in Abortion Argument Look past Court in Political Battle', *New York Times*, 20 April 1992, p. A1
88. Robert Shogan, 'GOP's Comeback Trail Looms as Long, Bumpy', *Los Angeles Times*, 15 November 1992, p. 1.
89. 'Pro-Life Advocate', a publication of the Christian Action Council, 1989.
90. Interview with Clive Calver, 11 May 1989.
91. Elizabeth Hann Hastings and Philip K. Hastings (eds), *Index to International Public 1980–1981* (Westport, CT: Greenwood Press, 1981), p. 392.
92. Elizabeth Hann Hastings and Philip K. Hastings (eds), *Index to International Public 1985–1986* (Westport, CT: Greenwood Press, 1986), p. 501.

93. George Gallup, *George Gallup Polls America on Religion*, pp. 55–6; and George Gallup, *The International Gallup Polls* (Wilmington, Delaware: Scholarly Resources, 1981), p. 26.

94. Donald Alexander Downs, *The New Politics of Pornography* (Chicago: University of Chicago Press, 1989).

95. M.A. McCarthy and R. A. Moodie, 'Parliament and Pornography: The 1978 Child Protection Act', *Parliamentary Affairs* 34 (Winter, 1981): 47–62.

96. Michael Granberry, 'Bibles and the Board – a Skirmish Brews', *Los Angeles Times*, 21 January 1993, p. 3.

97. For good discussions of the church–state conflict in education, see James E. Wood (ed.), *Religion, the State and Education* (Waco, Texas: Baylor University Press, 1984); James E. Wood (ed.), *Religion and the State: Essays in Honor of Leo Pfeffer* (Waco, Texas: Baylor University Press, 1985); and Linda Greenhouse, 'New Term to Test Supreme Court's New Majority', *New York Times*, 7 October 1991, p. 14.

98. *The Congressional Quarterly Annual Almanac, 1984* (Washington, DC: Congressional Quarterly, 1985), pp. 245–7.

99. John E. Chubb and Terry M. Moe, *A Lesson in School Reform from Great Britain* (Washington, DC: The Brookings Institution, 1992).

100. John Burn and Colin Hart, *The Crisis in Religious Education* (London: The Education Research Trust, 1988), p. 29.

101. 'Becoming a School Governor', undated publication of CARE.

7 THE FUTURE OF EVANGELICAL SOCIAL MOVEMENTS

1. Robin Toner, 'Atwater Urges Softer Abortion Line', *New York Times*, 20 January 1990, p. 17; Robinn Toner, 'Umbrella on Abortion Delays G.O.P. Decision', *New York Times*, 24 January 1990, p. 14; and Gwen Ifill, '2 Republican Factions on Abortion Gird for Battle on Party's '92 Platform', *New York Times*, 30 September 1991, p. 16.

2. Carlos V. Lozana and Ralph Frammolino, 'Christian Right Tries to Take over State GOP, *Los Angeles Times*, 18 October 1992, p. 1; Adam Clymer, 'Colorado's Test for the Religious Right', *New York Times*, 23 October 1992, p. 12; and Timothy Egan, 'Oregon G.O.P Faces Schism over Agenda of Christian Right', *New York Times*, 14 November 1992.

3. Allen D. Hertzke, *Echoes of Discontent: Jesse Jackson, Pat Robertson and the Resurgence of Populism* (Washington, DC: Congressional Quarterly Press, 1993).

4. Seth Mydans, 'Evangelicals Gain with Covert Candidates', *New York Times*, 27 October 1992, p. 1; and Michael Granberry, 'Bibles and the Board – a Skirmish Brews', *Los Angeles Times*, 21 January 1993, p. 3.

Index

DATE DUE

JUL 7 '99			
NOV 22 '01			
JUN 0 8 2006			
			Printed in USA